The Motets of Carissimi
Volume 2

by
Andrew V. Jones

UMI RESEARCH PRESS
Ann Arbor, Michigan

Copyright © 1982
Andrew V. Jones
All rights reserved

Produced and distributed by
UMI Research Press
an imprint of
University Microfilms International
Ann Arbor, Michigan 48106

Library of Congress Cataloging in Publication Data

Jones, Andrew V.
   The motets of Carissimi.

   (British studies in musicology ; no. 5)
   A revision of the author's thesis, Oxford University,
1980.
    1. Carissimi, Giacomo, 1605-1674. Motets. 2. Motets.
I. Title. II. Series.
ML410.C3268J6 1982   783.4'092'4   81-16363
ISBN 0-8357-1243-5 (set)   AACR2
ISBN 0-8357-1258-3 (v.2)

Contents

Volume Two: Appendices A, B, C, and D

Appendix A: Thematic and Source Catalogue of all Motets Attributed to Carissimi   *1*

Appendix B: The Printed Sources (1642-1978)   *131*
 Section 1: 1642-1675   *132*
 Section 2: 1693-1726   *141*
 Section 3: 1825-1978   *142*

Appendix C: The Manuscript Sources: Holdings of Individual Libraries   *147*

Appendix D: Transcriptions of Motets   *219*
 Introduction   *219*
 "Alma Redemptoris Mater" (SSB bc)   *221*
 "Anima nostra sustinet Dominum" (SS bc)   *229*
 "Annunciate gentes" (SSATB bc)   *236*
 "Ardens est cor nostrum" (SATB bc)   *250*
 "Audite sancti" (SSB bc)   *260*
 "Benedictus Deus et Pater" (SSS bc)   *269*
 "Cantabo Domino" (SS bc)   *274*
 "Confitebor tibi Domine" (SSB bc)   *281*
 "Desiderata nobis" (ATB bc)   *299*
 "Dicite nobis" (SSAT bc)   *308*
 "Domine, Deus meus" (S bc)   *319*
 "Domine, quis habitabit" (SST bc)   *327*
 "Emendemus in melius" (mSAT bc)   *338*
 "Exulta, gaude, filia Sion" (SS bc)   *345*
 "Exurge cor meum" (S VV vlne bc)   *354*
 "Hymnum jucunditatis" (SS bc)   *364*
 "Insurrexerunt in nos inimici nostri" (mSAT bc)   *372*
 "Laudemus virum gloriosum" (SS bc)   *382*
 "Militia est vita hominis" (SSB VV vdg bc)   *389*
 "Mortalis homo quid non recordaris" (S bc)   *407*
 "O dulcissimum Mariae nomen" (SS bc)   *413*

vi Contents

"O ignis sancte" (SS bc)   *417*
"O quam pulchra es" (S bc)   *424*
"Plaudite caelestes chori" (S bc)   *433*
"Quis est hic vir" (SSS bc)   *438*
"Quomodo facti sunt impii" (SSB bc)   *449*
"Salve Regina" (SSB bc)   *455*
"Si qua est consolatio" (SSB bc)   *464*
"Sicut stella matutina" (S bc)   *472*
"Suscitavit Dominus" (ATB VV vdg bc)   *482*
"Timete Dominum" (SSATB bc)   *495*
"Turbabuntur impii" (ATB bc)   *504*
"Viderunt te Domine" (SB bc)   *517*

Appendix A

Thematic and Source Catalogue of All Motets Attributed to Carissimi

This catalogue contains all motets known to the present writer which are attributed to Carissimi. It is tempting to divide a catalogue such as this into two halves: one half containing motets known or believed to be authentic, and the other containing those known or believed not to be authentic. There are indeed motets which can be said with complete conviction to be by Carissimi, and others which, with equal certainty, can be said not to be by him. But for a sizable group of motets the problem of authenticity cannot be reduced to such a 'black and white' issue: there exist many shades of grey. One could not hope, however, to devise a system of symbols which would adequately cover all the varying degrees of possibility and probability. It seems preferable, therefore, to use only three symbols (see below), and to present all the attributed motets in a single catalogue. In this way it will be easier, in the light of future research, to make any corrections which are necessary. Problems of authenticity and the reasons behind the conclusions are explained in the correspondingly numbered sections of chapter three.

Some features of the catalogue require explanation:

Title of motet

The following symbols are used with these meanings:

i) <u>Title</u>   A motet definitely or probably by Carissimi.
ii)   ? Title   A motet possibly or probably not by Carissimi.
iii)   x Title   A motet definitely not by Carissimi.
iv)   ...Title... A fragment of a motet. The dots may precede or follow the title, or both, depending on the position of the fragment in the complete motet.

Voices and instruments

The abbreviations (in parenthesis after the title) are explained in the general list of abbreviations at the beginning of volume 1. Unless otherwise stated, all motets employ a *basso continuo*.

Sources

Sources are arranged in the following order:

i) Manuscript sources, arranged according to the alphabetical sequence of libraries.
ii) Manuscript fragments.

iii) Printed sources, arranged chronologically.
iv) Printed fragments.

When appropriate, a printed attribution which conflicts with an incorrect manuscript attribution is included in the list of sources. Thus, for example, "Crucior in hac flamma," ascribed to Carissimi in GB Lk and Och, is in fact by Maurizio Cazzati, under whose name it was printed at Bologna in 1660. (Second and third editions appeared at Antwerp in 1663 and 1669.)

Addenda

There is a list of addenda at the end of the catalogue.

x A Domino factum est (SAT)

    D-brd Mbs: Mus. ms. 104
    D-brd MÜs: Sant. Hs. 902

x Ad cantus, ad melos (AA)

    GB Cfm: 32 G 30, 16^V-18^V

    M. Cazzati, <u>Tributo di sagri concerti...op.23</u> (Bologna, 1660; 2/Antwerp, 1663; 3/Antwerp, 1669)

? Ad dapes salutis venite (ATB)

    F LYm: 28329, 1-6

x Ad festum venite mortales
  (SS)

GB Cfm: 32 G 30, 25-8

M. Cazzati, <u>Tributo di sagri concerti...op.23</u> (Bologna, 1660; 2/Antwerp, 1663; 3/Antwerp, 1669)

? Ad te levavi animam meam
  (AT)

D-brd MÜs: Sant.Hs.1206, 159^v-60^v

? Adeste mortales (S)

F Pc: Rés.F.934^b, 148-54

x Adoremus Christum (SSB)

F Pc: Rés.F.934[b], 25-35

F. Foggia, Litanie et Sacrae Cantiones...op.4 (Rome, 1652)

x Adoro te (ATB)

GB T: 310, 213-17

x Ah Deus ego amo te (SSA VV vc)

GB T: 936, 106-32

J. H. Wilderer, Modulationi sacre... (Amsterdam, n.d.)

[VV and vc are silent in first section]

x Ah quid obdormis... (S VV vc)

GB T: 936, 48-54

Fragment:

...Convertimini ad me (SB VV vc)
GB T: 936, 54-64

J. H. Wilderer, <u>Modulationi sacre...</u> (Amsterdam, n.d.)

x Ah vide Domine (SATB VV vc)

GB T: 936, 149-78

J. H. Wilderer, <u>Modulationi sacre...</u> (Amsterdam, n.d.)

Ed. Jack Pilgrim [attributed to Carissimi] (Hilversum: Harmonia-Uitgave, 1971)

[STA ~~enter in bars 5, 7 and 9 respectively~~]

Alleluia. Jesum nostrum laudate (SSB)

See 'Alma Redemptoris Mater'

? Alleluia. O beatae caeli mentes (SB)

GB Cfm: 32 G 30, 7-8^v

? Alma Redemptoris Mater (SATB)

D-brd Müs: Sant.Hs.1202, 130-4

Alma Redemptoris Mater (SSB)

D-brd Mbs: Mus.ms.105
D-brd Müs: Sant.Hs.2748, 31^v-34^v
GB Cfm: 2 F 22, 3^v-6^v
GB T: 713, 169-75
I TLP: Ms.40.M, 51-
S Uu: Tab.Caps.83:no.5 (to the words 'Alleluia. Jesum nostrum laudate')
S Uu: Vok.mus. i hdskr. Caps.11: no.1 (to the words 'Alleluia. Jesum nostrum laudate')

[continued...

[continuation of 'Alma
Redemptoris Mater']

S Uu: Vok.mus. i hdskr. Caps.
   53: no.10/7

Floridus modulorum hortus...
(Rome, 1647)

x Amo te (ST VV vc)

GB T: 936, 1-13

J. H. Wilderer, Modulationi
sacre... (Amsterdam. n.d.)

x Angelus et Anima (AB)

See 'Crucior in hac flamma'

x Anima mea in aeterna
  dulcedine (SB)

  GB Lbl: Add.17835, 87-88ᵛ
  GB Lbl: Add.30382, 62ᵛ-64
  GB Lbl: Add.31479
  GB Lbl: Add.33234, 70-72
  GB Lbl: Add.33235, 92-4
  GB Ob: Mus.Sch.c.11, 175-70
       [sic]
  GB Ob: Mus.Sch.c.12-19
  GB Och: 43, 10-11ᵛ
  GB Och: 621, 9ᵛ-11
  GB Och: 623-26
  GB Och: 1178, 3ᵛ-4ᵛ

  E. Trabattone, <u>Concerti a
  2. 3. è 4 Voci. Libro
  Secondo... Opera Quarta</u>
  (Venice, 1629)

  See <u>Roger North on Music</u>,
  ed. John Wilson (London,
  1959), pp.113-14: attributed to Carissimi.

? Anima mea in dolore est
  (SSATB)

  F LYm: 28329, 7-14
  F Pn: Vm¹.1267, no.10

[SSAB are silent at the opening]

x Anima mea liquefacta est
(SAB)

GB Lam: 42, 154-9

F. M. Marini, Concerti
spirituali... (Venice,
1637)

Anima nostra sustinet Dominum
(SS)

F Pn: Vm¹.1268, no.2
GB Lam: 40, 197-202
GB Lam: 42, 171-80
GB Lbl: Add.31477, 63-64ᵛ
GB Ob: Mus.d.26, 5-13
GB Ob: Mus.Sch.c.9, 37-44
GB Och: 55, 25-9

Carissimi, Arion Romanus...
(Konstanz, 1670)

x Animae amantes (ATB)

F Pc: Rés.Vmᵇ.ms.6, 34-5

M. Cazzati, Tributo di sagri
concerti... op.23 (Bologna,
1660; 2/Antwerp, 1663;
3/Antwerp, 1669)

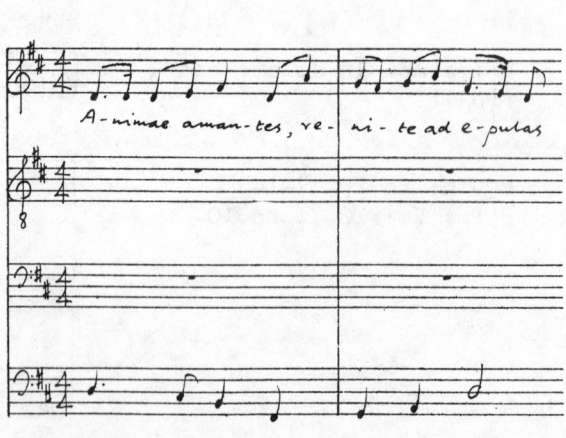

Annos aeternos (a 2)

No musical source known.

Performed by J. P. Krieger, Trinity I, 1693, at Weissenfels; see DdT, vol.53, p.liv.

Annunciate gentes (SSATB)

D-brd MÜs: Sant.Hs.905
F Pc: Rés.F.934c, 186-95
F Pc: Rés.2182(I), no.10
GB Cfm: 32 G 30, 141v-45v
GB Ckc: 206, 94v-98
GB Lam: 41, 79-94
GB Lbl: Add.17835, 18-22
GB Lbl: Add.31409, 46v-50v
GB Lbl: Add.31472, 91-95v
GB Lcm: 1101, 80-86v
GB Ob: Mus.Sch.c.9, 148-55
GB Ob: Mus.Sch.c.12-19
GB Och: 13, 73-9
GB Och: 53, 156-66
GB T: 1245, 20-39
GB T: 1260, no.5
GB Y: M 35/1 (S) [SSA and incomplete bc only]

Carissimi, Sacri concerti musicali... (Rome, 1675)

Ed. Niels Martin Jensen, Orbis Chori, iii (Egtved: Musikhojskolens Vorlag, 1967)

Ardens est cor nostrum/meum
(SATB)

A Wn: SA.68.Aa.111
A Wn: S.m.1550, 34-36ᵛ
D-brd Mbs: Cod.lat.1512/3, 63-6
D-brd Mbs: Mus.MS.565
D-brd Mbs: Mus.MS.720/1
D-brd MÜs: Sant.Hs. 900 (bc only)
D-brd MÜs: Sant.Hs. 2758, 11-15
D-ddr Bds: 3101, no.2
F Pc: Rés.2182(I), no.12
GB T: 746, 27-30
I Mc: (to the words 'Arde il cor nel petto')

R. Floridus...istas alias sacras cantiones... (Rome, 1664)
['Ardens est cor nostrum']

Carissimi, Arion Romanus... (Konstanz, 1670)
['Ardens est cor meum']

Sammlung...herausgegeben von F. Rochlitz (Mainz, Paris, Antwerp, 1835 ff.), ii, 9-12

? Audi Domine (S)

F LYm: 28329, 23-4
F Pc: Rés.F.934ᵇ, 164-8

12

x Audite gentes (ATB)

GB Cfm: 32 G 30, 22-24^v

M. Cazzati, <u>Tributo di sagri concerti... op.23</u> (Bologna, 1660; 2/Antwerp, 1663; 3/Antwerp, 1669)

Fragment:

x ...O felix anima... (ATB)

<u>The Fitzwilliam Music...published by Vincent Novello</u> (London, 1825), v, 26

<u>Recueil des Morceaux de Musique ancienne, ...</u> Paris, 1843 ff.), vi

<u>Echos du monde religieux</u> (Paris, 1859), 104-5

<u>Musica Sacra</u> (1874-5), no.14 (Paris, 1875)

Ed. A. Gastoué (Paris, 1932)

Ed. Maffeo Zanon (Basel, 1951)

Ed. Aimé Steck (Strasbourg, 1954)

Ed. Zanon-Vené (New York, 1957)

(In the publications from 1825 onwards it is attributed to Carissimi.)

<u>Audite justi</u> (SSB)

See 'Audite sancti'

Audite mortales (a 9)

No musical source known.

Bought by J. P. Krieger from the Marienkirche, Halle, in 1680; see DdT, vol.53, p.xvii.

See Addenda

x Audite omnes quodquod estis (SSB)

   S Uu: Tab.Caps.78: no.85
   S Uu: Vok.mus. i hdskr.
        Caps. 11: no.4

x Audite peccatores (SSB VV vc)

   GB T: 936, 133-48

   J. H. Wilderer, Modulationi sacre... (Amsterdam, n.d.)

[SS VV vc are silent at the opening]

Audite sancti (SSB)

F Pc: Rés.F.934^c, 56-63
F Pc: Rés.Vm^b.ms.6, 20-21
F Pn: Vm^1.1268, no.7
GB Bu: 5002, 191-7
GB Lam: 41, 105-14
GB Lbl: Add.30382, 13^v-15^v
GB Lbl: Add.31472, 27-30
GB Lbl: Add.31479
GB Lbl: Add.33234, 112-15
GB Lbl: Harley 1501, 48-52
GB Lcm: 1064, 5^v (B only)
GB Ob: Mus.Sch.c.9, 51-5
GB Ob: Mus.Sch.c.12-19
GB Ob: Mus.Sch.c.24-7 (SSB only)
GB Och: 43, 12-14
GB Och: 53, 65-70
GB Och: 623-6
GB T: 335, 70-78
S Uu: Tab.Caps.77: no.95 (to the words 'Audite justi')
S Uu: Vok.mus. i hdskr. Caps. 11: no.3 (to the words 'Audite justi')
S Uu: Vok.mus. i hdskr. Caps. 53: no.10/14

R. Floridus...has alteras sacras cantiones... (Rome, 1645)

R. Floridus...has sacras cantiones... (Rome, 1651)

Scelta di motetti... (Rotterdam, 1656)

Carissimi, Arion Romanus... (Konstanz, 1670)

Harmonia sacra: ... The second book... (London, 1693), 59-66

Audivi vocem (SSS VV L Tb)

A KR: L 13, 8-15

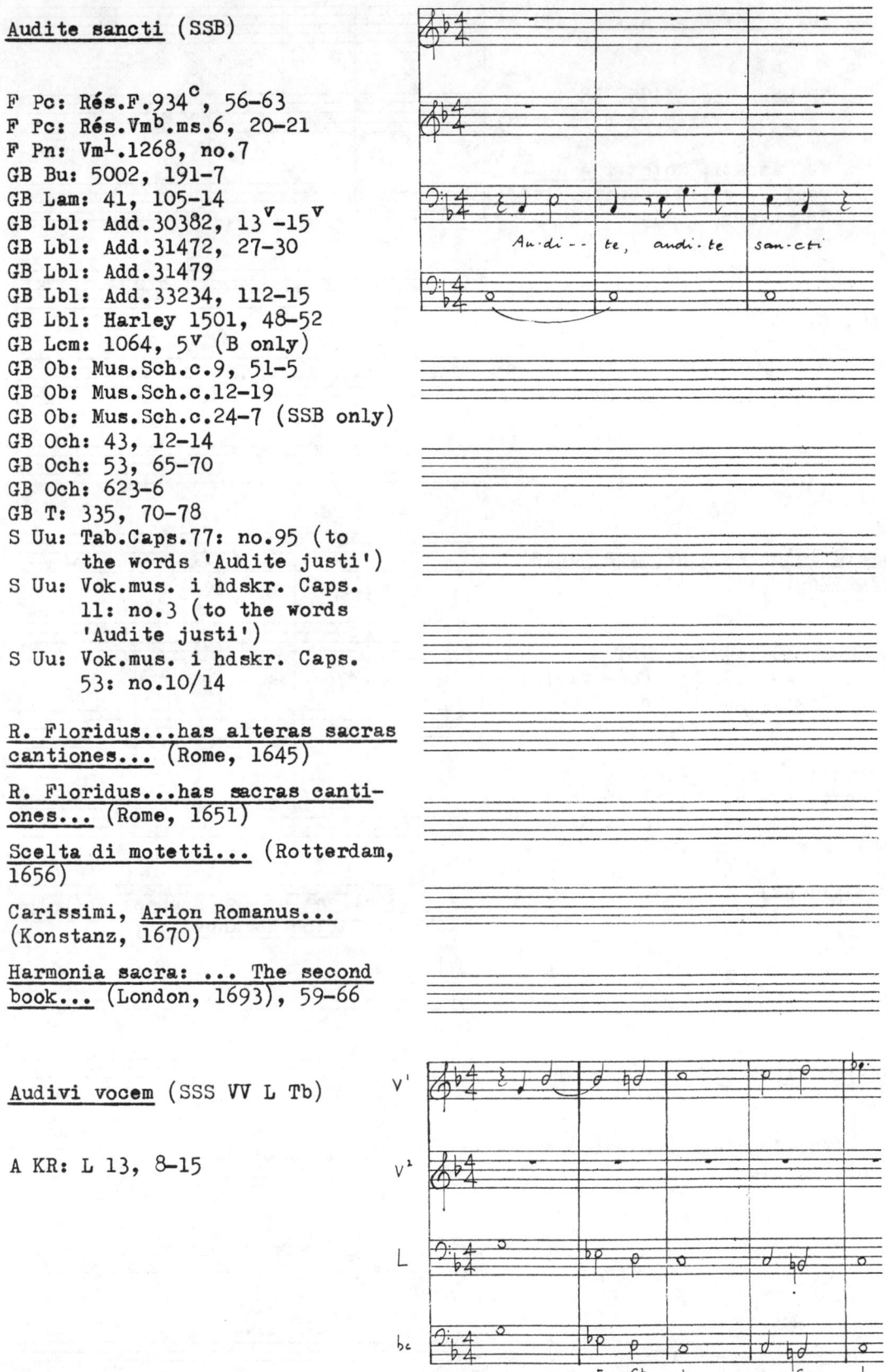

[The voices enter from bar 22 onwards with material derived from the above.]

15

x Ave dulcissima Maria (AT)

GB Lbl: Add.31475, 38^V
    (first 8½ bars only)

M. Cazzati, Motetti a due
voci... op.10 (Venice, 1648;
2/Antwerp, 1665)

[bc is left blank in GB Lbl Add.31475]

Ave dulcissime angelorum panis
sanctus (SST [VV])

GB Och: 13, 149-52 (SST)
I PS: B 25 n.3, [3] (one violin
    part, under the title
    'Ave dulcissime Jesu')

Carissimi, Arion Romanus...
(Konstanz, 1670) (SST VV; but
neither of the violin parts is
the same as that in I PS)

See Addenda

[VV are silent at the opening in both
I PS and Arion Romanus...]

Ave dulcissime Jesu ([SST] V[V])

See 'Ave dulcissime angelorum
panis sanctus'

x Ave verum corpus (SATB no bc)

F Pn: Vm^1.1267, [no.11a]
I Rsc: 2050

The Choir (London, 1852), i, 26

Ed. R. R. Terry (London, [1905])

? Beatus vir (A VV)

GB Cfm: 32 G 30, 61-74^v

? Beatus vir (S VV)

GB Cfm: 32 F 24, 8-12^v

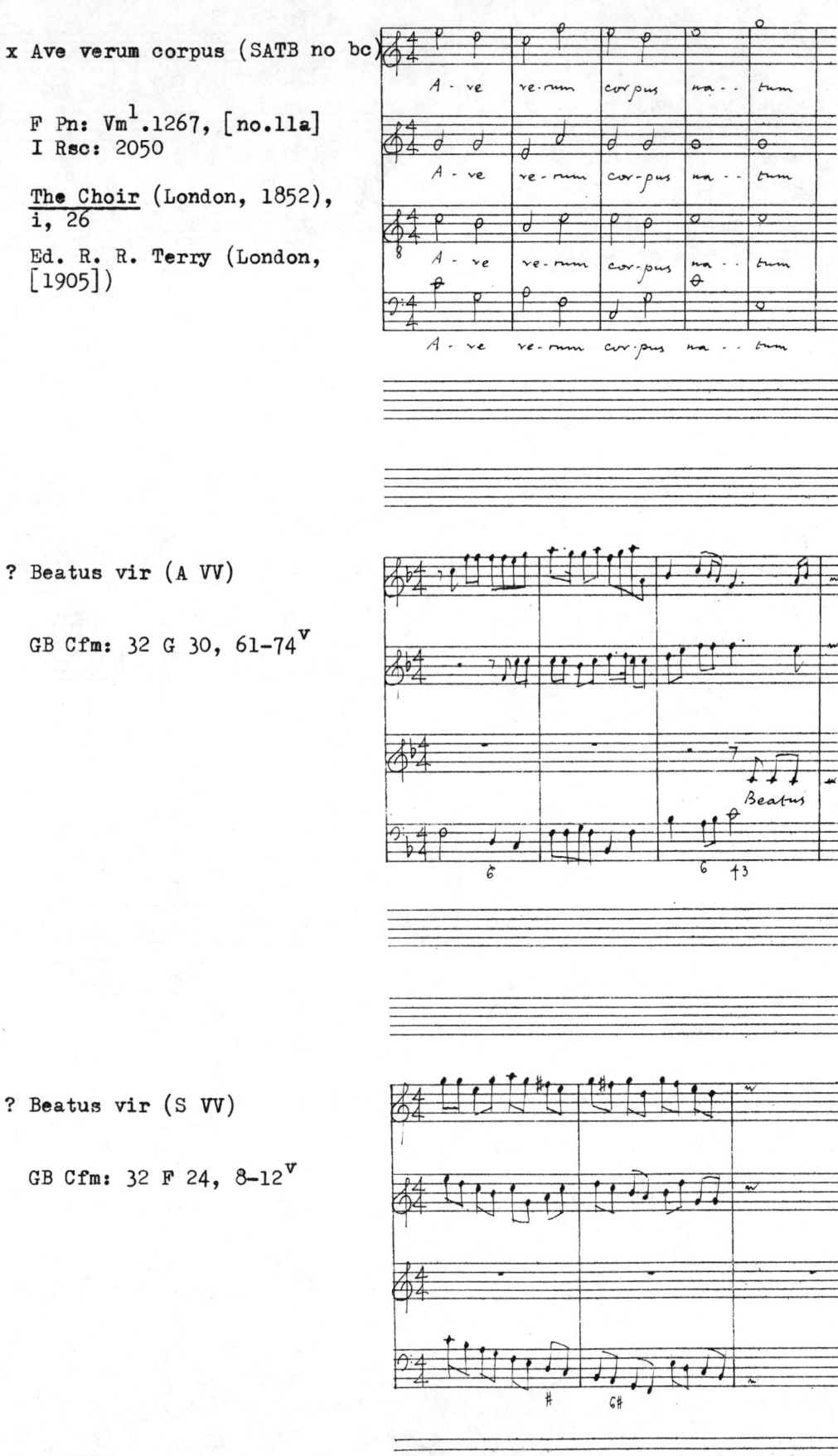

? Beatus vir (SATB SATB)

A Wn: Ms. 15621
D-brd Mbs: Mus.ms. 89
D-brd Müs: Sant.Hs. 893
GB T: 935

Ed. Jack Pilgrim (Hilversum: Harmonia-Uitgave, 1968)

? Beatus vir (SSATB)

GB Y: M.35/2(S)

Ed. Peter Seymour (London: Oxford University Press, 1975)

[B enters in bar 4; AT enter in bar 5.]

Benedicite gentes Deum nostrum (SSS)

Carissimi, Arion Romanus... (Konstanz, 1670)

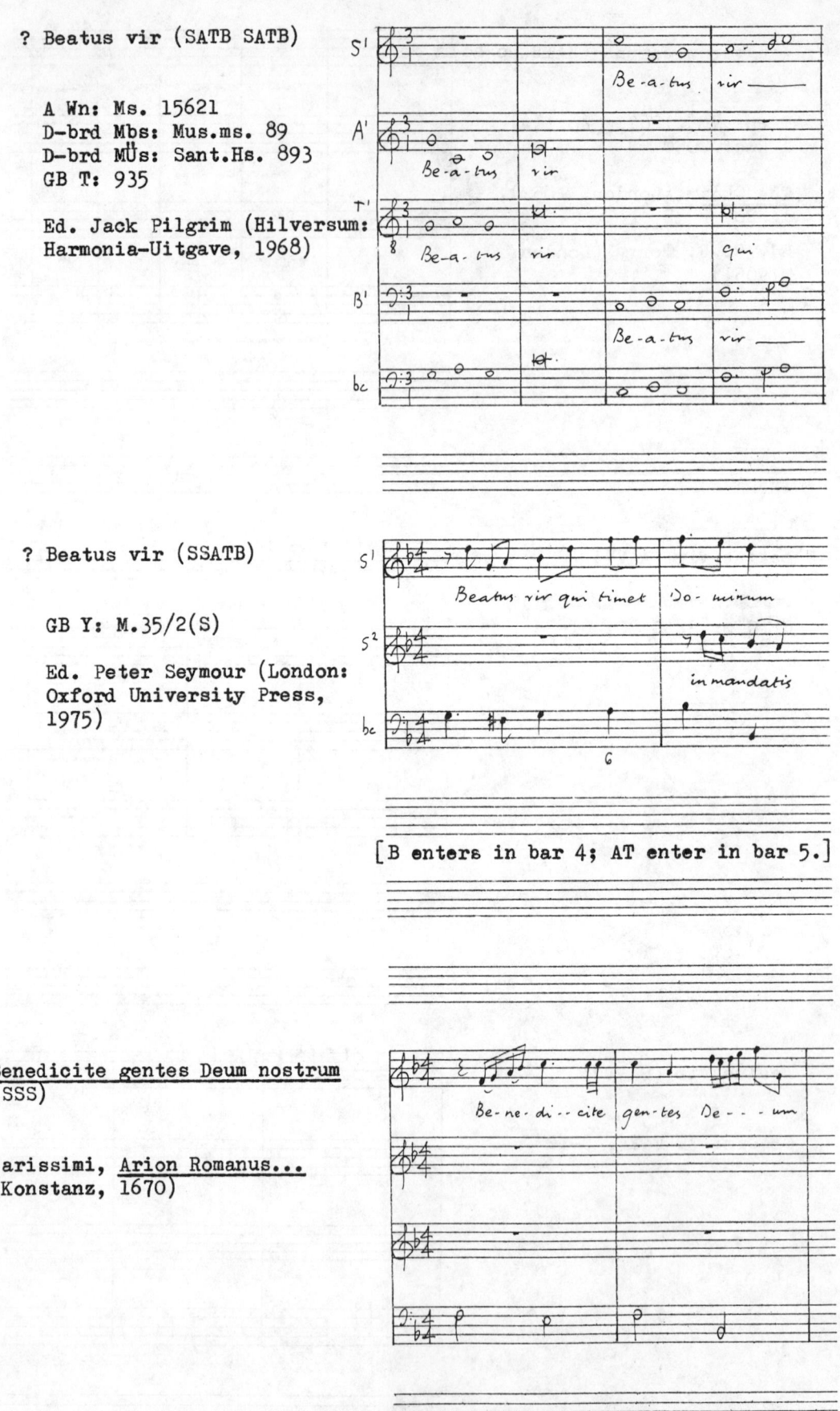

? Benedicite omnes angeli (ATB)

GB Och: 13, 221-5

Benedictus Deus et Pater (SSS)

D-brd Müs: Sant.Hs. 2748, 37-

R. Floridus...istas alias cantiones sacras... (Rome, 1668)

? Benedictus Redemptor (SS)

F Pc: Rés.Vm^b.ms.6, 54-5

x Benignissime Jesu (SST)

F LYm: 28329, 25-8
F Pc: Rés.F.934^b, 169-75
F Pc: Rés.Vm^b.ms.6, 28-9

B. Graziani, <u>Motetti...
libro terzo, op.7</u> (Rome,
1656; 2/Rome, 1657;
3/Rome, 1658)

Cantabo Domino (SS)

D-brd Mūs: Sant.Hs. 905
F Pc: Rés.2182(I), no.10
GB Cfm: 32 G 30, 120^v-23^v
GB Lam: 41, 24-9
GB Lbl: Add.17835, 30^v-33
GB Lbl: Add.29379, 16-18^v
GB Lbl: Add.31472, 12^v-15
GB Lbl: Add.37027, 19-21
GB Lcm: 1101, 36-9
GB Lgc: 455, 9^v
GB Ob: Mus.Sch.c.9, 175-9
GB Och: 13, 42-6
GB Och: 53, 46-52
GB T: 926, 38-45

Carissimi, <u>Sacri concerti
musicali...</u> (Rome, 1675)

Cantate Domino (a 2)

No musical source known.

Performed by J. P. Krieger,
Pentecost II, 1692, at Weissenfels; see <u>DdT</u>, vol.53, p.liv.

? Cantate Domino (SSB)

F LYm: 28329, 44-9
F Pc: Rés.F.934ᵇ, 176-84
F Pc: Rés.Vmᵇ.ms.6, 18-19

x Cantemus, jubilemus (ST)

GB Lbl: Add.31475, 27ᵛ-33

M. Cazzati, <u>Motetti a due voci... op.10</u> (Venice, 1648; 2/Antwerp, 1665)

[bc is left blank in GB Lbl Add.31475]

<u>Caro factum facta parens</u> (SS)

S Uu: Tab.Caps.83: no.61
S Uu: Vok.mus. i hdskr. Caps.11: no.5

Caro mea vere est cibus
(SmSATB VV)

F Pn: Mss.Latin 16830, 106ᵛ-10

[The voices enter in bars 49 and 50 with material related to the above.]

? Cernis panem (AB)

F Pc: Rés.F.934ᵇ, 1-12

? Christum regem adoremus
   (SATB no bc)

D-brd MÜs: Sant.Hs. 1206,
           143-43ᵛ

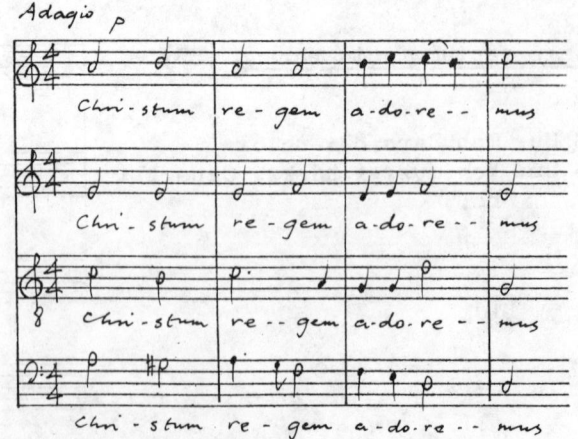

? Christus factus est (ATB)

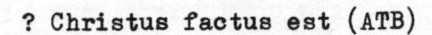

GB Cfm: 32 G 30, 11^v–12^v

x Christus factus est (SATB)

I Ls: B.251
I PAc:

Christus factus est (SSATB SATB)

I Rsg: II Settimana Santa, N.15

Ed. Lorenzo Feininger, <u>Documenta Liturgiae Polychoralis Sanctae Ecclesiae Romanae</u>, no.18 (Trent: Societas Universalis S. Ceciliae, 1964)

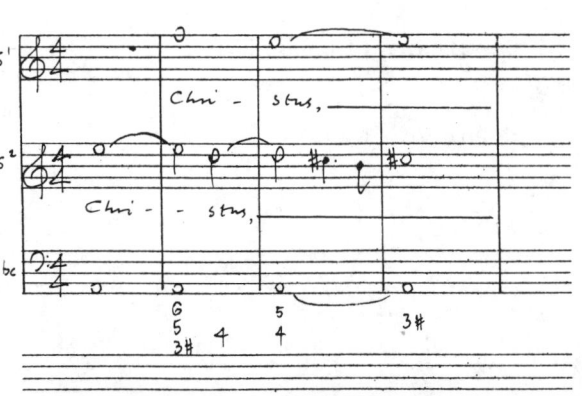

[The remaining voices enter in bar 40.]

Clama ne cesses (a 4)

No musical source known.

Mentioned in a letter dated 29 March 1642 from Friedrich, Landgrave of Hessen-Darmstadt, to Carissimi. It is not quite clear from the letter whether the motet had already been composed or whether Friedrich was suggesting a text for Carissimi to set. Since he specifies the number of voices (four) the former hypothesis seems more likely. A transcription and translation of the letter are printed in Thomas D. Culley, <u>Jesuits and Music:I...</u> (Rome/St Louis, 1970), pp.330-1 and 188-9 respectively.

? Concinant linguae (A)

F Pn: Vm^1.1306

Confitebor tibi Domine
(SSATB VV)

GB Lcm: 1179

[The remaining voices enter in bar 33.]

Confitebor tibi Domine (SSB)

F Pn: Vm^1. 1268, no.8
GB Lam: 40, 184-97
GB Lam: 42, 70-90
GB Lbl: Add.31477, 57-62^v
GB Lwa: CG 63, 209-21
GB Ob: Mus.d.26, 60-83
GB Ob: Mus.Sch.c.9, 156-68
GB Och: 13, 229-41
GB T: 335, 195-209
GB T: 1260, no.6
S Uu: Vok.mus. i hdskr. Caps. 53 no.10/3

Fragments:

'...Glory be to the Father'
GB Lbl: Add.31818, 20-21^v

'...Sicut erat in principio'
GB Lcm: 791, 30-31
GB Och: 75, 11 (bc only)

Printed (complete):

Motetti...Seconda raccolta di D. Benedetto Pace... (Loreto, 1646)

R. Floridus... Psalmos istos... (Rome, 1662)

25

Confitemini Domino (BB)

A KR: L 12, 17(-16)-19
F Pn: Vm¹. 1174, no.23

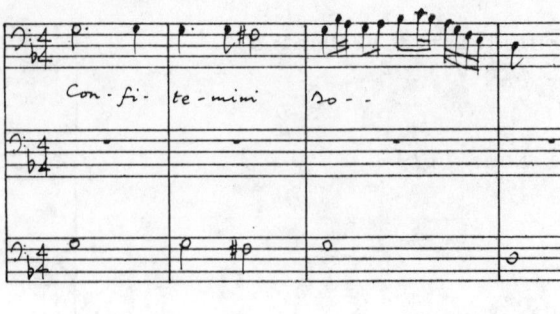

? Congratulamini, congaudete (S)

GB T: 1425, 43-8 (now in F Pn)

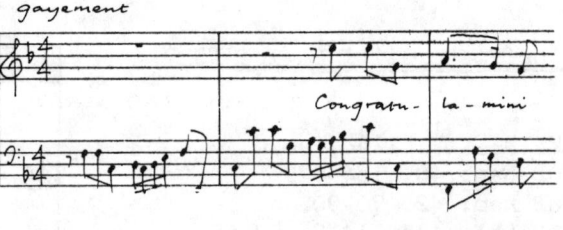

Convertere ad me (S)

F Pn: Vm¹.1306, 65-8

Carissimi, Arion Romanus...
(Konstanz, 1670)

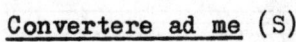

x ...Convertimini ad me
(SB VV vc)

See 'Ah quid obdormis'

x Crucior in hac flamma (AB)

GB Cfm: 32 G 30, 19-22
GB Lk: R.M.20.h.8, 127-25^v
     (sic)
GB Och: 1154, 2-4^v

M. Cazzati, <u>Tributo di sagri concerti... op.23</u> (Bologna, 1660; 2/Antwerp, 1663; 3/Antwerp, 1669)

? Cum audisset Gedeon (S)

F Pn: Vm^1.1306

(The scribe of GB Lbl: Add. 29292 probably considered it to be by Ercole Bernabei.)

Cum de sepulchro (a 8)

No musical source known.

Performed by J. P. Krieger, Easter Vespers, 1691, at Weissenfels; see DdT, vol. 53, p.liv.

Cum ingrederetur N./Cum reverteretur David (SSS) [i/ii]

D-brd MÜs: Sant.Hs.905	[ii]
F Pc: Rés.F.934c, 103-10	[ii]
F Pc: Rés.2182(I), no.10	[ii]
GB Cfm: 32 G 30, 129-32v	[i/ii]
GB Lam: 41, 44-53	[i/ii]
GB Lbl: Add.31472, 49v-53	[ii]
GB Lcm: 1101, 45v-49v	[ii]
GB Ob: Mus.Sch.c.9, 192-8	[ii]
GB Och: 13, 80-86	[ii]
GB Och: 53, 103-11	[i]
GB T: 310, 222-8	[ii]
GB T: 335, 136-43	[ii]
S Uu: Tab.Caps.83: no.2	[ii]
S Uu: Vok.mus. i hdskr. Caps.11: no.6	[ii]
S Uu: Vok.mus. i hdskr. Caps.53: no.10/11	[ii]

Carissimi, Sacri concerti musicali... (Rome, 1675) [i/ii]

x Deduxit illum Dominus (SSB)

S Uu: Bd.80, no.59

Attributed to F. Foggia in the anthology *R. Floridus ...has alteras sacras cantiones...* (Rome, 1645)

Attributed to Carissimi in the collection *Arion Romanus ...* (Konstanz, 1670) (to the words 'Gaudete cum Maria' (q.v.))

Desiderata nobis (ATB)

D-brd Mbs: Mus.ms.565, 33^v-
D-brd Mbs: Mus.ms.720/2
D-brd MÜs: Sant.Hs. 2758, 15-22
D-ddr Bds: 3101, no.3
F Pc: Rés.2182(I) no.12
F Pn: Vm^1.1174, no.8
GB Lbl: Add.31479
GB T: 746, 30^v-36
S Uu: Tab.Caps.77: no.101
S Uu: Vok.mus. i hdskr. Caps.11: no.7
S Uu: Vok.mus. i hdskr. Caps.53: no.10/26

Fragment:

'...Gaudeat ergo...' (no bc)
DK Kk: Rungs Musik Archiv Nr.196

Scelta de'motetti... (Rome, 1667)

? Deus Dominus (BB)

F Pn: Vm^1.1267, no.1

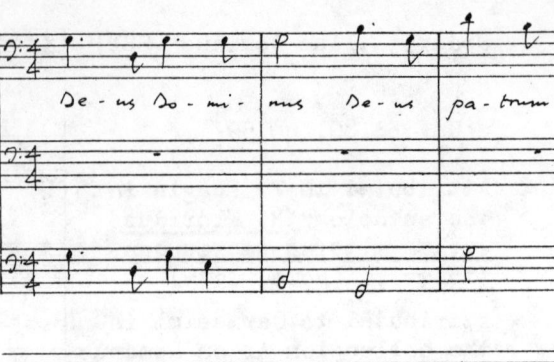

? Deus meus, ad te de luce (SST)

D-brd Mbs: Sant.Hs. 1206, 157^v-59^v

x Deus quis similis erit tibi (ATB)

F LYm: 134025[A], 23-4
F Pc: Rés.F.934^b, 155-63

G. Tricarico, in the anthology R. Floridus...istas alias sacras cantiones... (Rome, 1664)

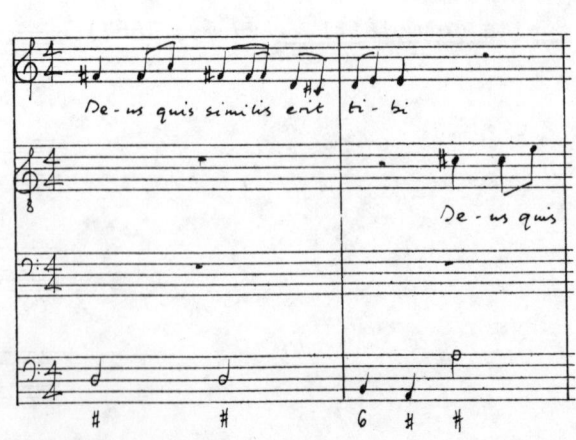

[In F LYm it is a tone lower, ~~and is scored for SSB: SS are a seventh~~ higher than AT.]

? Dextera Domini (a 2)

No manuscript source is known.

<u>Publicazione periodica di musica sacra</u> (Rome, 1881)

Dicite nobis (SSAT)

F Pc: Rés.F.934^c, 162-72
GB Cfm: 32 G 30, 136^v-41
GB Ckc: 207
GB Lam: 41, 65-78
GB Lbl: Add.17835, 13-17^v
GB Lbl: Add.31472, 79-84
GB Lcm: 1101, 73^v-79^v
GB Och: 13, 64-72
GB Och: 53, 132-42

Fragment:
'Dicite nobis...'
B Bc: 1057

Carissimi, <u>Sacri concerti musicali...</u> (Rome, 1675)

...Dies felicitatis aeternae (SS)

See 'Exulta, gaude, filia Sion'

? Diffusa est gratia (SATB)

D-brd MÜs: Sant.Hs.1206, 54ᵛ-55ᵛ

[bc is blank except for occasional figuring and 2 notes in bar 21]

x Dilatatae sunt tribulationes (SS)

GB T: 1423, 46-52 (now in F Pn)

A. M. Abbatini, in the anthology R. Floridus... cantiones alias sacras... (Rome, 1649; 2/Venice, 1649)

Dixit Dominus (SATB SATB)

See over

Dixit Dominus (SATB SATB)

GB Lcm: 1178
I PS: B 25 n.3 (B2 part-book
     only)
S Uu: Vok.mus. i hdskr. Caps.
     11: no.8

Dixit Dominus (SSATB)

CS KR: III 83
GB Lk: R.M.22.c.2
GB Och: 55, 1-18
GB Y: M.35/3(S)

Ed. Jack Pilgrim (Hilversum:
Harmonia Uitgave, 1968)

See Addenda

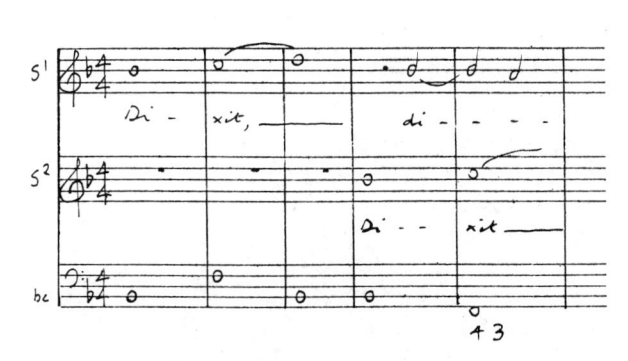

[ATB enter in bar 16]

Doleo et poenitet me (SSTB 3 viols)

S Uu: Vok.mus. i hdskr. Caps. 11: no.10

[Voices enter in bars 13 (B), 24 (SS) and 38 (T)]

? **Dominator Domine** (A VV)

GB Cfm: 32 G 30, 75-83^v

Domine, Deus meus (S)

B Bc: 1057
F Pc: Rés.F.934^c, 5-13
F Pn: Vm^1.1306
GB Lbl: Add.17835, 9-12^v
GB Lbl: Add.31472, 4-7^v
GB Och: 13, 17-24
GB Och: 53, 9-17
I COd: I-V-8

R. Floridus...has alteras sacras cantiones... (Rome, 1663)

[continued...

[continuation of
'Domine, Deus meus']

Carissimi, <u>Arion Romanus</u>...
(Konstanz, 1670)

Ed. Rudolf Ewerhart, <u>Cantio
Sacra</u>, viii (Cologne: Edmund
Bieler, 1956)

See Addenda

x Domine, Deus virtutum (SAT)

D-brd MÜs: Sant.Hs.902

x Domine, Dominus noster
   (SSB VV)

F LYm: 134025[A], 11-16
   (anon; see section X
   in Chapter 3)

x Domine, ne in furore tuo
(SSB)

F Pc: Rés.F.934^b, 211-22

B. Graziani, Motetti...
[op.1] (Rome, 1650);
2/Motetta... (Antwerp, 1652);
3/Motetti... (Rome, 1654).

B. Graziani, Motetti...
[no opus number] (Rome, 1667)

Domine, quis habitabit (SST)

D-brd MÜs: Sant.Hs.905
F Pc: Rés.F.934^c, 125-33
F Pc: Rés.2182(I), no.10
GB Cfm: 32 G 30, 132^v-36^v
GB Lam: 41, 53-64
GB Lbl: Add.31472, 60^v-64^v
GB Lcm: 1101, 68^v-73
GB Och: 13, 56-64
GB Och: 53, 94-102
GB T: 335, 157-65
GB Y: M.36, 3^v-5

Carissimi, Sacri concerti
musicali... (Rome, 1675)

x ...Dulce Te sum [sic; should
be 'Jesum'] dulce bonum...(T)

See 'Venite fideles'

x Dulcis amor Jesu (SS)

GB Lbl: Add.31475, 5^v-8^v

M. Cazzati, Motetti a due voci... op.10 (Venice, 1648; 2/Antwerp, 1665)

[bc is left blank in GB Lbl Add.31475]

? Duo ex discipulis (SST)

F LYm: 134025[A], 16-22
    (anon; see section X
    in Chapter 3)
F Pc: Rés.F.934^b, 86-101

Ed. Henri Quittard, Concerts Spirituels (Série Ancienne) ... (Paris: Schola Cantorum, [c.1905]), i, 13-17 (excerpt)

x Ecce in dolore (SSSATB)

F LYm: 134025[A], 43-7
    (anon; see section X
    in Chapter 3)

[SSATB are silent at the opening]

Ecce nos reliquimus omnia (TTB)

GB Lam: 42, 159-69
GB Ob: Mus.d.26, 84-100
GB Och: 9, 7-10 (anon.)
GB Y: M.35/4(S)
S Uu: Vok.mus. i hdskr. Caps.53: 10/25

? Ecce nunc benedicite Dominum (SSS)

GB Cfm: 32 G 30, 84-90

x Ecce sonuerunt inimici tui (ATB)

F Pc: Rés.Vm^b.ms.6, 36-8

G. M. Pagliardi, in the anthology <u>Scelta de'motetti ...</u> (Rome, 1667)

Ecce sponsus venit (SA)

F Pc: Rés.F.934^b, 67-74
F Pc: Rés.Vm^b.ms.6, 52-3
F Pn: Vm^1.1268, no.1

R. Floridus... Has alias cantiones sacras... (Rome, 1654)

Carissimi, Arion Romanus... (Konstanz, 1670)

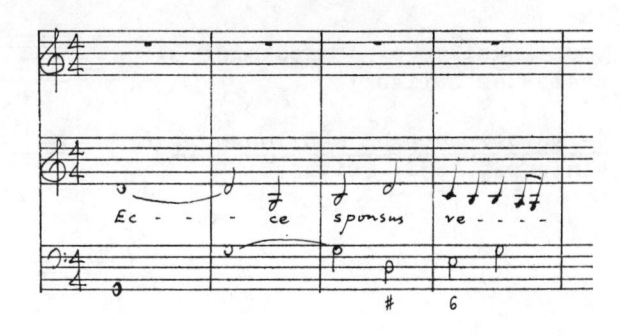

x **Ego sum panis vivus** (SSB)

GB Och: 688

O. Benevoli, in the anthology Sacrarum modulationum... (Rome, 1642)

Egredimini caelestes curiae (SSS)

F Pc: Rés.F.934^c, 64-9
GB Lbl: Add.31472, 30^v-33^v
GB Ob: Mus.Sch.c.9, 198-203
GB Och: 13, 125-8
GB Och: 53, 52-8
GB T: 335, 144-9
GB T: 739

Fragment:

'...in sonitu tubae'
GB Lcm: 2074, 24 (one S part only)

[continued...

39

[continuation of 'Egredimini caelestes curiae']

Delectus sacrarum cantionum...
(Antwerp, 1652) (with VV)

Egredimini filiae Sion et admiramini (S)

I Bc: Q 45, 23-25^v

Egredimini filiae Sion et videte (SSS)

Carissimi, Arion Romanus...
(Konstanz, 1670)

? Eia plebs fidelium laetare
(B VV vdg)

GB Cfm: 32 G 30, 49-55ᵛ

Elevatis manibus benedixit eis
(SAT)

I Rc: 5394

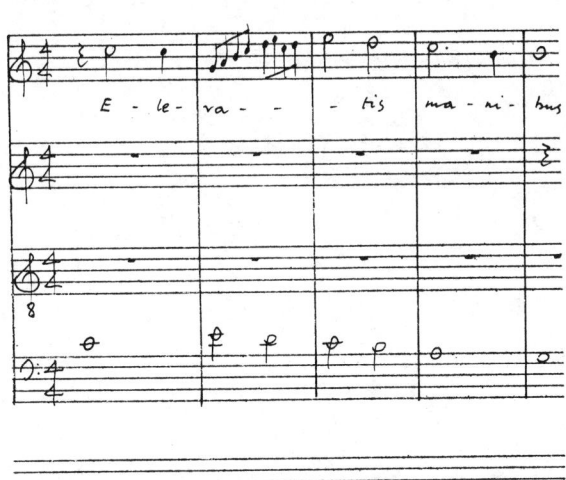

Emendemus in melius (mSAT)

F Pc: Rés.Vmᵇ.ms.6, 4-5
F Pn: Vm¹.1267, no.2
I Bc: X 233, 16ᵛ(-18)-17ᵛ
S Uu: Tab.Caps.83: no.13a
S Uu: Vok.mus. i hdskr. Caps.11: no.11
S Uu: Vok.mus. i hdskr. Caps.53: no.10/19

Scelta di motetti... (Rome, 1643)

? **Errate per colles** (SATB)

F Pc: Rés.F.934ᵇ, 51-66

x ...**Et sic laudabimus**... (ST)

See 'Venite fideles'

Euge, serve bone (AT)

GB Lam: 42, 169-70 (anon.)
GB Lcm: 1101, 50 (anon.)
GB Och: 9, 10-10ᵛ (anon.)
GB Y: M.35/5(S) (attributed to Carissimi)

Exulta, gaude, filia Sion (SS)

D-brd Mūs: Sant.Hs.905
F Pc: Rés.F.934c, 33-9
F Pc: Rés.2182(I), no.10
F Pn: Vm1.1174, no.7
GB Cfm: 2 F 22, 9-12
GB Lam: 41, 1-7
GB Lbl: Add.17835, 33v-36
GB Lbl: Add.31472, 15v-18v
GB Lbl: Add.37027, 21v-24
GB Lcm: 1101, 25-8
GB Ob: Mus.Sch.c.9, 170-5
GB Och: 13, 24-9
GB Och: 53, 42-6

Fragment:

'...dies felicitatis aeternae'
GB Cfm: 32 G 30, 112-13v

Carissimi, *Sacri concerti musicali...* (Rome, 1675)

Six Cantatas by Carissimi. Edited ...by Ridley Prentice (London: Lamborn Cock, 1877), 32-41

Exultabunt justi (SSS)

D-brd Hs: M C/270, 147-71
F Pc: Rés.F.934c, 88-102
GB Lam: 40, 151-61
GB Lam: 42, 1-17
GB Lbl: Add.31472, 42v-49
GB Lbl: Add.31477, 21v-26
GB Lcm: 1101, 100-05v
GB Ob: Mus.d.26, 145-63
GB Ob: Mus.Sch.c.9, 128-36
GB Och: 13, 195-202
GB Och: 53, 80-94

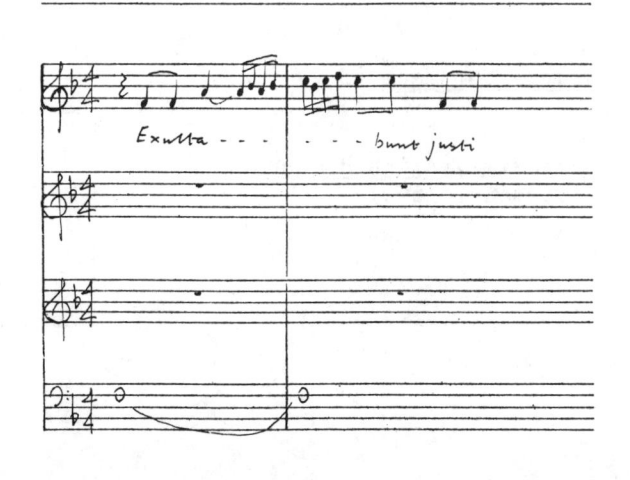

[continued...

[continuation of
'Exultabunt justi']

GB T: 335, 173-83
GB T: 1423, 17-45^v (now in F Pn)
I COd: I-V-9 (with VV)

Fragment:

'...O felix gloria'
B Bc: 1057

Ed. Carlo Dell'Argine (Florence: OTOS, 1972)

? Exultate colles (B VV vc)

GB Cfm: 32 G 30, 37-44

[B enters in bar 11 with material derived from the above.]

Exurge cor meum (S VV vlne)

Carissimi, Arion Romanus...
(Konstanz, 1670)

Felicitas beatorum (SSS)

See 'Exultabunt justi'

Feriae quintae in coena Domini
(mS and S)

See 'Lamentationes Jeremiae
Prophetae' (mS and S)

x **Fideles animae** (SB)

F Pc: Rés.Vm^b.ms.6, 70-1
GB Cfm: 32 G 30, 28-31

M. Cazzati, <u>Tributo di sagri
concerti... op.23</u> (Bologna,
1660; 2/Antwerp, 1663;
3/Antwerp, 1669)

? **Filiae Jerusalem** (SSSB VV)

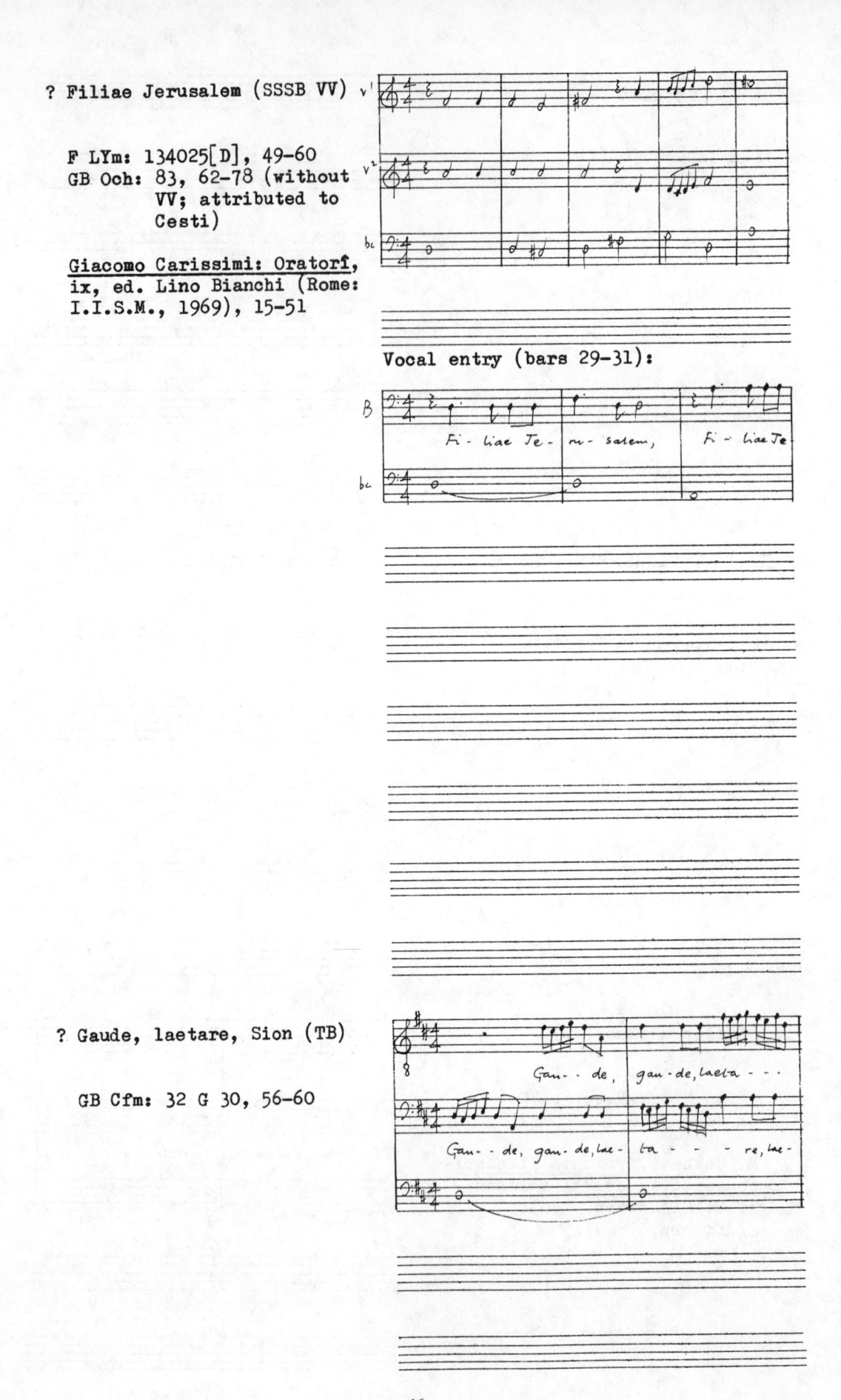

F LYm: 134025[D], 49-60
GB Och: 83, 62-78 (without
    VV; attributed to
    Cesti)

<u>Giacomo Carissimi: Oratori</u>,
ix, ed. Lino Bianchi (Rome:
I.I.S.M., 1969), 15-51

Vocal entry (bars 29-31):

? **Gaude, laetare, Sion** (TB)

GB Cfm: 32 G 30, 56-60

x Gaudeamus omnes (SATB)

GB Cfm: 32 G 30, 99-105^v

M. Cazzati, Tributo di sagri concerti... op.23 (Bologna, 1660; 2/Antwerp, 1663; 3/Antwerp, 1669)

The Fitzwilliam Music...published by Vincent Novello (London, 1825), i, 35-41

Recueil des Morceaux de Musique ancienne, ... (Paris, 1843 ff.), viii

Ed. Malcolm L. Lawson (London, [1880])

Ed. ? (London, [1903])

Ed. Aimé Steck (Paris, 1955)

(In the publications from 1825 onwards it is attributed to Carissimi.)

...Gaudeat ergo... (ATB no bc)

See 'Desiderata nobis'

Gaudeat terra (SS)

S Uu: Vok.mus. i hdskr. Caps. 11: no.12

x **Gaudete cum Maria** (SSB)

Attributed to F. Foggia in the anthology <u>R. Floridus ...has alteras sacras cantiones...</u> (Rome, 1645) (to the words 'Deduxit illum Dominus' (q.v.))

Attributed to Carissimi in the collection <u>Arion Romanus ...</u> (Konstanz, 1670) (to the words 'Gaudete cum Maria')

? **Gaudete exercitus** (SSB)

GB Och: 13, 163-4
GB Och: 53, 118-21

x Gaudia felices (SS)

F Pc: Rés.F.934^b, 121-5

B. Graziani, Motetti...
libro terzo, op.7 (Rome,
1656; 2/Rome, 1657;
3/Rome, 1658)

...Gloria Patri (ATB VV)

See 'In te Domine speravi'

x Gloria Patri (SSTB no bc)

GB Ob: Mus.Sch.c.9, 86

Attributed to Matthew Locke
in:
GB Bu: M.5002, 242

See Rosamond E. M. Harding,
A Thematic Catalogue of the
Works of Matthew Locke...
(Oxford, 1971), p.26, no.35

...Glory be to the Father (SSB)

See 'Confitebor tibi' (SSB)

x Haec dies quam fecit Dominus (SS)

GB Cfm: 32 G 30, 31-3

M. Cazzati, <u>Tributo di sagri concerti... op.23</u> (Bologna, 1660; 2/Antwerp, 1663; 3/Antwerp, 1669)

<u>Hodie Salvator mundi</u> (SSATB VV vdg)

S Uu: Bd.79, no.1

Vocal entry (bars 21-6):

Hodie Simon Petrus (TT)

B Bc: 1057
F Pc: Rés.F.934c, 53-6
GB Lam: 107, 124-6
GB Lbl: Add.17835, 7v-8v
GB Lbl: Add.31412, 59v-60v
GB Lbl: Add.31472, 25v-27
GB Och: 13, 121-3
GB Och: 53, 25-8
GB T: 900, 6-9
GB Y: M.35/6(S) (scored for SS)

<u>Giacomo Carissimi: Messe e Mottetti</u>, ed. Lino Bianchi (Rome: I.I.S.M., 1960), 68-73

Hymnum jucunditatis (SS)

F Pn: Vm¹.1268, no.3

<u>R. Floridus...has alteras sacras cantiones...</u> (Rome, 1645)

Carissimi, <u>Arion Romanus...</u> (Konstanz, 1670)

Immensus coeli conditor (SS)

A KR: L 12, 20-25
F Pn: Vm¹.1268, no.5
I Bc: Q 45, 95v-99v

x In memoriam suorum
  mirabilium (SAT)

D-brd MÜs: Sant.Hs.901

...In sonitu tubae (S[SS])

See 'Egredimini caelestes curiae'

In te, Domine, speravi
(ATB VV vdg)

F Pn: Vm¹.1267, no.12
F Pn: Vm¹.1638-39
GB Lcm: 1064, 2ᵛ-3ᵛ (B only)
GB Ob: Mus.c.24, 32-40ᵛ
GB Ob: Mus.Sch.c.12-19 and 20-23
GB Och: 4
GB T: 335, 226-37

Fragment:

...Gloria Patri
GB Och: 53, 166-71

[continued...

[continuation of 'In te, Domine, speravi']

Carissimi, Missa a quinque et a novem, cum selectis quibusdam cantionibus... (Cologne, 1666)

? In te, Domine, spes mea (SS)

F Pc: Rés.Vm^b.ms.6, 60-2

x In tribulationibus (SS)

F Pn: Vm^1.1738

A. Antonelli, in the anthologies *Scelta di motetti...* (Rome, 1647) and *Delectus sacrarum cantionum...* (Antwerp, 1652)

? In voce exultationis
(SSATTB)

D-ddr Bds: 3103 (score)
D-ddr Bds: 3103/1 (parts)

Incipit lamentatio Jeremiae
Prophetae (mS)

See 'Lamentationes'

x Incipit lamentatio Jeremiae
Prophetae (SA VV)

GB Ob: Mus.d.215

Incipit oratio Jeremiae Prophetae
(S)

A KR: L 146, 84-5 (Alessandro
      Poglietti, Compendium...
      (1676))

Inclinavit caelos Dominus (TT)

F Pn: Vm¹.1174, no.24

A copy of the motet was owned by
the St. Michaelisschule at Lüneburg while F. E. Praetorius was
Kantor there (1655-95); see Max
Seiffert, 'Die Chorbibliothek
der St. Michaelisschule in Lüneburg zu Seb. Bach's Zeit',
SIMG, ix(1907-08), 593-621, and
in particular 602.

**Insurrexerunt in nos inimici
nostri** (mSAT)

F Pc: Rés.F.934ᵃ, 205-16
F Pc: Rés.Vmᵇ.ms.6, 10-11
F Pn: Vm¹.1267, no.3
GB Lam: 41, 115-25
GB Lbl: Add.31479
GB T: 1425, 34-42 (now in F Pn)
I Bc: X 233, 24ᵛ-26
S Uu: Tab.Caps.83: no.13
S Uu: Vok.mus. i hdskr. Caps.
      11: no.13

[continued...

[continuation of 'Insurrexerunt in nos inimici nostri']

S Uu: Vok.mus. i hdskr. Caps. 53: no.10/20

Sacrarum modulationum... (Rome, 1642)

Teatro musicale de concerti ecclesiastici... (Milan, 1649)

R. Floridus...has sacras cantiones... (Rome, 1651)

Teatro musicale... (2/Milan, 1653)

? Ipse praeibit ante illum (SSTB)

A Wn: SA.68.Aa.111
D-brd Mbs: Mus.ms.565, 30^v-33^v
D-brd Mbs: Mus.ms.720, 9^v-
D-brd MÜs: Sant.Hs.896
D-ddr Bds: 3101, no.1
F Pc: Rés.2182(I), no.12
GB T: 746, 23-7
NL At: Ms-Cari-2, [76-81]

x Iste sanctus pro lege Dei sunt (ATB)

F Pc: Rés.F.934^a, 239-45

F. Foggia, Sacrae cantiones ...op.8 (Rome, 1665)

? Isti sunt triumphatores et amici Dei (ATB)

F Pc: Rés.Vm^b.ms.6, 22-3

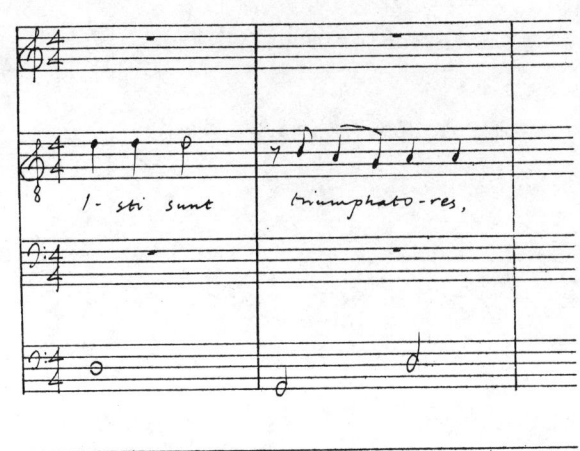

? Isti sunt triumphatores sancti (SSATB)

S Uu: Vok.mus. i hdskr. Caps.11:2

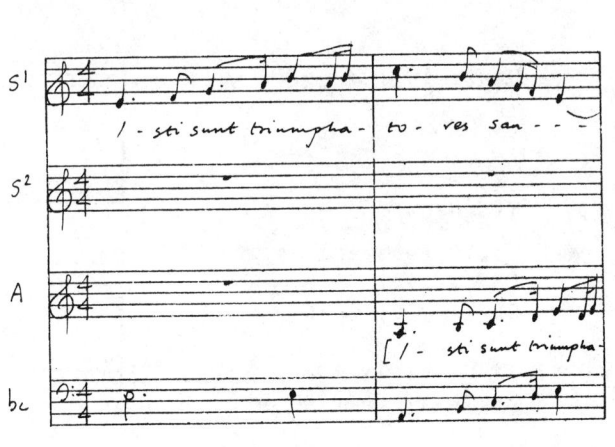

Jubilemus omnes (SSB)

S Uu: Vok.mus. i hdskr. Caps.11: no.14

Ed. Ebbe Selén (Kassel: Bärenreiter, 1973)

57

? Laeta caelestibus (S VV)

F Pc: Rés.Vm^b.ms.6, 84-8

[S enters in bar 15]

x Laetamini... (S VV vc)

GB T: 936, 36-41

Fragment:

'...O veneranda Aurora'
(SS VV vc)
GB T: 936, 42-8

J. H. Wilderer, Modulationi sacre... (Amsterdam, n.d.)

Lamentatio damnatorum

See 'Turbabuntur impii'

Lamentationes Jeremiae Prophetae
(Feriae Quintae in coena Domini)

Lectio Prima: 'Incipit lamentatio Jeremiae Prophetae' (mS)

I Bc: Q 43, 1-4^v

Lectio Seconda: 'Vau. Et egressus
est a filia Sion' (S)

I Bc: Q 43, 5-6^v

? Lapides praetiosi (SmSAT
no bc)

A Wn: SA.68.Aa.111
D-brd Mbs: Mus.ms.2944, 40-41^v
D-brd MÜs: Sant.Hs.1525,
    221-4
D-ddr Bds: 3101, no.4
F Pc: Rés.2182(I), no.12
GB T: 746, 36^v-39

? Lauda Sion (SAB)

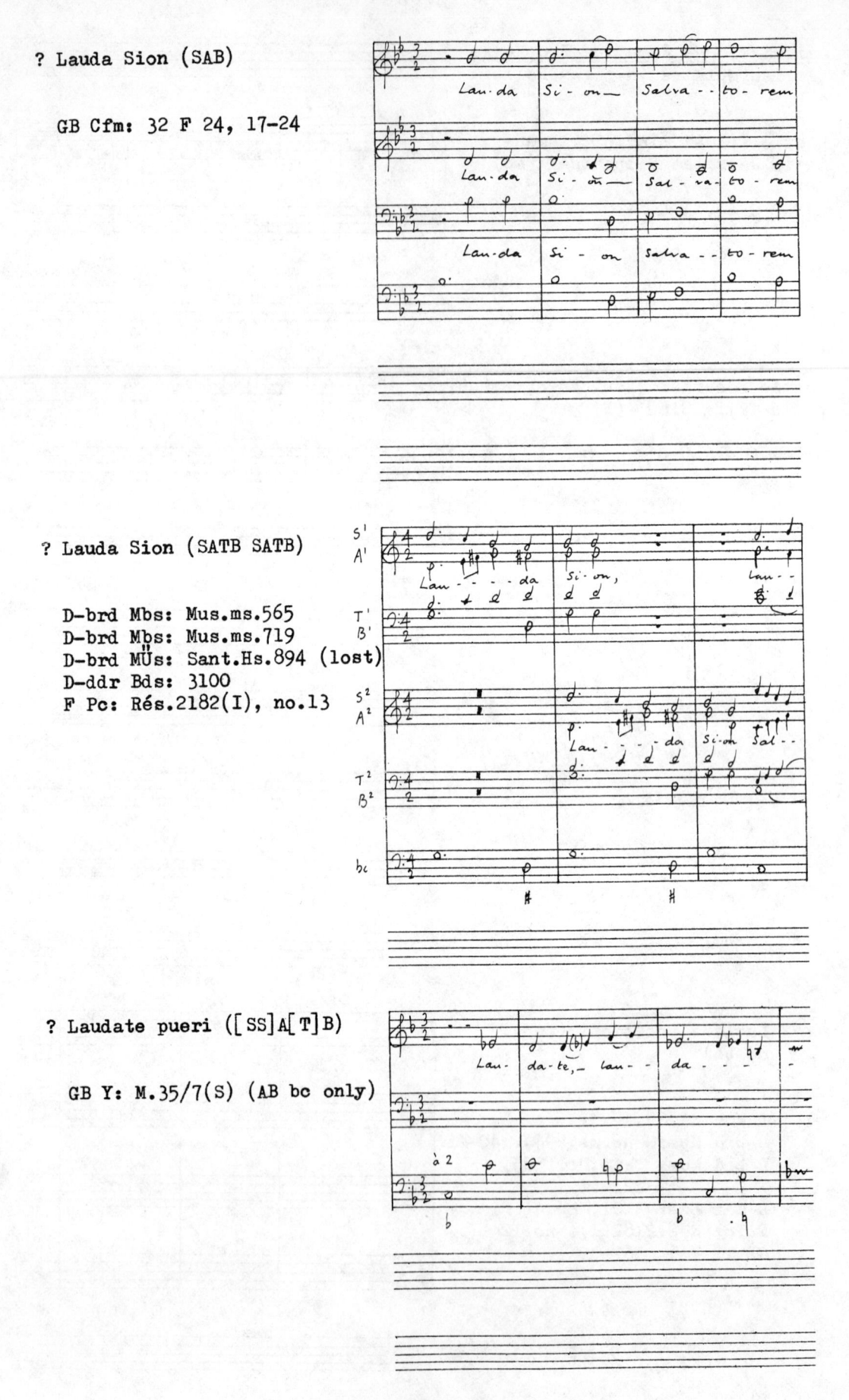

GB Cfm: 32 F 24, 17-24

? Lauda Sion (SATB SATB)

D-brd Mbs: Mus.ms.565
D-brd Mbs: Mus.ms.719
D-brd MÜs: Sant.Hs.894 (lost)
D-ddr Bds: 3100
F Pc: Rés.2182(I), no.13

? Laudate pueri ([SS]A[T]B)

GB Y: M.35/7(S) (AB bc only)

? **Laudate pueri** (SSB)

GB Y: M.35/8(S)

Laudate pueri (SSS)

A Wn: SA.67.C.19
CS KR: III 120
D-brd MÜs: Sant.Hs.895

See Addenda

The incipit on the right is from D-brd MÜs; the CS KR version is given in the Addenda at the end of Appendix A.

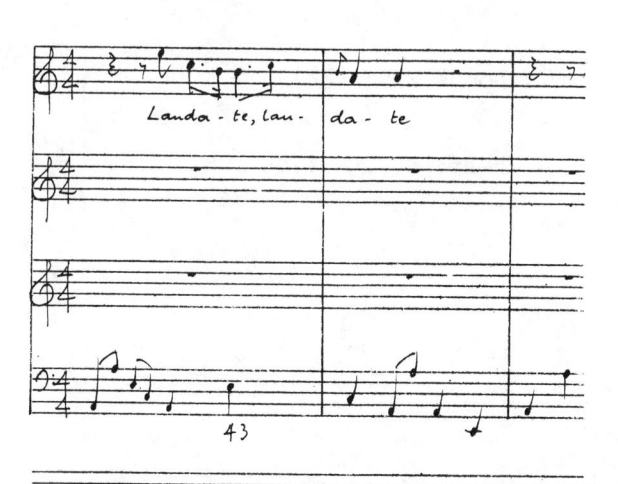

Laudemus virum gloriosum (SS)

F Pc: Rés.F.934^c, 47-52
F Pc: Rés.Vm^b.ms.6, 68-9
GB Cfm: 2 F 22, 12-14^v
GB Cfm: 32 G 30, 113^v-16
GB Lam: 41, 8-13
GB Lbl: Add.17835, 5^v-7^v
GB Lbl: Add.31472, 22^v-25
GB Lcm: 1101, 28-30^v
GB Ob: Mus.Sch.c.9, 187-91
GB Och: 13, 30-4
GB Och: 53, 36-41

[continued...

[continuation of 'Laudemus virum gloriosum']

GB T: 926, 46-52

<u>Scelta di motetti...</u> (Rotterdam, 1656)

Carissimi, <u>Arion Romanus...</u> (Konstanz, 1670)

Carissimi, <u>Sacri concerti musicali...</u> (Rome, 1675)

See Addenda

x Locus iste (SA)

D-brd Mbs: Mus.ms.105

Lucifer (B [or S])

F LYm: 133989, 85-9
F Pc: Rés.F.934^c, 13-17
F Pn: Vm^1.1306
GB Bu: 5002, 252-5
GB Cfm: 24 F 4, 82^v-84^v
GB Cmc: 2803, 80^v-87^v
GB Lam: 41, 133-7
GB Lbl: Add.22100, 56^v-58^v
GB Lbl: Add.31460, 5-7^v
GB Lbl: Add.31479
GB Lbl: Add.33234, 13-14^v
[continued...]

[continuation of 'Lucifer']

GB Lbl: Add.33235, 103-4^v
GB Lbl: Egerton 2960, 2-4
GB Och: 18, 23-5
GB Och: 23, 2^v-3^v
GB Och: 53, 5-9
GB Och: 598, 24-22 (voice part only)
GB T: 1031, 134-6

Harmonia sacra: ... The second book... (London, 1693; 2/London, 1714; 3/London, 1726)

Ed. Rudolf Ewerhart, Cantio Sacra, xxxvii (Cologne: Edmund Bieler, forthcoming)

x Magnificat anima mea Mariam (SA)

GB Lbl: Add.31475, 21^v-27

M. Cazzati, Motetti a due voci... op.10 (Venice, 1648; 2/Antwerp, 1665)

[bc is left blank in GB Lbl Add.31475]

Martyres (SST VV L)

See 'Tollite sancti mei'

? **Mihi autem nimis honorati sunt amici** (SSB)

D-brd MÜs: Sant.Hs.1206, 55^v-57^v

Militia est vita hominis (SSB [VV vdg])

D-brd Hs: M B/1979
F Pc: Rés.F.934^c, 80-88
F Pc: Rés.Vm^b.ms.6, 12-13
GB Lam: 41, 143-53
GB Lbl: Add.31472, 38^v-42
GB Lbl: Add.33235, 4-7
GB Lcm: 1064, 4-4^v (B only)
GB Ob: Mus.c.57, 92^v-96^v
GB Ob: Mus.Sch.c.12-19 and 20-23 (with VV vdg)
GB Och: 13, 145-8
GB Och: 53, 58-64
GB T: 335, 128-35
GB T: 728, 39^v-44
GB T: 926, 178-90
GB T: 958, 128-   (lost)
GB T: 1424, 44-51 (now in F Pn)
I PS: B 25 n.3, [3^v-4] (V only)

<u>Floridus concentus sacras continens laudes...</u> (Rome, 1643)

<u>Floridus...has sacras cantiones...</u> (Rome, 1652)

<u>Musica romana...</u> (Bamberg, 1665) (SSB VV)

<u>Carissimi, Missa a quinque et a novem, cum selectis quibusdam cantionibus...</u> (Cologne, 1666) (SSB VV vdg)

64

Mortalis homo quid non recordaris (S)

Carissimi, *Arion Romanus...* (Konstanz, 1670)

The music also survives as a cantata, set to the words 'No, no, mio core'. See Gloria Rose, *The Wellesley Edition Cantata Index Series, Fascicle 5* (Wellesley College, 1966), and Chapter Two of the present book.

Nigra es sed formosa (SS)

Recueil de motets choisis... (Paris, 1712)

Nigra sum sed formosa (SS)

D-ddr Bds: W.68
F Pn: Vm¹.1268, no.4
GB Lam: 41, 162-5
GB Lcm: 1076, 6ᵛ-7ᵛ
GB Lk: R.M.24.c.10(2), 69-72
GB Ob: Mus.c.57, 11-12ᵛ

R. Floridus...has alias sacras cantiones... (Rome, 1650)

65

x Nisi Dominus aedificaverit
   (S VV)

D-brd Mbs: Mus.ms.102

? Nisi Dominus aedificaverit
   (SATB SATB)

D-brd Müs: Sant.Hs.2333
            (lost)
  F Pc: L.11.897(3), 100ᵛ-07ᵛ

? Nisi Dominus aedificaverit
  (SSATB)

GB Cfm: 32 G 30, 106-11

Ed. Janet Beat (London: Novello, 1974)

x Non turbetur cor vestrum
  (SB)

GB Och: 688 (S and bc only)

...Nos quoque socii

See 'Quis est hic vir' (SSS)

? **Notus in Judaea Deus** (STB)

F Pc: Rés.F.934^b, 185-97

? **O admirabile commercium** (SSB)

F LYm: 28329, 38-44
F Pc: Rés.F.934^b, 126-34

x **O anima festina** (SATB VV vc)

GB T: 936, 210-54

J. H. Wilderer, <u>Modulationi sacre...</u> (Amsterdam, n.d.)

Ed. Jack Pilgrim [attributed to Carissimi] (Hilversum: Harmonia-Uitgave, 1971) x O anima mea suspira (SA)

GB Lbl: Add.31475, 14^v-21

M. Cazzati, Motetti a due voci... op.10 (Venice, 1648; 2/Antwerp, 1665)

[bc is left blank in GB Lbl Add.31475]

O anima mea suspira (SS/TT)

No musical source known.

A copy of the motet was owned by the St. Michaelisschule at Lüneburg while F. E. Praetorius was Kantor there (1655-95); see Max Seiffert, 'Die Chorbibliothek der St. Michaelisschule in Lüneburg zu Seb. Bach's Zeit', SIMG, ix(1907-08), 593-621, and in particular 602.

x O beata virgo Maria (SSS)

Carissimi, Arion Romanus... (Konstanz, 1670)

F. Foggia, Concentus ecclesiastici duarum, trium, quattuor et quinque vocum... (Rome, 1645)

F. Foggia, in the anthology Musica Romana... (Bamberg, 1665)

x O beatae caeli mentes (AA)

GB Cfm: 32 F 24, 24ᵛ-27

M. Cazzati, Sacri concerti di motetti a due voci... op.34 (Bologna, 1664)

O beatum virum (SSA)

Floridus concentus sacras continens laudes... (Rome, 1643)

Carissimi, Arion Romanus... (Konstanz, 1670)

x O bonitas, o amor (SSB)

F LYm: 134025[A], 7-11 (anon; see section X in Chapter 3)

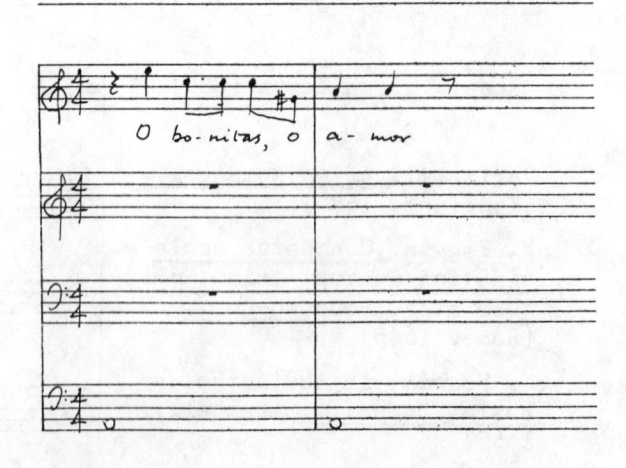

x O crux benedicta (ATB)

    GB Ob: Mus.Sch.c.12-19

    G. F. Sances, **Motetti...**
    (Venice, 1638)

x O crux nobilitata (AT)

    GB Lbl: Add.31475, 33ᵛ-38ᵛ

    M. Cazzati, **Motetti a due voci... op.10** (Venice, 1648; 2/Antwerp, 1665)

[bc is left blank in GB Lbl Add.31475]

O dulcissime Jesu (SS)

D-brd MÜs: Sant.Hs.3679, 117-20
F Pc: Rés.F.934ᵃ, 246-50
F Pc: Rés.Vmᵇ.ms.6, 50-51
GB T: 1423, 57-61 (now in F Pn)

Carissimi, **Arion Romanus...**
(Konstanz, 1670)

R. Floridus...**sacras cantiones...**
(Rome, 1672)

O dulcissimum Mariae nomen (SS)

D-brd MÜs: Sant.Hs.3298, 16-22
D-ddr Bds: W.103
GB Ob: Mus.d.26, 1-4
GB Och: 13, 117-18
GB T: 1423, 53-6 (now in F Pn)
S Uu: Tab.Caps.83: no.62a (to the words 'O mi chare Jesu Christe')

<u>Scelta di motetti...</u> (Rome, 1647)

<u>Delectus sacrarum cantionum...</u>
(Antwerp, 1652)

x ...**O felix anima**... (ATB)

See 'Audite gentes'

...**O felix gloria** (SSS)

See 'Exultabunt justi'

72

x O ignis qui semper ardes
(SST)

F Pc: Rés.Vm^b.ms.6, 24-5

F. Foggia, in the anthology
Sacrarum modulationum...
(Rome, 1642)

O ignis sancte (SS)

Fragment:

'...Veni consolator suspirantis'
D-brd MÜs: Sant.Hs.2758, 22-4

Printed (complete):

Scelta de'motetti... (Rome, 1667;
2/Rome, 1667, under the title
Sacras cantiones...)

? O impii mortales (ATB VV)

F Pn: Vm^1.1639

O mi chare Jesu Christe (SS)

See 'O dulcissimum Mariae nomen'

x O miracula, o prodigia (S)

F Pn: Vm7.3, 37-47

P. P. Vannini, in the anthology R. Floridus...has alias sacras cantiones... (Rome, 1659)

? O miraculum miraculorum (SB)

F Pc: Rés.F.934^b, 234-46
F Pc: Rés.Vm^b.ms.6, 63-5

x O mortalis quid mundanas (ATB)

F Pn: Vm¹.1175bis, 515-24

S. Durante, in the anthology R. Floridus...istas alias sacras cantiones... (Rome, 1664), to the words 'O mortalis nimis fralis'

? O piissime Jesu (ATB)

F Pc: Rés.F.934^b, 44-50

Ed. Charles Bordes, Concerts Spirituels (Série Ancienne)... (Paris, [c.1905]), v, 7-13 (transposed down a semitone)

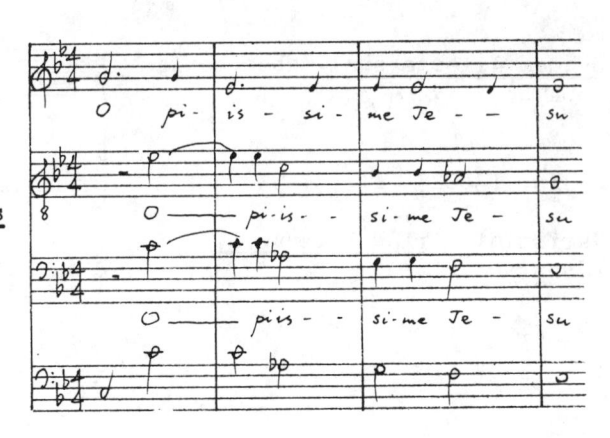

O pretiosum et admirandum convivium (S [V])

GB Lcm: 1180 (with V)
I COd: I-V-10 (S only)

x O quam clemens (SS)

F Pc: Rés.F.934^b, 37-43

Attributed to F. Foggia in
the manuscript source:
F Pn: Vm^1.1185

Attributed to A. Vermeren
in the printed anthology:
Florida verba... (Antwerp,
1661)

O quam dilecta sunt tabernacula
(SSATB)

F LYm: 134025 [A], 47-51

Carissimi, Arion Romanus...
(Konstanz, 1670)

O quam mirabilia sunt (SS)

GB Lam: 40, 202-6
GB Lam: 41, 138-43
GB Lam: 42, 183-88
GB Lam: 50, 46-55
GB Lbl: Add.31477, 65-66
GB Ob: Mus.d.26, 21-27
GB Ob: Mus.Sch.c.9, 31-37
GB Och: 55, 34-37

Scelta di motetti sacri...
(Rome, 1675)

O quam pulchra es (S)

GB Lbl: Add.29292, 46-57^v
GB Lcm: 2038, 31-34^v

Ed. Rudolf Ewerhart, Cantio Sacra, lvii (Cologne: Edmund Bieler, 1964)

x O quam pulchra et casta es (SS)

GB Lbl: Add.31475, 1-5

M. Cazzati, Motetti a due voci... op.10 (Venice, 1648; 2/Antwerp, 1665)

[bc is left blank in GB Lbl Add.31475]

? O quam suave (SSS)

GB Lbl: Add.31477, 18^v-21^v (later attribution to Carissimi)
GB Och: 83, 117-24 (later attribution to Carissimi)
GB T: 926, 126-37 (original attribution to Carissimi)

[continued...

[continuation of 'O quam suave']

Other sources, either anonymous or with an attribution to Bassani:
    GB Lbl: Add.31399, 95-99ᵛ
        (original attribution to Bassani)
    GB Lcm: 995, 87-

    GB Ob: Mus.Sch.c.9, 87-94
        (later attribution to Bassani)
    GB T: 335, 209-
        (original attribution to Bassani)

Cf. Chapter Three, section XIX

Probably a fragment:
    '...Stillate rores'
    GB T: 958, 146-   (lost)

x O quam terribilis est (SS)

    S Uu: Vok.mus. i hdskr. Caps.11: no.16 (The original scribe attributes it to Vincenzo Albrici; the attributions to Carissimi are made by later hands. It is attributed to Albrici also in S Uu Tab.Caps.29: 8a.)

x O Regina coeli (SA)

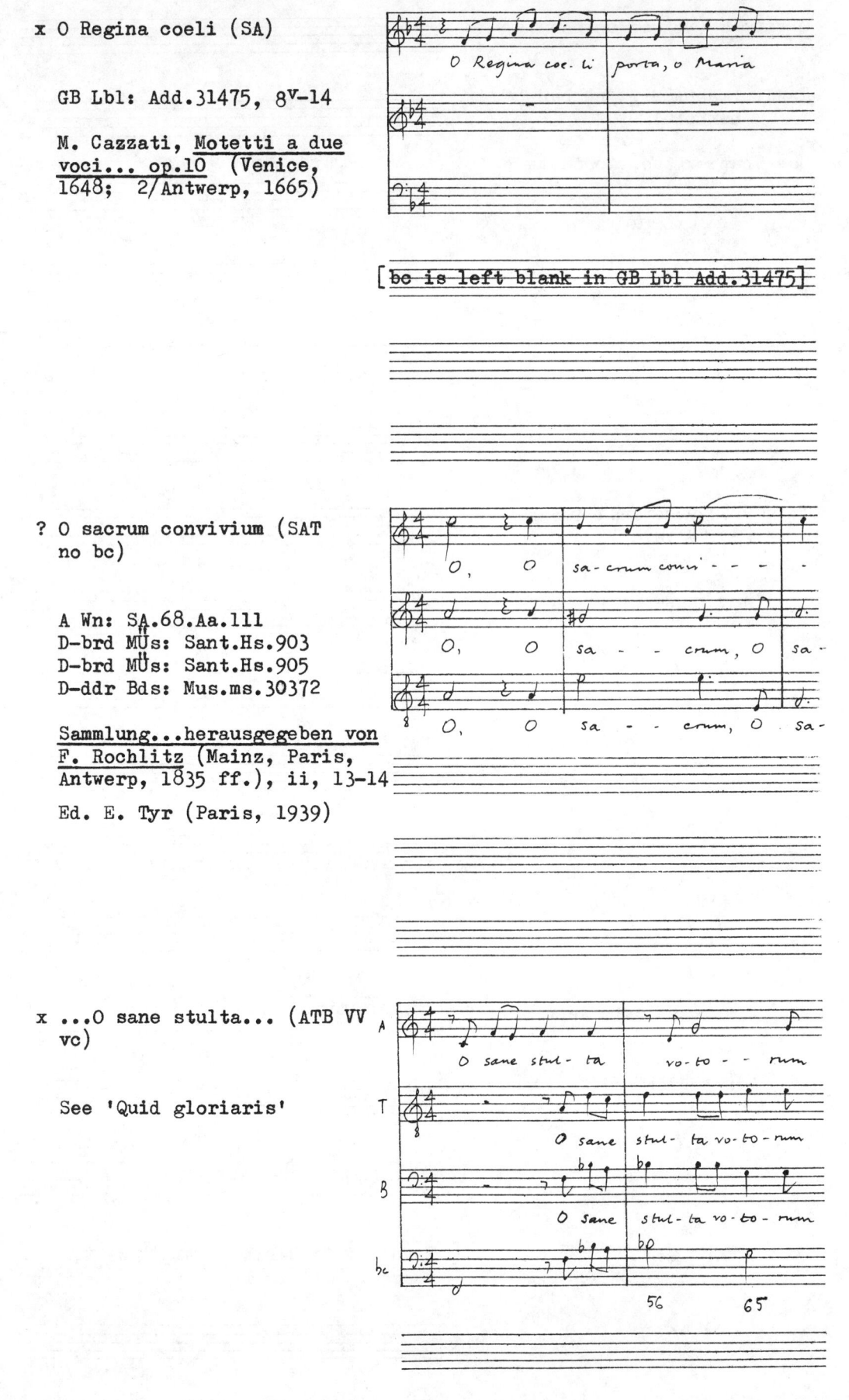

GB Lbl: Add.31475, 8^v-14

M. Cazzati, *Motetti a due voci... op.10* (Venice, 1648; 2/Antwerp, 1665)

[bc is left blank in GB Lbl Add.31475]

? O sacrum convivium (SAT no bc)

A Wn: SA.68.Aa.111
D-brd MÜs: Sant.Hs.903
D-brd MÜs: Sant.Hs.905
D-ddr Bds: Mus.ms.30372

Sammlung...herausgegeben von F. Rochlitz (Mainz, Paris, Antwerp, 1835 ff.), ii, 13-14

Ed. E. Tyr (Paris, 1939)

x ...O sane stulta... (ATB VV vc)

See 'Quid gloriaris'

79

O stupor (voices unknown)

I Ad: (manuscript number
         unknown)

See Chapter One, **footnote 7**.

x ...O veneranda Aurora
     (SS VV vc)

See 'Laetamini'

? O vere et care Jesu (TB VV)

F Pc: Rés.F.934^b, 13-24

[T enters in bar 12 with Vl's
  thematic material.]

? O vita cui omnia vivunt (A)

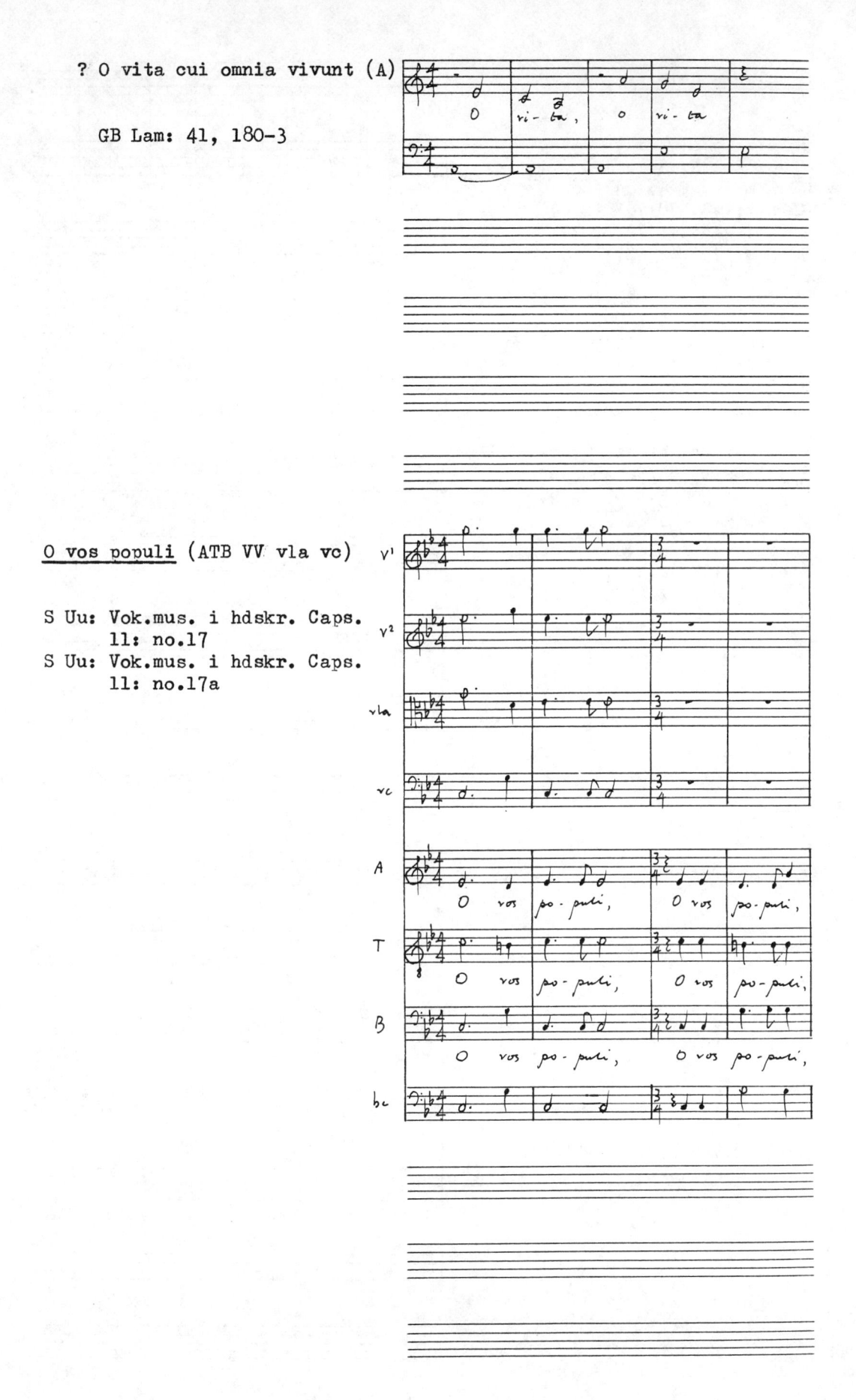

GB Lam: 41, 180-3

O vos populi (ATB VV vla vc)

S Uu: Vok.mus. i hdskr. Caps.
11: no.17
S Uu: Vok.mus. i hdskr. Caps.
11: no.17a

O vulnera doloris (B)

B Bc: 1057
F Pc: Rés.F.934c, 1-4
GB Cfm: 24 F 4, 84v-86
GB Lam: 43, 78-76v (sic)
GB Lbl: Add.31472, 2-3v
GB Lcm: 791, 25-27v
GB Lcm: 793, 5-6
GB Och: 13, 215-20 (for SSB a tone lower)
GB Och: 13, 123 (for B, incomplete)
GB Och: 46, 12v-14
GB Och: 53, 1-4
GB Och: 1210 (bc only)

Ed. Charles Bordes, Concerts Spirituels (Série Ancienne) ... (Paris, [c.1905]), v, 1-6

Ed. Rudolf Ewerhart, Cantio Sacra, xvi (Cologne: Edmund Bieler, 1958)

x Obstupescite redem[p]ti (ATB)

D-ddr Dl(b): Mus.1706-E-502

Francesco della Porta, Cantiones... Libri secundi op.3 (Venice, 1648; (2/Antwerp, 1650)

82

x Oleum effusum est (S)

GB Lam: 42, 143-53

...Omnes gentes gaudete...

See 'Quasi columba'

See Addenda

Omnes sancti

See 'Summi regis puerpera'

? Panem coelestem angelorum (SATB)

F Pn: Vm¹.1267, no.8

Panem coelestem angelorum (SS)

Carissimi, Arion Romanus...
(Konstanz, 1670)

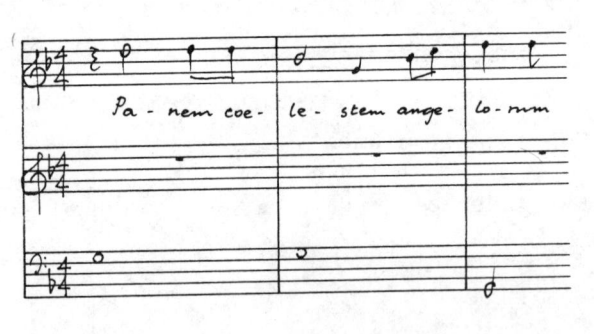

? Pange lingua (SAB)

GB Cfm: 32 G 30, 9-11ᵛ

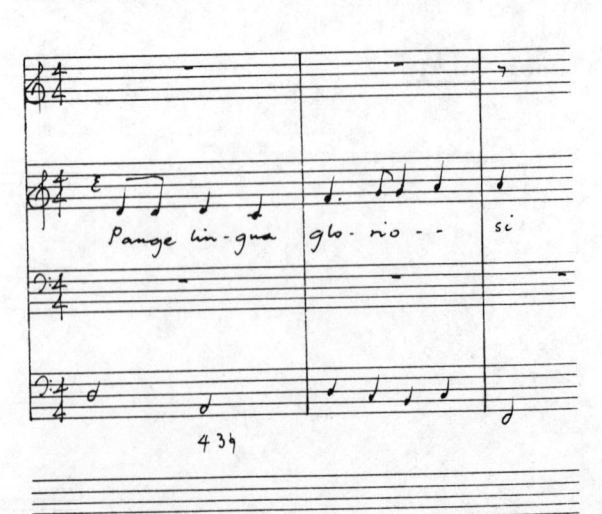

Paratum cor meum (S/B V)

I PS: B 25 n.3, [4^v] (V only)
S Uu: Vok.mus. i hdskr. Caps. 53: no.10/23

Parce, heu, parce jam (SSAB)

S Uu: Tab.Caps.85: no.30
S Uu: Vok.mus. i hdskr. Caps. 11: no.18

Ed. Jack Pilgrim (Hilversum: Harmonia-Uitgave, 1971)

x Pastores dum custodistis (S)

GB Och: 13, 5-11

B. Graziani, in the anthology R. Floridus...has alias sacras cantiones... (Rome, 1659)

x Peccaverunt habitatores
  (SATB)

  F Pc: Rés.Vm^b.ms.6, 88-9
  F Pn: Vm^1.1267, no.9

  Manuscript attribution to
  C. Cecchelli in:
  F Pn: Vm^1.1268^{bis}, no.1

  Printed attribution to
  C. Cecchelli in the
  anthology:
  R. Floridus...has alteras
  sacras cantiones... (Rome,
  1645)

x Peccavi Domine, et
  miserere mei (SAB)

  F LYm: 133721, 29-35
  F Pc: Rés.Vm^b.ms.6, 26-7

  G. Ferrari ('il Modondone'),
  in the anthology Teatro
  musicale... (Milan, 1649;
  2/Milan, 1653)

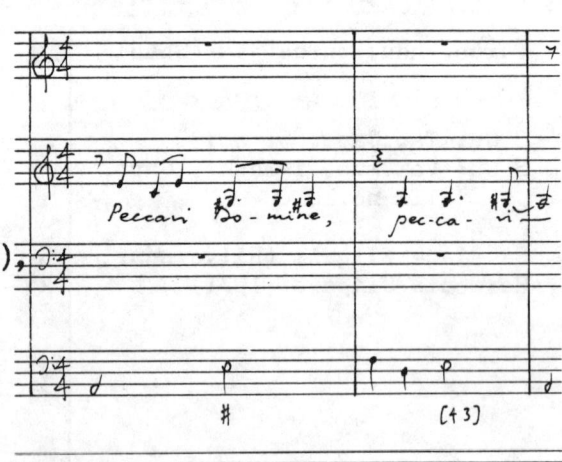

? Peccavi Domine, peccavi
  multum (SSB)

  GB T: 1424, 13-24 (now in
    F Pn)

86

? Peccavi super numerum (SA)

D-brd MÜs: Sant.Hs.1206,
255-8

x ...Per labores ad sudores...
(T VV vc)

See 'Quid gloriaris'

Plaudite caelestes chori (S)

I COd: I-V-12

Praevaluerunt in nos inimici
nostri (mSAT)

B Bc: 1057
D-ddr Bds: W.68
F Pc: Rés.F.934c, 118-25
GB Lbl: Add.31472, 56v-60
GB Ob: Mus.d.26, 28-39
GB Och: 13, 135-9
GB T: 335, 150-6
GB T: 958, 138- (lost)
I Rsc: 3749, 119-21

R. Floridus...Florida verba...
(Rome, 1648; 2/Venice, 1649)

R. Floridus...alias cantiones
sacras... (Rotterdam, 1657)

Florida verba... (Antwerp, 1661)

x Pulchra et decora (SATB)

I Bc: X 233, 6v-7

G. Ghizzolo, Il quarto
libro delli concerti...
op.16 (Venice, 1622;
2/Venice, 1640)

Ed. Francesco Vatielli
[attributed to Carissimi,
and scored for SAT bc only],
Antiche cantate spirituali,
vi (Turin, [1922])

x Quam pulchra es (SSB)

GB Lbl: Add.31479

G. Rovetta, Bicinia sacra
...Liber tertius (Antwerp,
1648; 2/Antwerp, 1668)

(On the differences between
the manuscript and printed
versions see section XIX in
Chapter Three.)

x Quando Jesus adest
(SA VV vc)

GB T: 936, 13-36

J. H. Wilderer, Modulationi sacre... (Amsterdam, n.d.)

? Quare fremuerunt (ATB)

F Pc: Rés.F.934ª, 165-84

x Quare suspiras (SSB)

F Pc: Rés.Vm^b.ms.6, 2-3
F Pn: Vm^l.1175bis, 365-78

F. Foggia, Concentus ecclesiastici binis,... (Rome, 1645; 2/Antwerp, 1658)

Quasi aquila (T VV fag)

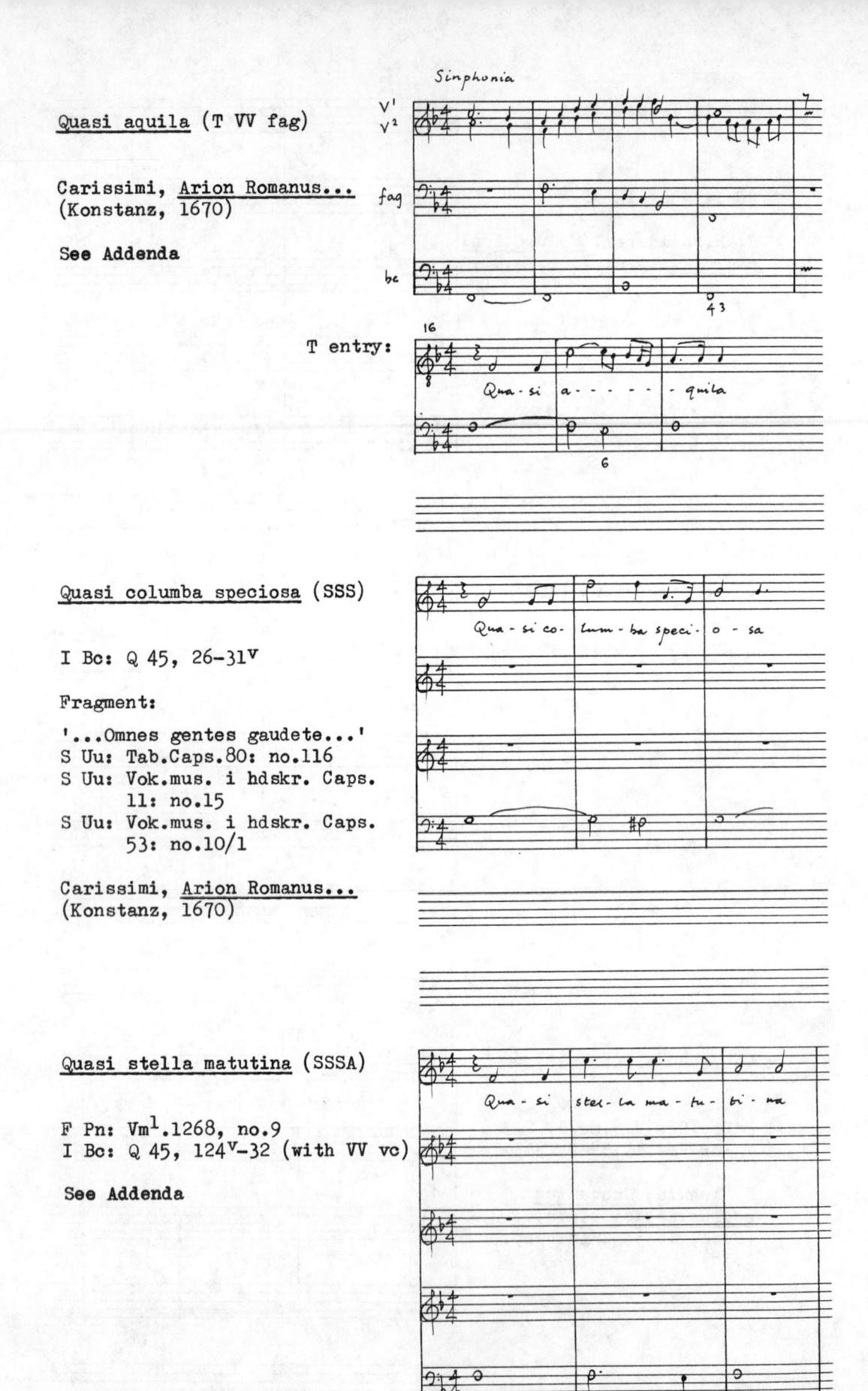

Carissimi, Arion Romanus...
(Konstanz, 1670)

See Addenda

T entry:

Quasi columba speciosa (SSS)

I Bc: Q 45, 26-31^v

Fragment:

'...Omnes gentes gaudete...'
S Uu: Tab.Caps.80: no.116
S Uu: Vok.mus. i hdskr. Caps.
    11: no.15
S Uu: Vok.mus. i hdskr. Caps.
    53: no.10/1

Carissimi, Arion Romanus...
(Konstanz, 1670)

Quasi stella matutina (SSSA)

F Pn: Vm^1.1268, no.9
I Bc: Q 45, 124^v-32 (with VV vc)

See Addenda

? Qui descendunt mare (BB)

F Pc: Rés.F.934ª, 217-26

? Qui non renuntiat (TTB)

F Pc: Rés.F.934ᵇ, 198-210

x Qui vult post me venire (SATB VV vc)

GB T: 936, 179-209

J. H. Wilderer, *Modulationi sacre...* (Amsterdam, n.d.)

x Quid agis cor meum (S)

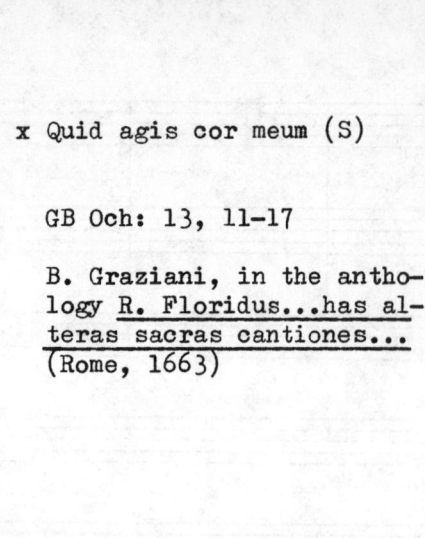

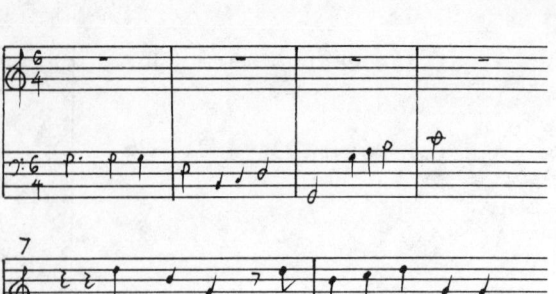

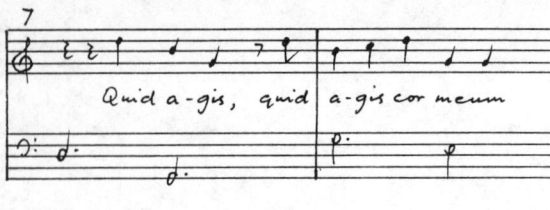

GB Och: 13, 11-17

B. Graziani, in the anthology R. Floridus...has alteras sacras cantiones... (Rome, 1663)

x Quid gloriaris... (ATB)

GB T: 936, 64-6

Fragments:

x '...Per labores ad sudores...' (T VV vc)
GB T: 936, 67-71

x '...O sane stulta...' (ATB VV vc)
GB T: 936, 72-90

x '...Vix homo nascitur' (ATB VV vc)
GB T: 936, 91-105

Printed (complete):

J. H. Wilderer, Modulationi sacre... (Amsterdam, n.d.)

Quid tandem sunt mundi deliciae (ATB)

D-ddr Dl(b): Mus.1706-E-501
S Uu: Vok.mus. i hdskr. Caps. 53: no.9

Quis est hic vir (AB)

Carissimi, Arion Romanus...
(Konstanz, 1670)

Quis est hic vir (SSS)

D-brd Mbs: Sant.Hs.3298, 42-50
D-ddr Bds: W.103
F Pc: Rés.F.934c, 70-79
GB Lbl: Add.31472, 34-38v
GB Och: 13, 129-34
GB Och: 53, 71-9
GB T: 335, 106-12

[continued...

[continuation of 'Quis est hic vir' (SSS)]

Fragment:

'...nos quoque socii' (one S part only)
GB Lcm: 2074, 25^v

Printed (complete):

<u>Motetti d'autori eccellentissimi</u>... (Loreto, 1646)

<u>Scelta di motetti</u>... (Rome, 1647)

<u>Delectus sacrarum cantionum</u>... (Antwerp, 1652)

Quo abiit dilectus meus (SA)

F Pc: Rés.Vm^b.ms.6, 56-9
GB T: 1425, 19-33 (now in F Pn)
I COd: I-V-13

See Addenda

Quo tam laetus (SS)

F Pc: Rés.F.934^c, 39-47
GB Cfm: 32 G 30, 116-20
GB Lam: 41, 13-23
GB Lam: 107, 119-24
GB Lbl: Add.17835, 2-5^v
GB Lbl: Add.31472, 18^v-22^v
GB Lcm: 1101, 31-35^v
GB Ob: Mus.Sch.c.9, 180-7
GB Och: 13, 34-41
GB Och: 53, 29-36

[continued...

[continuation of 'Quo tam laetus']

GB T: 1424, 1^v-12 (now in F Pn)
GB Y: M.35/9(S)
GB Y: M.36/1(S)

Fragment:

'Quo tam laetus...'
GB Cfm: 2 F 22, 14^v-16

Printed (complete):

Carissimi, Arion Romanus... (Konstanz, 1670) (for SST)

Carissimi, Sacri concerti musicali... (Rome, 1675)

See Addenda

Quomodo facti sunt impii (SSB)

F Pc: Rés.Vm^b.ms.6, 16-17
F Pn: Vm^1.1174, no.4
GB Och: 13, 226-9
GB T: 958, 149-[58] (lost)

R. Floridus... Has alias cantiones sacras... (Rome, 1654)

...Quomodo praevenerunt nos

See 'Turbabuntur impii'

? Regina coeli (SAT)

D-brd MÜs: Sant.Hs.1206, 145-45ᵛ

Regina coeli I (SATB no bc)

I Ac: ms N.5, 65ᵛ-66

Regina coeli II (SATB no bc)

I Ac: ms N.5, 76ᵛ-77

? Revertimini praevari-
catores (ATB)

F Pc: Rés.F.934ª, 227-38
F Pc: Rés.Vm^b.ms.6, 30-1
F Pn: Vm¹.1267, no.4

Sacerdotes Dei (SS)

S Uu: Tab.Caps.83: no.64
S Uu: Vok.mus. i hdskr.
   Caps.45: no.9

Salve amor noster (SS)

D-brd MÜs: Sant.Hs.3298,
   138-45
F Pn: Vm¹.1174, no.17
F Pn: Vm¹.1175bis, 288-301
GB Cfm: 32 G 30, 44^v-48

Fragment:

'Salve amor noster...'
GB Cfm: 2 F 22, 7-8^v

[continued...

97

[continuation of 'Salve amor noster']

Printed (complete):
Scelta de'motetti... (Rome, 1665)

x Salve Jesu spes nostra (SAB)

F Pc: Rés.F.934^b, 251-60

G. Carisio, Sacri concerti...op.1 (Venice, 1664)

[Key signature sic in the F Pc ms; there is no key signature in the 1664 publication.]

Salve puellule (S or T)

F Pn: Vm⁹.ms.8 (i), 160-77 (a copy of F Pc: Rés. Vm⁷.673, the Manuscrit Rost, which may not be seen) (for T VV bc)
F Pn: Vm¹.1267bis
GB Lbl: Add.29292, 16-25^v
GB Lcm: 2038, 35-38

Ed. Rudolf Ewerhart, Cantio Sacra, xlviii (Cologne: Edmund Bieler, 1961)

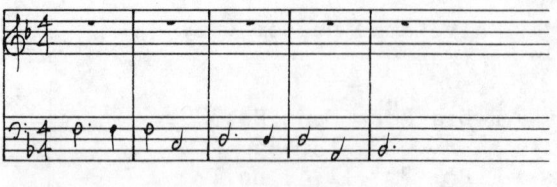

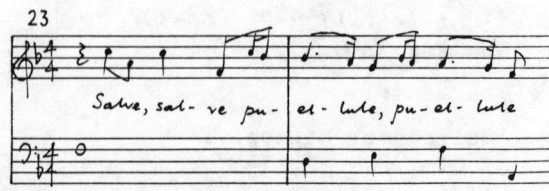

See Addenda

x Salve Regina (ATB)

GB Lbl: Add.31476, 4ᵛ-8ᵛ
GB Lbl: Add.31477, 54ᵛ-57
GB Lcm: 1064, 8ᵛ (bc only)
GB Ob: Mus.Sch.c.9, 46-50

N. Monferrato, *Motetti Concertati... Libro Primo. op.3* (Venice, 1655;
2/Venice, 1660;
3/Antwerp, 1660;
4/Antwerp, 1668)

Salve Regina (SATB SATB)

S Uu: Vok.mus. i hdskr. Caps. 11: no.19

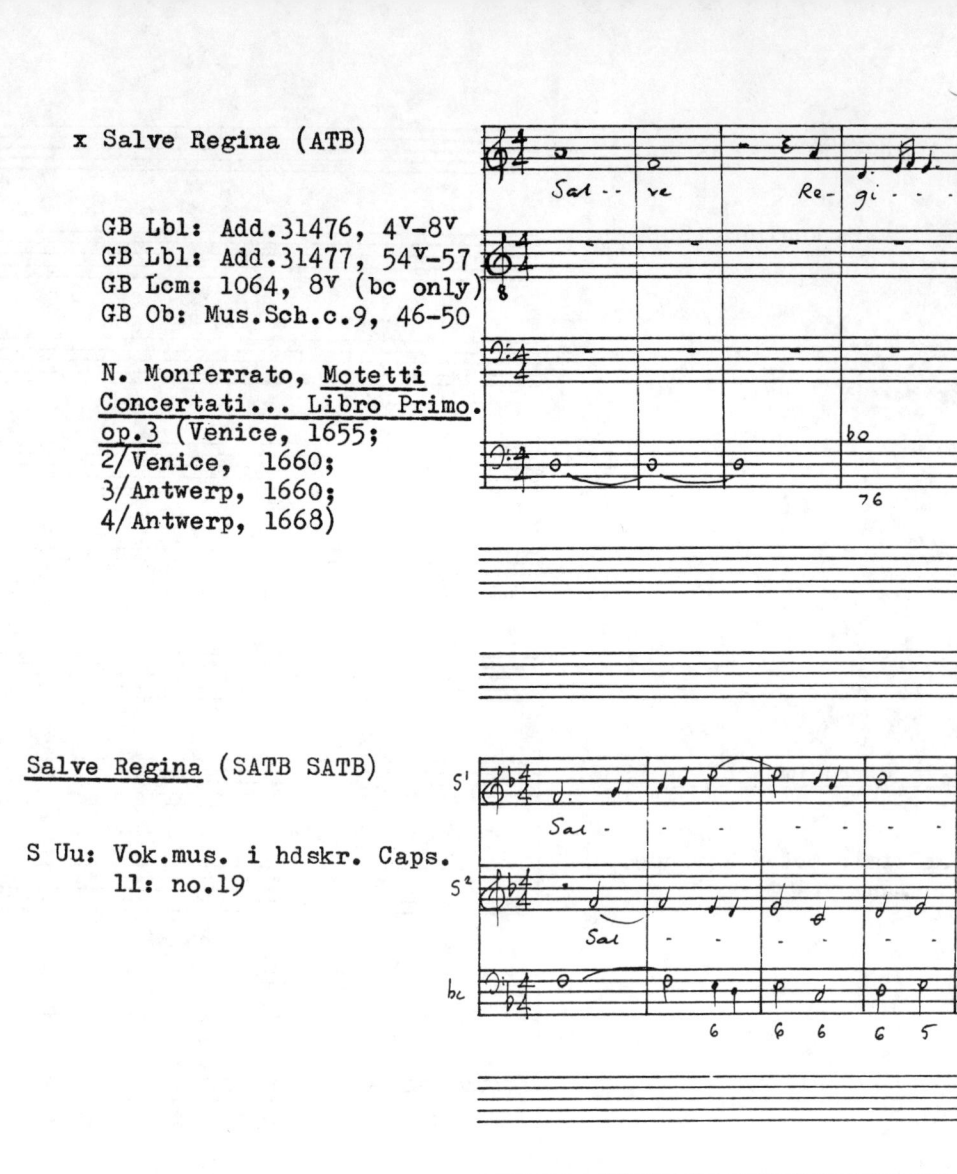

Salve Regina (SSB)

F Pc: Rés.Vmᵇ.ms.6, 32-3
F Pn: Vm¹.1174, no.3
F Pn: Vm¹.1268, no.6
S Uu: Tab.Caps.80: no.117
S Uu: Vok.mus. i hdskr.Caps. 11: no.20
S Uu: Vok.mus. i hdskr. Caps. 53: no.10/6

(In the S Uu manuscripts there is an alternative text: 'Salve Rex Christe'.)

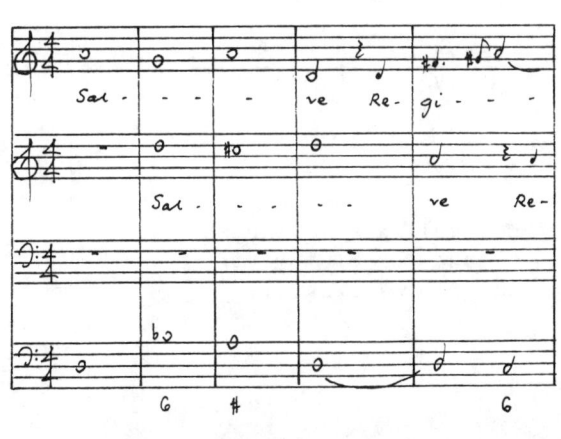

Salve Rex Christe (SSB)

See 'Salve Regina' (SSB)

Salve virgo immaculata (SSB)

Carissimi, *Arion Romanus...*
(Konstanz, 1670)

Sancta et individua Trinitas
(SS VV L or Tb)

A KR: L 13, 16-19

Ed. Wolfgang Fürlinger
(Neuhausen-Stuttgart:
Hänssler-Verlag, 1978)

[The voices enter in bars 21 and 26 with the same thematic material.]

? Sedente Salomone (SSB)

F LYm: 134025[A], 37-9
F Pc: Rés.Vm^b.ms.6, 40-1

? Serve bone et fidelis
(SSAT)

D-brd MÜs: Sant.Hs.
        4222, 90-98

x Si Deus pro nobis (SSB
VV)

S. Fabri, in the anthology R. Floridus...
Florida verba... (Rome, 1648) (SSB only)

S. Fabri, in the anthology Floridus...has sacras cantiones (Rome, 1652) (SSB only)

[continued...

[continuation of 'Si Deus pro nobis']

S. Fabri, in the anthology Scelta di motetti ... (Rotterdam, 1656) (SSB only)

Carissimi, Arion Romanus ... (Konstanz, 1670)

Si linguis hominum (SSS [VV])

F Pc: Rés.F.934ª, 189-204
F Pn: Vm¹.1267, no.6 (SST)
GB Och: 9, 11-14
GB Y: M.35/10(S) (SS[S] V[V]; S3, V2 and bc missing)
I PS: B 25 n.3, [1-1ᵛ] ([SSS] V[V]; only V1 is extant)
S Uu: Tab.Caps.83: no.67 (SSS VV)
S Uu: Vok.mus. i hdskr. Caps. 12: no.1 (SSS VV)

See Addenda

Si qua est consolatio (SSB)

GB Lam: 41, 125-33
I PS: B 25 n.3, [2ᵛ] (V only)
I Rc: 5397
S Uu: Tab.Caps.83: no.2b

Sacrarum modulationum... (Rome, 1642)

R. Floridus...has sacras cantiones... (Rome, 1651)

x Siccine te Domine (ATB)

GB Cfm: 32 G 30, 94-8

M. Cazzati, <u>Tributo di sagri concerti...op.23</u> (Bologna, 1660; 2/Antwerp, 1663; 3/Antwerp, 1669)

? Sicut cervus (SSB)

F Pc: Rés.F.934^b, 135-47

<u>...Sicut erat in principio</u>

See 'Confitebor tibi Domine' (SSB)

Sicut mater consolatur filios suos (SS)

F Pc: Rés.Vm^b.ms.6, 66-7
GB Ob: Mus.d.26, 14-20
GB Ob: Mus.Sch.c.9, 25-30
GB Och: 55, 30-33
GB T: 1225, 1^v-4

Carissimi, <u>Arion Romanus...</u>
(Konstanz, 1670)

Sicut stella matutina (S)

F Pc: Rés.F.934^c, 18-26
F Pn: Vm¹.1306
GB Lam: 43, 91^v-87^v (<u>sic</u>)
GB Lbl: Add.31472, 8-12
GB Och: 53, 17-25
GB Y: M.36/4(S)

Fragment:

'Sicut stella matutina...'
GB Och: 13, 105-7

Printed (complete):

<u>R. Floridus...has alias sacras cantiones...</u> (Rome, 1659)

Carissimi, <u>Arion Romanus...</u>
(Konstanz, 1670)

See Addenda.

Silentium tenebant (SST VV)

F Pc: Rés.Vm^b.ms.6, 80-81
Fragment:
'...Somne laborum dulce levamen'
F Pn: Vm^1.3123, 50-64 (lacks VV and bc)

Simile est regnum coelorum (SS)

S Uu: Tab.Caps.12: no.2
S Uu: Vok.mus. i hdskr. Caps. 53: no.10/12

...Somne laborum dulce levamen
(SSB no bc)

See 'Silentium tenebant'

? Sonent organa (SAB VV)

GB Cfm: 32 G 30, 1-6^v

[The voices enter in bar 11 with the same thematic material.]

? Sponsa Canticorum

See 'Filiae Jerusalem'

? ...Stillate rores

See 'O quam suave'

? Sub umbra Jesu (ATB)

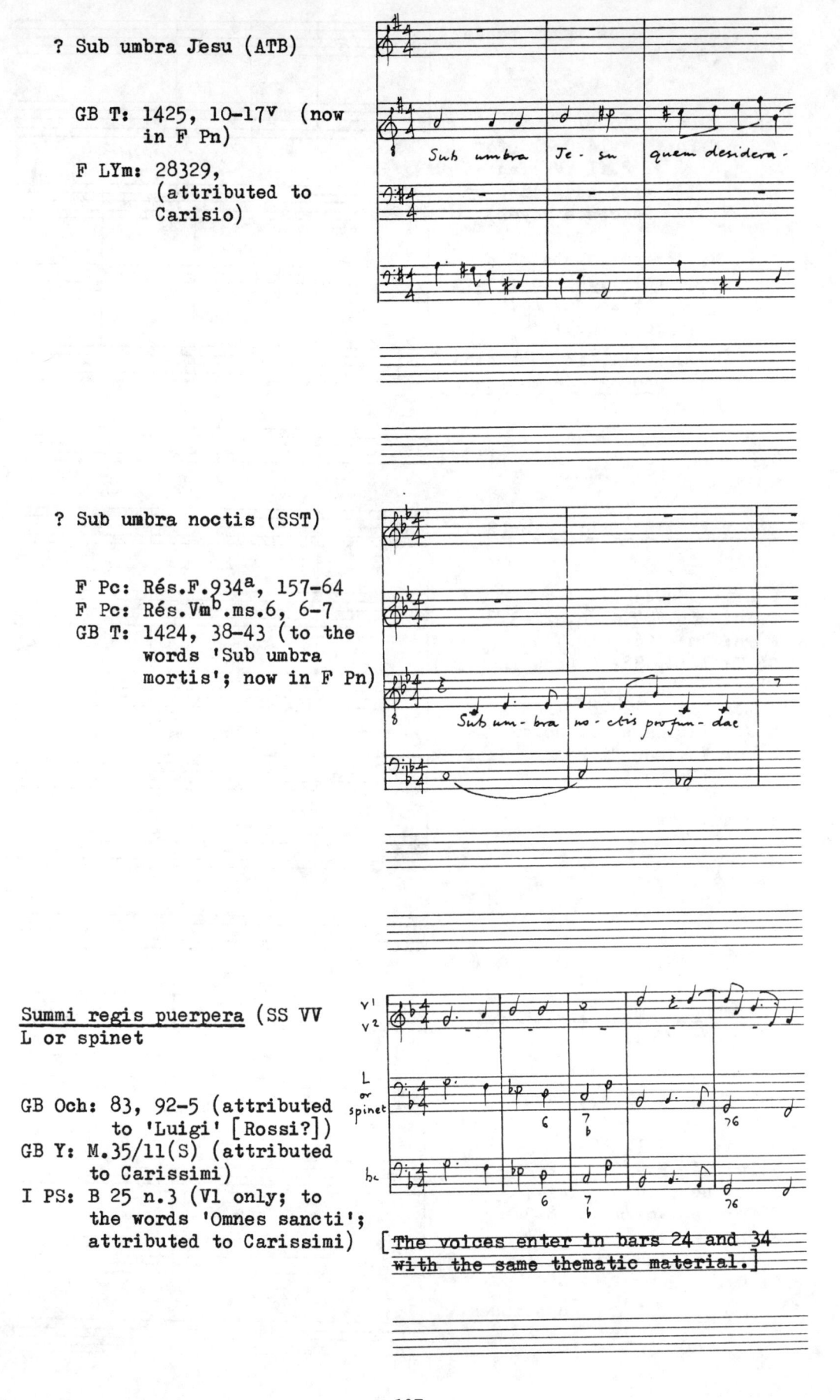

    GB T: 1425, 10-17ᵛ (now in F Pn)
    F LYm: 28329, (attributed to Carisio)

? Sub umbra noctis (SST)

    F Pc: Rés.F.934ᵃ, 157-64
    F Pc: Rés.Vmᵇ.ms.6, 6-7
    GB T: 1424, 38-43 (to the words 'Sub umbra mortis'; now in F Pn)

Summi regis puerpera (SS VV L or spinet

    GB Och: 83, 92-5 (attributed to 'Luigi' [Rossi?])
    GB Y: M.35/11(S) (attributed to Carissimi)
    I PS: B 25 n.3 (Vl only; to the words 'Omnes sancti'; attributed to Carissimi)

[The voices enter in bars 24 and 34 with the same thematic material.]

x Sunt breves mundi rosae
   (B VV)

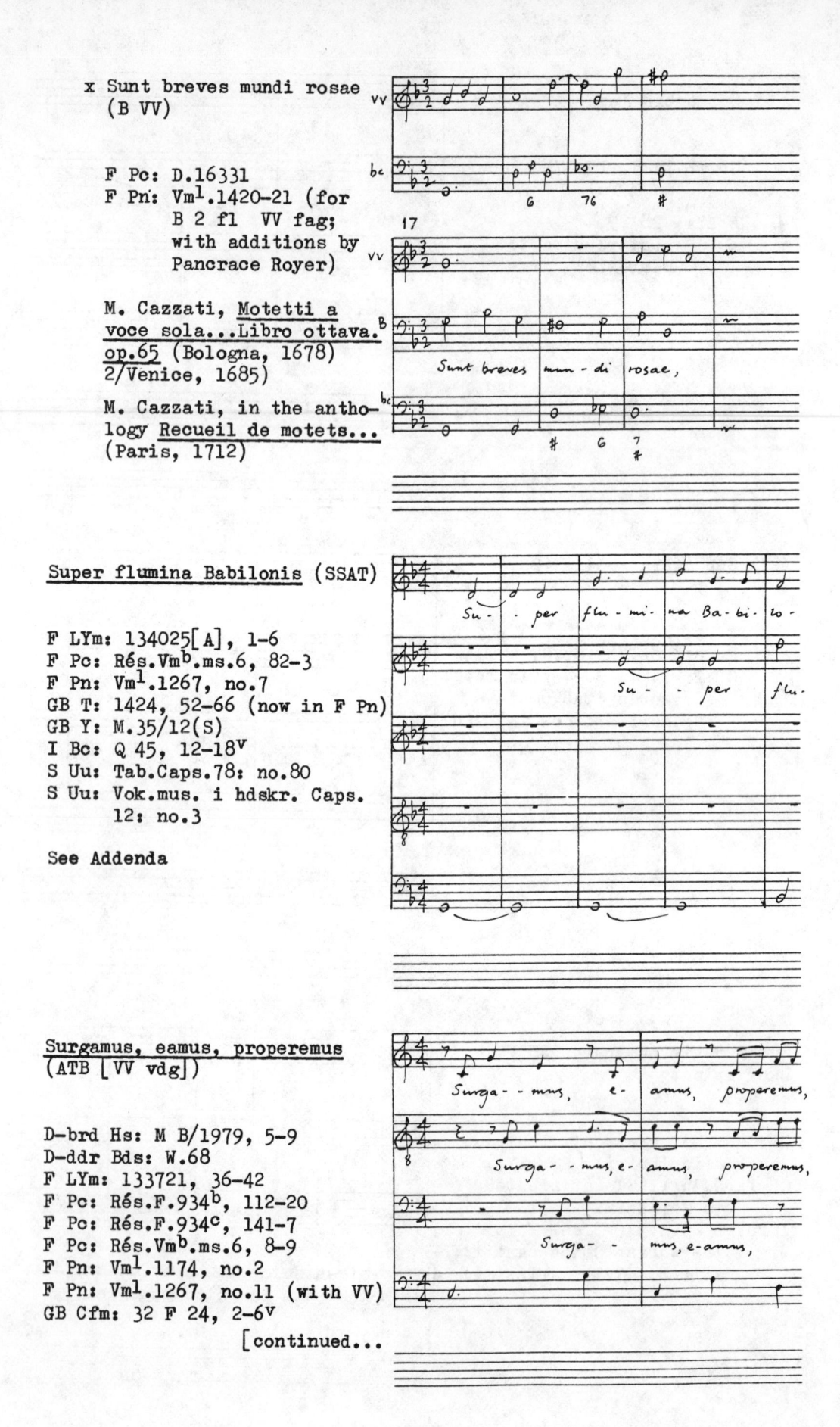

   F Pc: D.16331
   F Pn: Vm¹.1420-21 (for
      B 2 fl VV fag;
      with additions by
      Pancrace Royer)

M. Cazzati, Motetti a
voce sola...Libro ottava.
op.65 (Bologna, 1678)
2/Venice, 1685)

M. Cazzati, in the antho-
logy Recueil de motets...
(Paris, 1712)

Super flumina Babilonis (SSAT)

F LYm: 134025[A], 1-6
F Pc: Rés.Vm♭.ms.6, 82-3
F Pn: Vm¹.1267, no.7
GB T: 1424, 52-66 (now in F Pn)
GB Y: M.35/12(S)
I Bc: Q 45, 12-18ᵛ
S Uu: Tab.Caps.78: no.80
S Uu: Vok.mus. i hdskr. Caps.
    12: no.3

See Addenda

Surgamus, eamus, properemus
(ATB [VV vdg])

D-brd Hs: M B/1979, 5-9
D-ddr Bds: W.68
F LYm: 133721, 36-42
F Pc: Rés.F.934ᵇ, 112-20
F Pc: Rés.F.934ᶜ, 141-7
F Pc: Rés.Vm♭.ms.6, 8-9
F Pn: Vm¹.1174, no.2
F Pn: Vm¹.1267, no.11 (with VV)
GB Cfm: 32 F 24, 2-6ᵛ
       [continued...

[continuation of 'Surgamus, eamus, properemus']

GB Lam: 41, 153-62
GB Lam: 52, 6-9^v
GB Lbl: Add.31472, 68^v-71^v
GB Lbl: Add.31476, 1-4^v
GB Lbl: Add.33235, 33-6
GB Lcm: 793, 1-3^v
GB Lcm: 1059, 36^v-38^v
GB Lcm: 1064, 2-2^v (B only)
GB Ob: Mus.c.57, 107-11^v
GB Ob: Mus.Sch.c.12-19 and 20-23 (with VV vdg)
GB Och: 13, 159-62
GB Och: 53, 111-18
GB T: 335, 99-105
GB T: 958, 120- (lost)
GB T: 1226, 125-8

R. Floridus...cantiones alias sacras... (Rome, 1649; 2/ Venice, 1649)

Floridus...has sacras cantiones... (Rome, 1652)

Scelta di motetti... (Rotterdam, 1656)

Carissimi, Missa a quinque et a novem, cum selectis quibusdam cantionibus... (Cologne, 1666) (ATB VV vdg)

? Surge, propera (S)

GB T: 1425, 49-55 (now in F Pn)

Surrexit pastor bonus (SSS)

S Uu: Tab.Caps.80: no.115
S Uu: Vok.mus. i hdskr. Caps. 12: no.4
S Uu: Vok.mus. i hdskr. Caps. 53: no.10/2

Suscitavit Dominus (ATB [VV vdg])

D-brd Hs: M B/1979, 1-4
D-brd MUs: Sant.Hs.3298, 186-93
F Pc: Rés.F.934c, 111-17
F Pn: Vm¹.1174, no.5
GB Lbl: Add.31472, 53ᵛ-56ᵛ
GB Lbl: Add.33235, 30ᵛ-32ᵛ
GB Lcm: 1064, 1ᵛ-2 (B only)
GB Ob: Mus.d.26, 40-48
GB Ob: Mus.Sch.c.12-19 and 20-23 (with VV vdg)
GB Och: 13, 140-44
GB T: 335, 166-72
S Uu: Tab.Caps.79: no.41 (with VV)
S Uu: Vok.mus. i hdskr. Caps. 12: no.5 (with VV)

Scelta de'motetti... (Rome, 1665)

Carissimi, **Missa a quinque et a novem, cum selectis quibusdam cantionibus...** (Cologne, 1666) (ATB VV vdg)

See Addenda

? Tecum principium in die
(ATB)

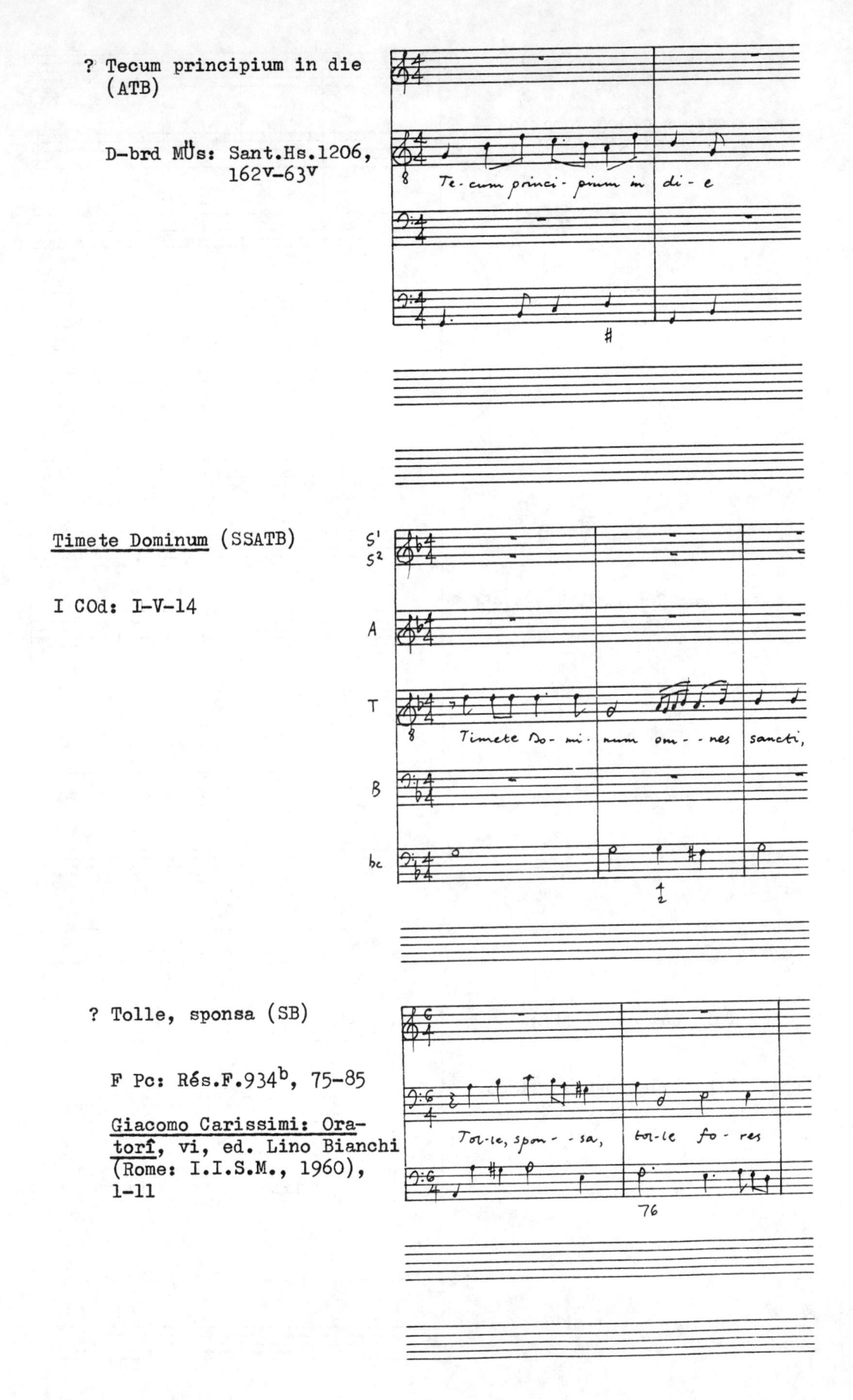

D-brd MÜs: Sant.Hs.1206,
162ᵛ–63ᵛ

Timete Dominum (SSATB)

I COd: I-V-14

? Tolle, sponsa (SB)

F Pc: Rés.F.934ᵇ, 75-85

Giacomo Carissimi: Oratorî, vi, ed. Lino Bianchi (Rome: I.I.S.M., 1960), 1-11

Tollite sancti mei (SST)

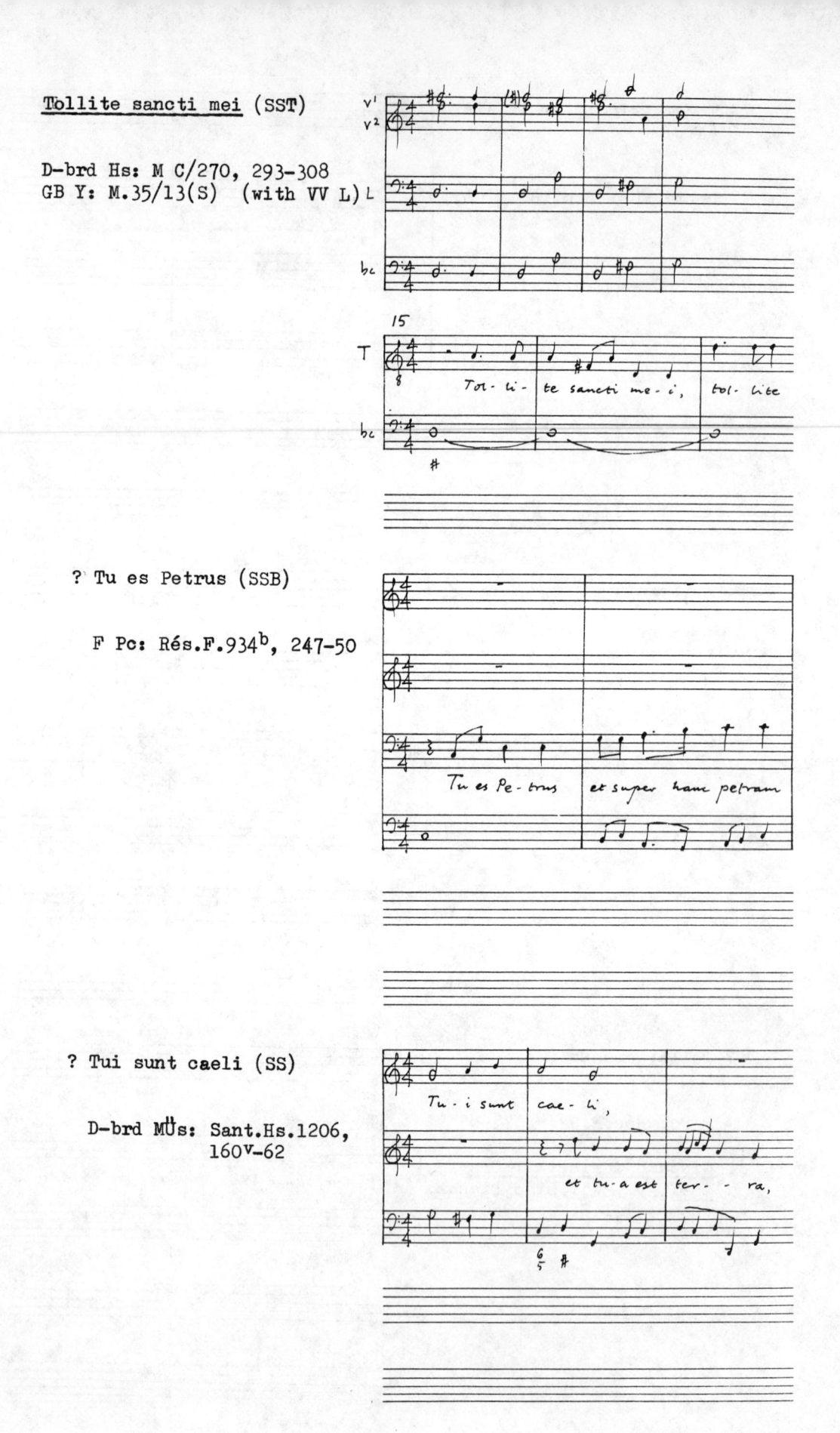

D-brd Hs: M C/270, 293-308
GB Y: M.35/13(S) (with VV L)

? Tu es Petrus (SSB)

F Pc: Rés.F.934ᵇ, 247-50

? Tui sunt caeli (SS)

D-brd MÜs: Sant.Hs.1206, 160ᵛ-62

Turbabuntur impii (ATB [VV vdg])

A Wn: SA.68.Aa.112
D-brd Hs: M C/270, 277-89
D-brd MÜs: Sant.Hs.905
D-brd MÜs: Sant.Hs.1206, 85-90
D-ddr Bds: 3110
D-ddr Dl(b): Mus.1706-E-500
      (with VV)
F LYm: 134025[A], 39-43
F LYm: 134025[B], 11-12^v
F Pc: Rés.F.934^a, 117-43 (+ VV)
F Pc: Rés.F.934^c, 151-61
F Pc: Rés.2182(I), no.10
F Pn: Vm^1.1469 (with VV)
F Pn: Vm^1.1641 (B only)
GB Cfm: 32 G 30, 123^v-28^v
GB Lam: 41, 30-44
GB Lbl: Add.31472, 73^v-78^v
GB Lcm: 792, 1-6^v
GB Lcm: 1064, 6-6^v (B only)
GB Lcm: 1101, 39-45^v
GB Ob: Mus.e.34 (ATB VV fag)
GB Ob: Mus.Sch.c.12-19
GB Och: 13, 47-56
GB Och: 53, 121-32
GB T: 335, 118-27 (with VV)
GB T: 746, 45-55
GB T: 1423, 1^v-16 (with VV;
    now in F Pn)
I Mc: (ms number unknown)

Carissimi, *Missa a quinque et a novem, cum select s quibusdam cantionibus...* (Cologne, 1666) (ATB VV vdg)

Carissimi, *Sacri concerti musicali...* (Rome, 1675)

Sammlung vorzüglicher Gesängstücke...herausgegeben von F. Rochlitz (Mainz, Paris, Antwerp, 1835 ff.), ii, 5-8 (incomplete)

Concerts Spirituels (Série Ancienne)..., ed. Henri Quittard (Paris, [c.1905]), i. 27-37

Ed. Carlo Dell'Argine (Florence: OTOS, 1972) (ATB VV vdg)

[continued...]

[continuation of 'Turbabuntur impii']

Fragment:

'...Quomodo praevenerunt nos' (ATB VV fag)
Raymund Schlecht, Geschichte der Kirchenmusik... (Regensburg, 1871), 447-56

See Addenda

Valete mundi delitiae (SS/TT)

No musical source known.

A copy of the motet was owned by the St. Michaelisschule at Lüneburg while F. E. Praetorius was Kantor there (1655-95); see Max Seiffert, 'Die Chorbibliothek in Lüneburg zu Seb. Bach's Zeit', SIMG, ix(1907-08), 593-621, and in particular 602.

Valete risus, valete cantus (SS/TT)

No musical source known.

See 'Valete mundi delitiae'.

? **Vanitas vanitatum** (SS)

F LYm: 28329, 32-8
F Pc: Rés.F.934^b, 102-11
<u>Giacomo Carissimi: Oratori</u>, x, ed. Lino Bianchi (Rome: I.I.S.M., 1973), 1-17

<u>**Vau. Et egressus**</u> (S)

See 'Lamentationes Jeremiae Prophetae'

<u>**...Veni consolator suspirantis**</u> (SS)

See 'O ignis sancte'

Veni dilecta mea (SS)

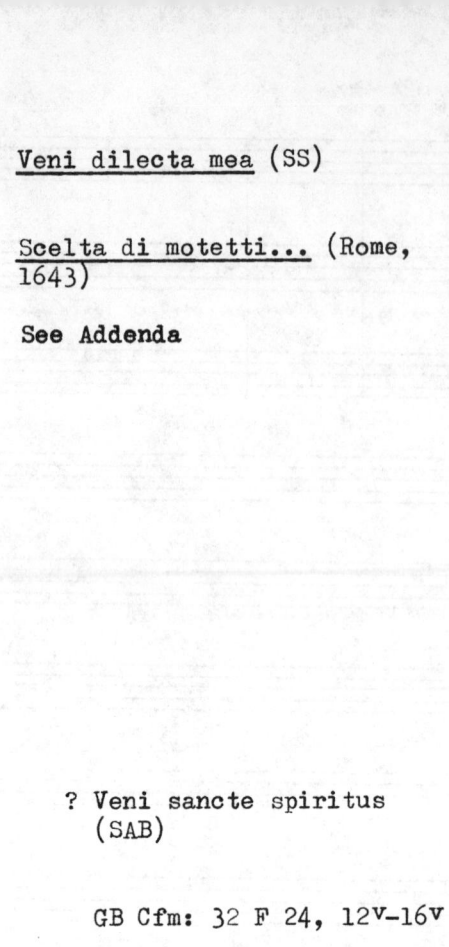

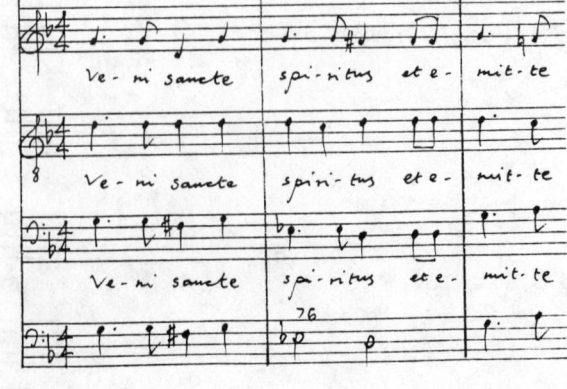

Scelta di motetti... (Rome, 1643)

See Addenda

? Veni sancte spiritus (SAB)

GB Cfm: 32 F 24, 12^v-16^v

x Veni sancte spiritus (SATB)

D-brd MÜs: Sant.Hs.899

? **Veni sancte spiritus**
(SSA)

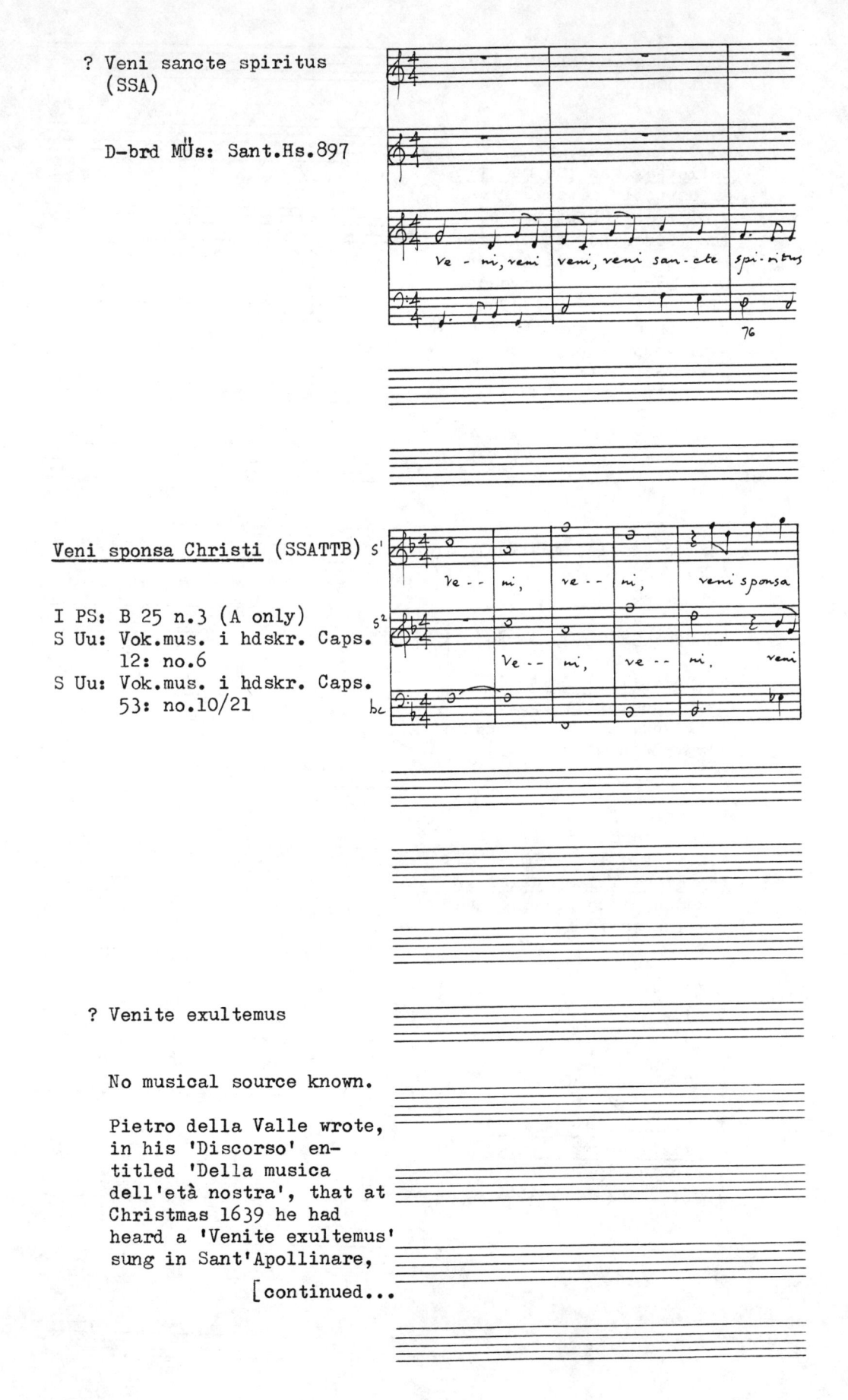

D-brd Müs: Sant.Hs.897

Veni sponsa Christi (SSATTB)

I PS: B 25 n.3 (A only)
S Uu: Vok.mus. i hdskr. Caps. 12: no.6
S Uu: Vok.mus. i hdskr. Caps. 53: no.10/21

? **Venite exultemus**

No musical source known.

Pietro della Valle wrote, in his 'Discorso' entitled 'Della musica dell'età nostra', that at Christmas 1639 he had heard a 'Venite exultemus' sung in Sant'Apollinare,

[continued...

[continuation of 'Venite exultemus']

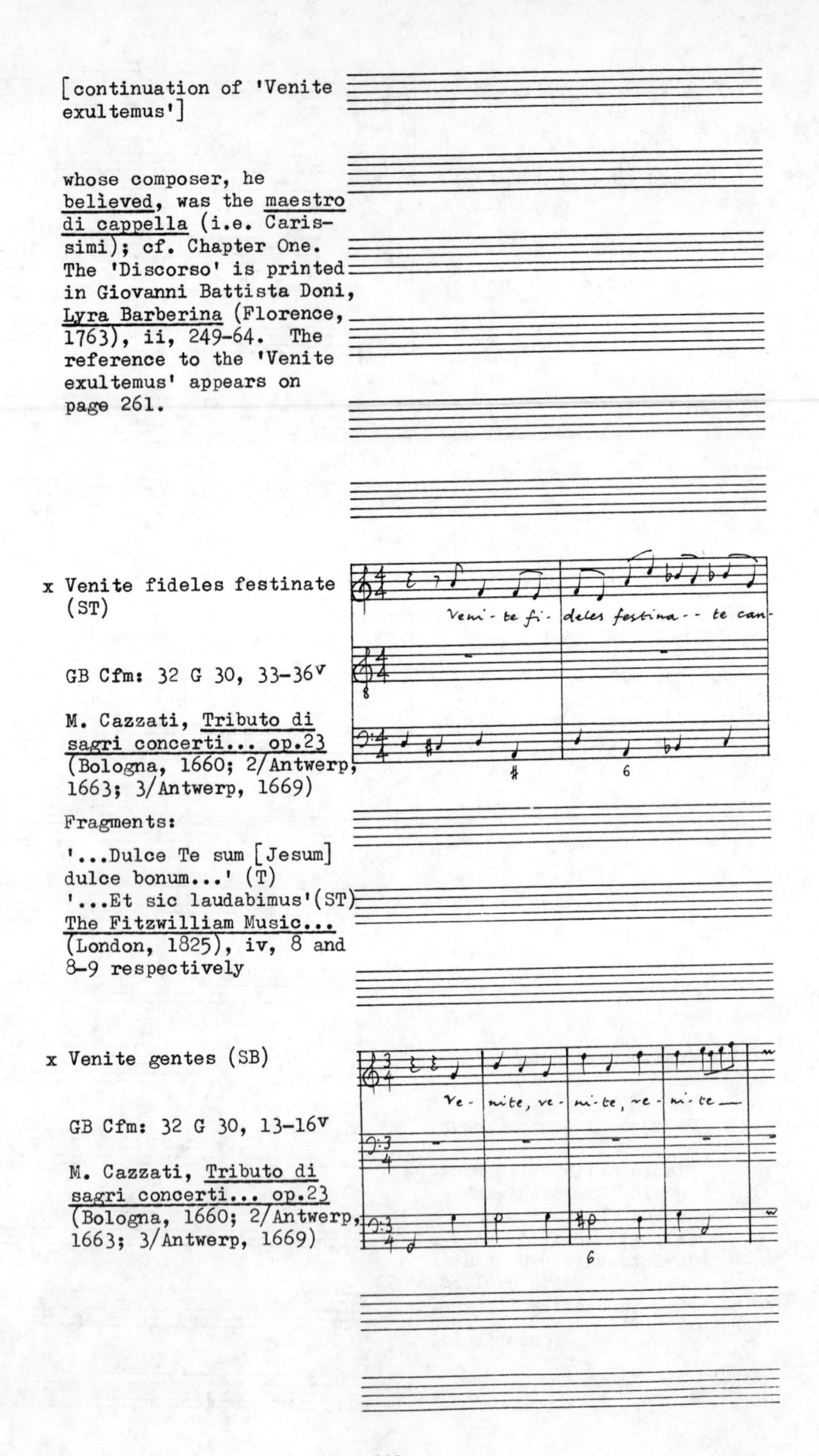

whose composer, he believed, was the maestro di cappella (i.e. Carissimi); cf. Chapter One. The 'Discorso' is printed in Giovanni Battista Doni, Lyra Barberina (Florence, 1763), ii, 249-64. The reference to the 'Venite exultemus' appears on page 261.

x Venite fideles festinate (ST)

GB Cfm: 32 G 30, 33-36^v

M. Cazzati, Tributo di sagri concerti... op.23 (Bologna, 1660; 2/Antwerp, 1663; 3/Antwerp, 1669)

Fragments:
'...Dulce Te sum [Jesum] dulce bonum...' (T)
'...Et sic laudabimus'(ST)
The Fitzwilliam Music... (London, 1825), iv, 8 and 8-9 respectively

x Venite gentes (SB)

GB Cfm: 32 G 30, 13-16^v

M. Cazzati, Tributo di sagri concerti... op.23 (Bologna, 1660; 2/Antwerp, 1663; 3/Antwerp, 1669) x Venite pastores (S)

GB Och: 13, 1-5

B. Graziani, *Il quarto libro de mottetti a voce sola... op.10* (Rome, 1665; 2/Rome, 1677)

B. Graziani, in the anthology *Harmonia sacra: ... The second book...* (London, 1693; 2/London, 1714; 3/London, 1726)

x Veritas mea (SA)

D-brd Mbs: Mus.ms.103

? Viam mandatorum tuorum (SATB)

D-brd Müs: Sant.Hs.2968 (lost)

Viderunt te Domine (SB)

D-ddr Bds: 3102
GB Cfm: 2 F 22, 1-3^v
S Uu: Vok.mus. i hdskr. Caps.
    53: no.10/13

Floridus modulorum hortus...
(Rome, 1647)

Carissimi, *Arion Romanus...*
(Konstanz, 1670)

Vidi impium (ATB)

F LYm: 134025[D], 45-9
F Pc: Rés.F.934^a, 145-56
F Pc: Rés.F.934^c, 134-40
F Pc: Rés.Vm^b.ms.6, 14-15
F Pn: Vm^1.1267, no.5 (VV
    added by Brossard)
F Pn: Vm^1.1641, 5-6 (B only)
GB Lam: 41, 95-105
GB Lbl: Add.31472, 65-8
GB Ob: Mus.d.26, 49-59
GB Och: 13, 153-8
GB T: 335, 113-18
GB T: 926, 168-77
GB T: 958, 111- (lost)
GB T: 1425, 1^v-9 (now in F Pn)
I COd: I-V-15

*R. Floridus...alias cantiones
sacras...* (Rome, 1655)

*R. Floridus...alias cantiones
sacras...* (Rotterdam, 1657)

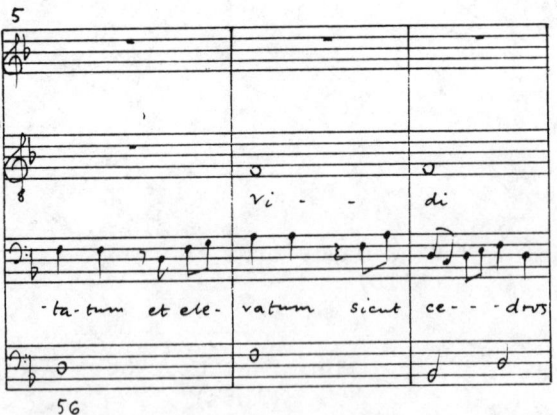

x Vir frugi et pater
  familias (TTB)

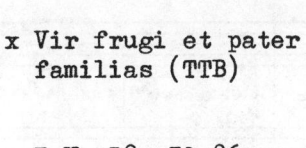

F V: 58, 73-86
GB T: 1424, 25-37 (now
    in F Pn)

<u>Giacomo Carissimi: Ora-
tori</u>, ii, ed. Lino Bianchi
(Rome: I.I.S.M., 1953),
23-41

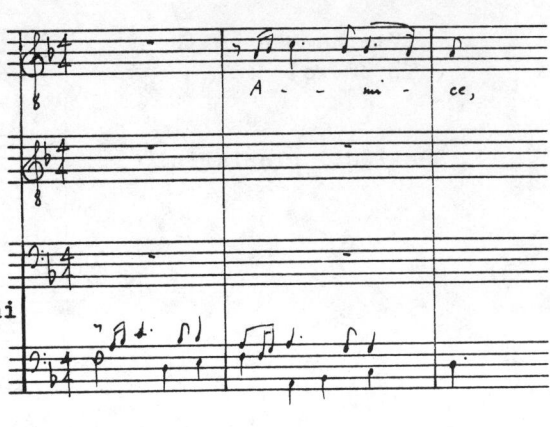

? Viri Galilaei (SSB)

D-ddr Bds: 3101, no.5
F Pc: Rés.2182(I), no.12
GB T: 746, 39^v-43

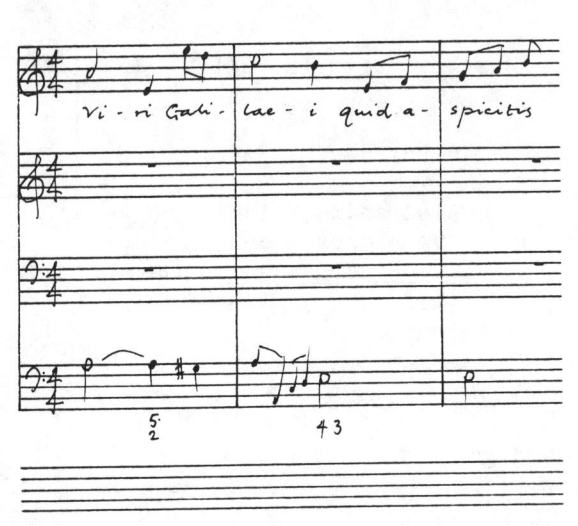

x Vivat laeta triumphalis
  (ATB)

GB Cfm: 32 G 30, 91-93^v

M. Cazzati, <u>Tributo di
sagri concerti...op.23</u>
(Bologna, 1660; 2/Antwerp,
1663; 3/Antwerp, 1669)

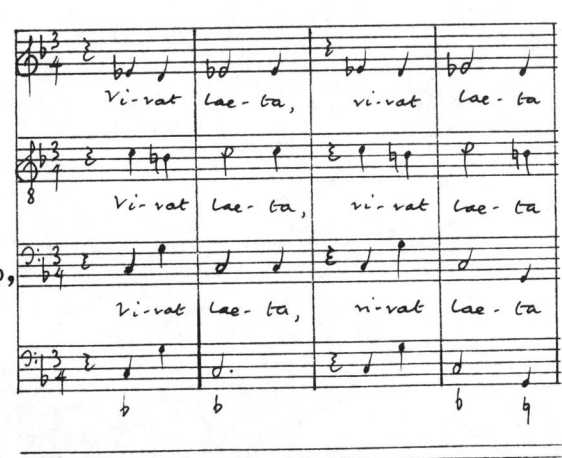

x ...Vix homo nascitur
(ATB VV vc)

See 'Quid gloriaris'

x Vox turturis (SA)

F Pc: Rés.F.934^b, 223-33

Alessandro Melani, <u>Delec-
tus sacrorum concentuum
... Liber secundus</u> (Rome,
1673)

APPENDIX A: ADDENDA

The following information is derived from two sources: that concerning the music at Kroměříz (CS KR) is from Craig A. Otto, <u>Seventeenth-Century Music from Kroměříz, Czechoslovakia: A catalog of the Liechtenstein Music Collection on microfilm at Syracuse University</u> (Syracuse, N.Y., 1977); that concerning the Ansbach inventory of 1686 is from Richard Schaal, <u>Die Musikhandschriften des Ansbacher Inventars von 1686</u> (Wilhelmshaven, 1966). As yet no musical sources are known for numbers 1, 18-27 and 30.

<u>ADDITIONAL SOURCES FOR MOTETS WHICH APPEAR ALREADY IN APPENDIX A</u>

1   <u>Audite mortales</u> (6 voices and 3 instruments)

    Ansbach inventory, f.1015 (In F major.)

2   <u>Ave dulcissime [angelorum] panis</u> (SST VV)

    Ansbach inventory, f.1015

3   <u>Dixit Dominus</u> (SSATB)

    CS KR: III 83

        N.B. The date of the manuscript (seventeenth century) and the attribution ("da Sig^{re} Charissimi") suggest that this motet should probably be accepted as an authentic composition of Carissimi.

123

4   <u>Domine, Deus meus</u> (S)

Ansbach inventory, f.1015

5   <u>Laudate pueri</u> (SSS VV)

CS KR: III 120

N.B. The incipit indicates that the version given in Appendix A is almost certainly the same motet but that the vocal and bc parts have been modified (possibly by Santini) and the violin parts omitted. The attribution on the manuscript ("Authore Sig. Charissimo") and the date (1681) suggest that the motet in its original form should probably be accepted as an authentic composition of Carissimi.

6   <u>Laudemus virum gloriosum</u> (SS)

CS KR: II 184 (Missing and without attribution; hence not definitely Carissimi's motet of this name.)

7   <u>...Omnes gentes...</u> (SSS)

Ansbach inventory, f.1016

8   **Quasi aquila** (T V vdg)

    CS KR: II 134 (anonymous)
    CS KR: II 298 ("del Sig:re Charissimo")

9   **Quo abiit dilectus meus** (SA)

    CS KR: II 160

10 **Quo tam laetus** (SS)

    CS KR: II 131 (anonymous)
    CS KR: II 300 ("dal Charissimo")

11 **Salve puellule** (T VV)

    CS KR: II 133 (anonymous)

12 **Si linguis hominum** (SSS VV)

    CS KR: II 2   (Missing and without attribution; hence not
                    definitely Carissimi's motet of this name.)
    CS KR: II 166

13 **Sicut stella matutina** (S)

    CS KR: II 132   (Missing but attributed to Carissimi.)
    CS KR: II 295   (Missing and without attribution; hence not
                    definitely Carissimi's motet of this name.)

14   Super flumina Babilonis (SSAT)

   Ansbach inventory, f.1015

15   Suscitavit Dominus (ATB)

   Ansbach inventory, f.1015

16   Turbabuntur impii (ATB VV vdg)

   Ansbach inventory, f.1016 ("à 5. Voc.")
   CS KR: II 301 (for ATB VV L bc)

17   Veni dilecta mea (SS)

   Ansbach inventory, f.1015

SOURCES FOR ADDITIONAL MOTETS WHICH DO NOT APPEAR IN APPENDIX A

18   Ad coelestem Jerusalem (S)

   Ansbach inventory, f.1032

19   Ad fontem (3 voices)

   Ansbach inventory, f.1015   (In C major.)

20   Audite sancti (6 voices and 5 instruments)

   Ansbach inventory, f.1015 (In C major.)

21   Beatus vir (5 voices)

   Ansbach inventory, f.1015 (In A.)

22   Estote fortes in bello (3 voices)

   Ansbach inventory, f.1015

23   Iratus sum (3 voices)

   Ansbach inventory, f.1015 (In C major.)

24   Jesus noster (2 voices and 2 instruments)

   Ansbach inventory, f.1015 (In G minor.)

25   O cor meum (T)

   Ansbach inventory, f.1015

26 **O felix felicitas** (3 voices and 2 instruments)

Ansbach inventory, f.1015 (In C major.)

27 **O sanctissimum Sacramentum** (3 voices)

Ansbach inventory, f.1016 (In C major.)

28 **Sustinuimus pacem** (SSATTB)

CS KR: II 164

29 **Usquequo peccatores** (SSS SAT SATB VV L)

    CS KR: II 188 (Missing and without attribution; hence not definitely Carissimi's motet of this name.)

    CS KR: II 287 ("del Sig^re Charissimo")

30 **Venite socii** (4 voices)

    Ansbach inventory, f.1015 (In F.)

Appendix B

The Printed Sources (1642–1978)

This chronological list is divided into three sections. Section 1 constitutes the most important period of publication: from 1642 until 1675 (the year after Carissimi's death). It is with this period that chapter two is concerned. Section 2 contains a handful of late seventeenth- and early eighteenth-century publications for which *RISM* information (that is, principally, information about library sources) is available. A few publications containing arrangements by Henry Aldrich, in which music from more than one composition is combined with free material in a setting of English words, are omitted from this appendix.

The method used for denoting an opinion on a motet's authenticity is the same as that used in Appendices A and C; details are given in the introduction to Appendix A. In sections 1 and 2 *RISM* numbers are given on the right of the page after a single square bracket; in section 2, "XVIIIe" is an abbreviation for the *RISM* volume entitled *Recueils imprimés: XVIIIe siècle,* in which the entries are arranged not chronologically, as in the volume covering the sixteenth and seventeenth centuries, but alphabetically. Unless otherwise stated, all motets have a *basso continuo;* in several nineteenth- and twentieth-century publications it may be realized (sometimes very freely).

Sections 1 and 2 of this appendix have been compiled from the three relevant volumes of *RISM* (which never give the titles of motets), from library catalogues (which rarely give the titles) and from personal investigation in libraries throughout Europe. Those items marked with an asterisk are omitted from *RISM;* among the more serious omissions are three complete collections: those of 1651, 1652 *(Delectus sacrarum cantionum...)* and 1657. It is possible that they are second editions (with alterations in all cases) of, respectively, *RISM* 1642[1], 1647[1] and 1655[1].

SECTION 1: 1642-1675

1642   Sacrarum modulationum ex variis selectis auctoribus [1642¹
       collectarum selectio prima studio et diligentia
       Dominici Blanci quae partim binis ac ternis partim
       vero quaternis quinisque vocibus concinuntur.
       (Rome: L. Grignani, 1642)

       'Insurrexerunt in nos' (mSAT)
       'Si qua est consolatio' (SSB)

       I Bc, COd, Rsgf*

1643   Floridus concentus sacras continens laudes a   [1643¹
       celeberrimis musices erudites auctoribus, binis,
       ternis, quaternis, quinisque vocibus suavissimis
       modulis concinnatas, quas in unum collegit R.
       Floridus canonicus de Sylvestris a Barbarano.
       (Rome: A. Fei, 1643)

       'Militia est vita' (SSB)
       'O beatum virum' (SSA)

       A Wn;* I Bc, CEc (SB)

1643   Scelta di motetti di diversi eccellentissimi autori [1643²
       raccolti da Filippo Berretti a 2, 3, 4 e 5 voci,
       dedicati all'ill^{mo} et rev^{mo} signore monsignor Gio.
       Maria Roscioli coppiero di N.S. et canonico di S.
       Pietro in Vaticano. (Rome: L. Grignani, 1643)

       'Emendemus in melius' (mSAT)
       'Veni dilecta mea' (SS)

       I Bc (Abc), COd, Rsgf (SST)*

1645   R. Floridus canonicus de Sylvestris a Barbarano has [1645²
       alteras sacras cantiones in unum ab ipso collectas
       suavissimis modulis ab excellentissimis auctoribus
       concinnatas binis, ternis, quaternis vocibus cura-
       vit in lucem edendas. (Rome: L. Grignani, 1645)

       'Audite sancti' (SSB)
       'Hymnum jucunditatis' (SS)

       I Bc, Rsgf (B)*

1646   Motetti d'autori eccellentissimi, a 2.3.4.5. e 6   [1646²
       voci. Con un Laudate à 3. et un Confitebor à 4.
       et un Dialogo a quattro in ultimo. Seconda
       raccolta di D. Benedetto Pace monaco silvestrino.
       (Loreto: P. & G. B. Serafini, 1646)

       [Despite the title, the 'Laudate' is for four voices,
       and the 'Confitebor' (Carissimi's) for three.]

       'Confitebor tibi Domine' (SSB)
       'Quis est hic vir' (SSS)

       D-brd Rp (S1); F Pc (bc only; pp.29-51 are damaged)

1647   Scelta di motetti de diversi eccellentissimi autori   [1647¹
       a 2, 3, 4 e 5 voci da potersi cantare in diverse
       feste dell'anno, si per monache, come anche per voci
       ordinarie, raccolti da Antonio e Giovanni Poggioli.
       (Rome: L. Grignani, 1647)

       [There are two slightly different editions of this
       publication in I Bc: the first has a dedication
       which is dated 29 July 1647, and the second a
       different dedication dated 31 July 1647. There are
       differences also in the contents: each edition con-
       tains four motets which are not present in the
       other. The two Carissimi motets are common to both
       editions.]

       'O dulcissimum Mariae nomen' (SS)
       'Quis est hic vir' (SSS)

       I Bc, COd

1647   Floridus modulorum hortus ab excellentissimis   [1647²
       musices auctoribus, binis, ternis, quaternisque
       vocibus modulatus. Quorum tertiam selectionem
       R. Floridus canonicus de Sylvestris a Barbarano
       in unum ab ipso collectam in lucem curavit edendam.
       (Rome: A. Fei, 1647)

       'Alma Redemptoris Mater' (SSB)
       'Viderunt te Domine' (SB)

       D-brd Mūs (SATB); GB Lcm,* Lwa; I Bc, Bsp (ATBbc),
       Rsgf;* P La; S Uu

1648　　R. Floridus canonicus de Sylvestris a Barbarano　　[1648¹
　　　　Florida verba a celeberrimis musices auctoribus
　　　　binis, ternis, quaternisque vocibus curavit in
　　　　lucem edenda. (Rome: G. B. Robletti, 1648)

　　　　'Praevaluerunt in nos' (mSAT)

　　　　GB Lwa; I Bc (ATBbc), Rc

1649　　Teatro musicale de concerti ecclesiastici a due,　　[1649¹
　　　　tre, e quattro voci di diversi celebri e nomati
　　　　autori con una Messa, Antifone et Letanie della
　　　　B. Virgine Maria nuovamente esposto alla luce da
　　　　Giorgio Rolla musico milanese... (Milan: G. Rolla,
　　　　1649)

　　　　'Insurrexerunt in nos' (mSAT)

　　　　I COd, Md

1649　　R. Floridus canonicus de Sylvestris a Barbarano　　[1649²
　　　　cantiones alias sacras ab excell. auctoribus
　　　　concinnatas suavissimis modulis binis, ternis,
　　　　quaternisque vocibus in lucem edendas curavit.
　　　　(Rome: L. Grignani, 1649)

　　　　'Surgamus, eamus, properemus' (ATB)

　　　　B Br; I Bc, Bsp, Nf, PCd (lacks S1), Rc (S2),
　　　　Rsgf (S1TB)*

1649　　= 1649²　R. Floridus... (Venice: A. Vincenti,　　[1649³
　　　　1649)

　　　　I Bc; S Uu

1649　　= 1648¹　R. Floridus... (Venice: A. Vincenti,　　[1649⁴
　　　　1649)

　　　　I Bc; S Uu

1650　　R. Floridus canonicus de Sylvestris a Barbarano,　　[1650¹
　　　　has alias sacras cantiones, ab excellentissimis
　　　　musices auctoribus suavissimis modulis binis,
　　　　ternis, quaternisque vocibus concinnatas, in lucem
　　　　edendas curavit. (Rome: L. Grignani, 1650)

　　　　'Nigra sum sed formosa' (SS)

　　　　F Pc; GB Lbl(bm), Lwa

1651　　R. Floridus canonicus de Sylvestris a Barbarano　　[*
　　　　has sacras cantiones ... in lucem denuo curavit
　　　　edendas. Pars prima. (Rome: V. Mascardi, 1651)

　　　　'Audite sancti' (SSB)
　　　　'Insurrexerunt in nos' (mSAT)
　　　　'Si qua est consolatio' (SSB)

1652　　Delectus sacrarum cantionum duarum, trium, quatuor, [*
　　　　ac quinque vocum ex optimis quibusque ac recentis-
　　　　simis huius aevi auctoribus. Per Antonium Poggioli.
　　　　(Antwerp: P. Phalèse, 1652)

　　　　'Egredimini caelestes curiae' (SSS VV)
　　　　'O dulcissimum Mariae nomen' (SS)
　　　　'Quis est hic vir' (SSS)

　　　　GB Och

1652　　Floridus canonicus de Sylvestris a Barbarano has　　[1652¹
　　　　sacras cantiones ab excellentissimis musicae auc-
　　　　toribus, binis, ternis, quaternisque vocibus sua-
　　　　vissimis modulis concinnatas in lucem denuo
　　　　curavit edendas. Pars secunda... (Rome: V. Mas-
　　　　cardi, 1652)

　　　　'Militia est vita' (SSB)
　　　　'Surgamus, eamus, properemus' (ATB)

　　　　I COd; NL DHgm (ATB)

1653　　= 1649¹ Teatro musicale... (Milan: G. Rolla, 1653) [1653¹

　　　　F Pc (bc lacks pp.43-48); GB Lk(R.M.15.g.15, and **not**
　　　　R.M.15.d.10 as in the catalogue)

1654   R. Floridus canonicus de Sylvestris a Barbarano.   [1654²
        Has alias cantiones sacras ab excellentissimis
        musices auctoribus binis, ternis, quaternisque
        vocibus suavissimis modulis concinnatas, in lucem
        edendas curavit. (Rome: V. Mascardi, 1654)

        'Ecce sponsus venit' (SA)
        'Quomodo facti sunt impii' (SSB)

        I Bc, Nf

1655   R. Floridus canonicus de Silvestris a Barbarano   [1655¹
        alias cantiones sacras ab excellentissimis musi-
        ces auctoribus concinnatas suavissimis modulis
        tribus vocibus paribus cum organo in lucem edendas
        curavit. (Rome: M. Cortellini, 1655)

        'Vidi impium' (ATB)

        F Pm (bc); I Bc, FZac, Rsgf (ATB)*

1656   Scelta di motetti di diversi eccellentissimi   [1656²
        autori raccolti da Gio. Van Geertsom. A due,
        e tre voci. Con il basso continuo par l'organo
        clavicembalo spinetto o altro instrumento.
        (Rotterdam: J. Van Geertsom, 1656)

        'Audite sancti' (SSB)
        'Laudemus virum gloriosum' (SS)
        'Surgamus, eamus, properemus' (ATB)

        B Br (S2 bc); GB DRc

1657   R. Floridus canonicus de Silvestris a Barbarano   [*
        alias cantiones sacras ab excellentissimis musi-
        ces auctoribus concinnatas suavissimis modulis
        tribus vocibus cum organo in lucem edendas curavit.
        (Rotterdam: J. Van Geertsom, 1657)

        'Praevaluerunt in nos' (mSAT)
        'Vidi impium' (ATB)

        B Br (A bc); GB Och

1659   R. Floridus canonicus de Silvestris a Barbarano   [1659¹
       has alias sacras cantiones ab excellentissimis
       musices auctoribus suavissimis modulis unica voce
       contextas in lucem edendas curavit. (Rome:
       F. Moneta, 1659)

       'Sicut stella matutina' (S)

       GB Och;* I Bc

1661   Florida verba. A celeberrimis musices auctoribus   [1661¹
       binis, ternis, quaternis, quinisque tam vocibus
       quam instrumentis. Suavissimis modulis concinnata.
       (Antwerp: P. Phalèse, 1661)

       'Praevaluerunt in nos' (mSAT)

       GB Lbl(bm), Och; US Wc

1662   R. Floridus canonicus de Sylvestris a Barbarano.   [1662²
       Psalmos istos ab excellentissimis musices aucto-
       ribus suavissimis modulis tribus diversis vocibus
       concinnatos in lucem edendos curavit. (Rome:
       I. de Lazzari, 1662)

       'Confitebor tibi Domine' (SSB)

       I Af,* Md, Rvat-giulia, Td (TB)

1663   R. Floridus canonicus de Silvestris a Barbarano   [1663¹
       has alteras sacras cantiones ab excell. musices
       auctoribus suavissimis modulis unica voce contex-
       tas in lucem edendas curavit. Pars secunda.
       (Rome: I. de Lazzari, 1663)

       'Domine, Deus meus' (S)

       GB Och,* Lcm; I Bc (S bc), Ls (S)

1664   R. Floridus canonicus de Silvestris a Barbarano   [1664¹
       istas alias sacras cantiones ab excellentissimis
       musices auctoribus, unica, binis, ternis, quater-
       nisque vocibus suavissimis modulis concinnatas,
       in lucem edendas curavit. (Rome: I. de Lazzari,
       1664)

       'Ardens est cor nostrum' (SATB)

       D-brd Mūs; I Bc

1665 Scelta de'motetti da cantarsi a due e tre voci [1665[1]
composti in musica da diversi eccellentissimi
autori romani, raccolti dal molto Rev. Sig. D.
Francesco Cavallotti, benefiziato della Basilica
di S. Lorenzo in Damaso. E dati alle stampe da
Gio. Battista Caifabri. Parte prima. (Rome:
G. Fei, 1665)

  'Salve amor noster' (SS)
  'Suscitavit Dominus' (ATB)

  CH E (B bc); I Bc, Bof, Nc (bc)

1665 Musica romana D. D. Foggiae, Charissimi, Gratiani, [1665[3]
aliorumque excellentissimorum authorum, hactenus
tribus duntaxat vocibus decantata, nunc verò ad
plurimorum instantiam duobus instrumentis, vulgò
violinis ad libitum exornata & aucta per R. P.
Spiridionem à monte Carmeli,... (Bamberg:
J. E. Höffling, 1665)

  'Militia est vita' (SSB VV)

  D-ddr Dl (vox I, II incomplete; III); F Pn

1666 Missa a quinque et a novem, cum selectis quibusdam [C 1220
cantionibus ([A2, T2:]... novem, trium vocum et
duorum instrumentorum, cum secundo choro IV. vocum
ad libitum). (Cologne: F. Friesser, 1666 (T1: 1665))

  'In te Domine speravi' (ATB VV vdg)
  'Militia est vita' (SSB VV vdg)
  'Surgamus, eamus, properemus' (ATB VV vdg)
  'Suscitavit Dominus' (ATB VV vdg)
  'Turbabuntur impii' (ATB VV vdg)

  F Pn; GB Lbl(bm) (some parts damaged: Sl, B, Vl, bc)

1667 Scelta de'motetti a 2, e 3 voci, composti da [1667[1]
diversi eccellentissimi autori, dati in luce
da Gio. Battista Caifabri. Parte seconda...
(Rome: A. Belmonte, 1667)

  'Desiderata nobis' (ATB)
  'O ignis sancte' (SS)

  CH E (bc); D-brd Müs (SSB); I ASc (Sl B bc), Bc,
  Rvat-giulia

1667　　Sacras cantiones ab excellentissimis nusices　　[1667²
　　　　auctoribus binis, ternisque vocibus... Jo.
　　　　Baptista Caifabrius in lucem edendas curavit.
　　　　Secunda pars... (Rome: A. Belmonte, 1667)

　　　　= 1667¹ Scelta de'motetti...

　　　　CH E (SS)

1668　　R. Floridus canonicus de Sylvestris a Barbarano　　[1668¹
　　　　istas alias cantiones sacras ab excellentissimis
　　　　musices auctoribus tribus diversis vocibus sua-
　　　　vissimis modulis concinnatas in lucem curavit
　　　　edendas. (Rome: G. Fei (A. Poggioli), 1668)

　　　　'Benedictus Deus et Pater' (SSS)

　　　　D-brd Müs; GB Lbl(bm); I Bc (SS bc)

1670　　Arion Romanus sive Liber primus sacrarum cantionum [C 1221
　　　　I.II.III.IV.V. vocibus vel instrumentis concinen-
　　　　darum. (Konstanz: D. Hautt jun., 1670)

　　　　'Anima nostra sustinet Dominum' (SS)
　　　　'Ardens est cor meum' (SATB)
　　　　'Audite sancti' (SSB)
　　　　'Ave dulcissime Angelorum panis sanctus' (SST)
　　　　'Benedicite gentes' (SSS)
　　　　'Convertere ad me' (S)
　　　　'Domine, Deus meus' (S)
　　　　'Ecce sponsus venit' (SA)
　　　　'Egredimini filiae Sion' (SSS)
　　　　'Exurge cor meum' (S VV vlne)
　　　　 x 'Gaudete cum Maria' (SSB)   [by Foggia]
　　　　'Hymnum jucunditatis' (SS)
　　　　'Laudemus virum gloriosum' (SS)
　　　　'Mortalis homo' (S)
　　　　 x 'O beata virgo Maria' (SSS)   [by Foggia]
　　　　'O beatum virum' (SSA)
　　　　'O dulcissime Jesu' (SS)
　　　　'O quam dilecta sunt tabernacula' (SSATB)
　　　　'...Omnes gentes gaudete...' (SSS)   [part of 'Quasi columba']
　　　　'Panem coelestem Angelorum' (SS)
　　　　'Quasi aquila' (T VV fag)
　　　　'Quis est hic vir' (AB)
　　　　'Quo tam laetus' (SS)
　　　　'Salve virgo immaculata' (SSB)
　　　　 x 'Si Deus pro nobis' (SSB VV)   [by Fabri]
　　　　'Sicut Mater consolatur' (SS)
　　　　'Sicut stella matutina' (S)
　　　　'Viderunt te Domine' (SB)

　　　　CH Zz

1672　　R. Floridus canonicus de Silvestris a Barbarano　　[1672[1]
　　　　sacras cantiones duabus, variis vocibus ab excel-
　　　　lentissimis musices auctoribus, suavissimis
　　　　modulis concinnatas in lucem edendas curavit.
　　　　(Rome: G. A. Mutii, 1672)

　　　　'O dulcissime Jesu' (SS)

　　　　GB Lwa; I Bc

1675　　Scelta di motetti sacri raccolti da diversi eccel-　　[1675[3]
　　　　lentissimi autori à 2. e 3. voci, dedicati al
　　　　molto rev. mio in Christo osservandissimo il
　　　　Padre Simone Stiava... da Gio. Battista Caifabri.
　　　　(Rome: V. Mascardi, 1675)

　　　　'O quam mirabilia sunt' (SS)

　　　　D-brd Rp (S2); F Pc (S2); GB Lk; I ASc, Bc, Ls,
　　　　Rvat-giulia

1675　　Sacri concerti musicali a due, tre, quattro, e　　[C 1222
　　　　cinque voci. (Rome: V. Mascardi, 1675)

　　　　'Annunciate gentes' (SSATB)
　　　　'Cantabo Domino' (SS)
　　　　'Cum ingrederetur N.' or 'Cum reverteretur David' (SSS)
　　　　'Dicite nobis' (SSAT)
　　　　'Domine quis habitabit' (SST)
　　　　'Exulta, gaude, filia Sion' (SS)
　　　　'Laudemus virum gloriosum' (SS)
　　　　'Quo tam laetus' (SS)
　　　　'Turbabuntur impii' (ATB)

　　　　A Wgm (SSB bc); GB Lbl(bm), Lk, Och; I Bc, Ls (2 copies),
　　　　Od (B and bc incomplete), Rvat-giulia [?]

SECTION 2: 1693-1726

1693   Harmonia sacra: ... The second book...   [1693[1]
        (London: E. Jones, 1693)

        'Audite sancti' (SSB)   pp.59-66
        'Lucifer' (S)   pp.67-70

        B Bc; D-brd Hs; F Pc; GB A, Bu, Cfm, Ckc, Cmc, Cpl,
        Gc, Lam (2 copies), Lbl(bm) (2 copies), Lcm (2 copies),
        Lgc, Mp, Ob (2 copies), Och, Ouf (2 copies), T;
        US AA, BE, CA, IO, LA, PR, R, SF, SM, Wc, Ws

1712   Recueil de motets choisis... (Paris: [XVIII[e]: p.328
        C. Ballard, 1712)

        'Nigra es sed formosa' (SS)   vol.iii, pp.101-14

        F Pc (vols.i-ii), Pn; I Rsc

1714   Harmonia sacra: ... Book II. The 2nd edition... [XVIII[e]: p.196
        (London: W. Pearson, 1714)

        'Lucifer' (S)   pp.49-52

        A Wn; D-brd Mbs; F Pa, Pc (2 copies); GB Cfm, Ckc (2
        copies), Cu, Eu, Er, Gm, Lam, Lbl(bm), Lcm (2 copies),
        Lgc, Mp (2 copies), Ob, R; US AA, Bp, NH (66 pages),
        NE, NYp

1726   Harmonia sacra: ... Book II. The 3d [sic]   [XVIII[e]: p.196
        edition... (London: W. Pearson, 1726)

        'Lucifer' (S)   pp.49-52

        GB Ge, Lbl(bm)

SECTION 3: 1825-1978

1825   The Fitzwilliam Music...published...by Vincent Novello
        (London: Novello, 1825)

        'Surgamus, eamus, properemus' (ATB)   vol.i, pp.12-17
          x 'Gaudeamus omnes' (SATB)   vol.i, pp.35-41
            [by Cazzati]

          x '...Dulce Te sum [sic; should
            be 'Jesum'] dulce bonum...' (T)   vol.iv, p.8
            [by Cazzati; from 'Venite
            fideles]
          x '...Et sic laudabimus' (ST)   vol.iv, pp.8-9
            [by Cazzati; from 'Venite
            fideles']

          x '...O felix anima...' (ATB)   vol.v, p.26
            [by Cazzati; from 'Audite gentes']

1835   Sammlung vorzüglicher Gesängstücke...herausgegeben von
        F. Rochlitz (Mainz, Paris, Antwerp: Schott, 1835 ff.)

        'Turbabuntur impii...' (ATB)   vol.ii, pp.5-8
        'Ardens est cor meum' (SATB)   vol.ii, pp.9-12
          ? 'O sacrum convivium' (SAT, no bc)   vol.ii, pp.13-14
        ('Cantemus omnes Domino') (SSSATB)   vol.ii, pp.15-23
          [the latter part of Jephte]

1843   Recueil des Morceaux de Musique ancienne, ... (Paris:
        Pacini, 1843 ff.)

          x '...O felix anima...' (ATB)   vol.vi
            [see above, 1825]

          x 'Gaudeamus omnes' (SATB)   vol.viii
            [see above, 1825]
        'Surgamus, eamus, properemus' (ATB)   vol.viii

1852   The Choir (London: Burns and Lambert, 1852)

          x 'Ave verum corpus' (SATB, no bc)   part i, p.26
          x 'Serve bone' (ATB)   part iv, pp.104-5

1859   Echos du monde religieux (Paris: G. Flaxland, 1859)

          x '...O felix anima...' (ATB)   pp.104-5
            [see above, 1825]

1871   Raymund Schlecht, <u>Geschichte der Kirchenmusik...</u>
(Regensburg: Coppenrath, 1871)

    '...Quomodo praevenerunt nos' (ATB
      VV fag) [from 'Turbabuntur impii'] pp.447-56 (no.73)

1874-5 <u>Musica Sacra</u>. Première année. (1874-5)

    x '...O felix anima...' (ATB)   no.14
    [see above, 1825]

1875   x '...O felix anima...' (ATB) (Paris: Michelet, 1875)
    [see above, 1825]

1877   <u>Six Cantatas by Carissimi</u>. Edited...by Ridley Prentice
(London: Lamborn Cock, 1877)

    'Exulta, gaude, filia Sion' (SS)   pp.32-41
    x 'Anima mea in aeterna dulcedine'
      (SB) [by Trabattone]   pp.42-9

1880   x 'Gaudeamus omnes' (SATB) ed. Malcolm L. Lawson
    (London: Stanley Lucas, Weber & Co.,[1880])
    [see above, 1825]

1881   <u>Publicazione periodica di musica sacra</u> (Rome, 1881)

    x 'A Domino factum est' (SAT)
    ? 'Dextera Domini'

1903   x 'Gaudeamus omnes' (SATB) (London: Leonard & Co.,
    [1903]) [see above, 1825]

1905   <u>Concerts Spirituels (Série Ancienne)</u>..., ed. Henri
Quittard (vol.i) and Charles Bordes (vol.v) (Paris:
Schola Cantorum, [c.1905])

    ? 'Duo ex discipulis' (SST)   vol.i, pp.13-17
      [excerpt]
    'Turbabuntur impii' (ATB)   vol.i, pp.27-37

    'O vulnera doloris' (B)   vol.v, pp.1-6
    ? 'O piissime Jesu' (ATB)   vol.v, pp.7-13

1905   x 'Ave verum corpus' (SATB), ed. R. R. Terry
            (London: Carey & Co., [1905])

1913-14   Musique d'église des XVIIe et XVIIIe siècles...,
          ed. Charles Pineau (Paris, 1913-14)

            'O vulnera doloris' (B)

1922   x 'Pulchra et decora' (SAT; = 'Carissimi' [Ghizzolo]
            SATB), ed. Francesco Vatielli, Antiche cantate
            spirituali, vi (Turin: STEN [1922]) [by Ghizzolo]

1932   x '...O felix anima...' (ATB), ed. A. Gastoué
            (Paris: Maison de la Bonne presse, 1932)
            [see above, 1825]

1939   ? 'O sacrum convivium' (SAT, no bc), ed. E. Tyr
            (Paris: La Petite Maîtrise, 1939)

1951   x '...O felix anima...' (ATB), ed. Maffeo Zanon
            (Basel: Symphonia, 1951) [see above, 1825]

1953   Giacomo Carissimi: Oratori, ii, ed. Lino Bianchi
          (Rome: Istituto Italiano per la Storia della Musica,
          1953)

            x 'Vir frugi et pater familias' (TTB)   pp.23-41

1954   x '...O felix anima...' (ATB), ed. Aimé Steck
            (Strasbourg: F. X. Le Roux, 1954) [see above, 1825]

1955   x 'Gaudeamus omnes' (SATB), ed. Aimé Steck (Paris:
            L. Philippo, 1955) [see above, 1825]

1956   'Domine, Deus meus' (S), ed. Rudolf Ewerhart, Cantio
              Sacra, viii (Cologne: Edmund Bieler, 1956)

1957   x '...O felix anima...' (ATB), ed. Zanon-Vené (New
            York: Ricordi, 1957) [see above, 1825]

1958   'O vulnera doloris' (B), ed. Rudolf Ewerhart, <u>Cantio Sacra</u>, xvi (Cologne: Edmund Bieler, 1958)

1960   <u>Giacomo Carissimi: Messe e Mottetti</u>, ed. Lino Bianchi (Rome: I.I.S.M., 1960)

      'Hodie Simon Petrus' (TT)   pp.68-73
      'Cum reverteretur David' (SSS)   pp.74-91

1960   <u>Giacomo Carissimi: Oratorî</u>, vi, ed. Lino Bianchi (Rome: I.I.S.M., 1960)

    ? 'Tolle sponsa' (SB)   pp.1-11
    ? 'Duo ex discipulis' (SST)   pp.12-46

1961   'Salve puellule' (S), ed. Rudolf Ewerhart, <u>Cantio Sacra</u>, xlviii (Cologne: Edmund Bieler, 1961)

1964   'Christus factus est' (SSATB SATB), ed. Lorenzo Feininger, <u>Documenta Liturgiae Polychoralis Sanctae Ecclesiae Romanae</u>, no.18 (Trent: Societas Universalis S. Ceciliae, 1964)

1964   'O quam pulchra es' (S), ed. Rudolf Ewerhart, <u>Cantio Sacra</u>, lvii (Cologne: Edmund Bieler, 1964)

1967   'Annunciate gentes' (SSATB), ed. Niels Martin Jensen, <u>Orbis Chori</u>, iii (Egtved: Musikhojskolens Vorlag, 1967)

1968   ? 'Beatus vir' (SATB SATB), ed. Jack Pilgrim (Hilversum: Harmonia-Uitgave, 1968)

1968   'Dixit Dominus' (SSATB), ed. Jack Pilgrim (Hilversum: Harmonia-Uitgave, 1968)

1969   <u>Giacomo Carissimi: Oratorî</u>, ix, ed. Lino Bianchi (Rome: I.I.S.M., 1969)

    ? 'Sponsa Canticorum' (SSSB)   pp.15-51

1971   x 'Ah! vide Domine' (SATB VV vc), ed. Jack Pilgrim
        (Hilversum: Harmonia-Uitgave, 1971) [by J. H.
        Wilderer]

1971   x 'O anima festina' (SATB VV vc), ed. Jack Pilgrim
        (Hilversum: Harmonia-Uitgave, 1971) [by J. H.
        Wilderer]

1971   'Parce, heu parce iam' (SSAB), ed. Jack Pilgrim
        (Hilversum: Harmonia-Uitgave, 1971)

1972   <u>Felicitas beatorum</u> ['Exultabunt justi'] (SSS VV),
        ed. Carlo Dell'Argine (Florence: OTOS, 1972)

1972   <u>Lamentatio damnatorum</u> ['Turbabuntur impii'] (ATB VV vdg),
        ed. Carlo Dell'Argine (Florence: OTOS, 1972)

1973   <u>Giacomo Carissimi: Oratori</u>, x, ed Lino Bianchi
        (Rome: I.I.S.M., 1973)

        ? <u>Vanitas vanitatum I</u> ['Vanitas vanitatum']
        (SS)   pp.1-17
        (<u>Vanitas vanitatum II</u> ['Proposui in mente mea']
        (SSATB VV))   pp.18-68

1973   'Jubilemus omnes' (SSB), ed. Ebbe Selén (Kassel:
        Bärenreiter, 1973)

1974   ? 'Nisi Dominus' (SSATB), ed. Janet Beat (London:
        Novello, 1974)

1975   ? 'Beatus vir' (SSATB), ed. Peter Seymour (London:
        Oxford University Press, 1975)

1978   'Sancta et individua Trinitas' (SS VV L), ed. Wolfgang
        Fürlinger (Neuhausen-Stuttgart: Hänssler-Verlag, 1978)

Forthcoming:

        'Lucifer' (B), ed. Rudolf Ewerhart, <u>Cantio Sacra</u>,
        xxxvii (Cologne: Edmund Bieler,   )

        'Summi Regis puerpera' (SS VV spinet/lute), ed. Peter
        Seymour (London: Oxford University Press,   )

Appendix C

The Manuscript Sources: Holdings of Individual Libraries

The information in the following tables is based for the most part on original research. Of the forty-one library collections listed, twenty-one have been studied at first hand; these include all the important collections with the exception of S Uu, whose manuscripts have been studied on microfilm. Investigation of the remaining nineteen collections has been carried out by means of correspondence with librarians and the study of photocopies and microfilms, both of library card indexes and of the manuscripts themselves. Most of the collections are discussed in the correspondingly numbered sections of chapter three, where, among other matters, decisions regarding authenticity and the identification of scribes are explained.

Some features of the tables require explanation:

Column 2: Page or Folio Numbers

i) A few manuscripts have no page numbers, but instead the contents are numbered. Figures in column 2 preceded by "no." are such. Other figures (without "no.") are page or folio numbers.

ii) Where modern pagination has been added, often to remedy the inconsecutive or inconsistent nature of the original, this is given in column 2 in preference to the original. The sole exception to this practice is GB Lk, R.M.24.c.10(2), where the modern pagination is useless for purposes of identification, since it repeatedly returns to page 1.

iii) No page numbers are given either if the motet occupies a complete manuscript, or if the manuscript takes the form of a set of part books. The sole exception to the latter is F Pc, Rés.Vm^b.ms.6, in which the (original) pagination is arranged irregularly in order that the same motets should appear on the same pages in different volumes.

Column 3: Title of Motet

The following symbols are used with these meanings:

i) Title   A motet definitely or probably by Carissimi.
ii) (Title)   A composition by Carissimi other than a motet.
iii) Title   [J   A motet attributed to Carissimi by the present writer.
iv) ? Title   A motet possibly or probably not by Carissimi.
v) x Title   A motet definitely not by Carissimi.
vi) ...Title...   A fragment of a motet.

Column 4: Voices and Instruments

The abbreviations used in this column are explained in the general list of abbreviations at the beginning of volume 1. Unless otherwise stated, all motets employ a *basso continuo*.

Column 5: Hand

The abbreviations used in this column signify the following scribes. (The alphabetical sequence of the *full* names is followed below; the last column lists the libraries in which Carissimi transcriptions by each scribe have been found.)

Abbreviation	Full Name	Dates	Libraries
Ald	Henry Aldrich	1648–1710	GB Lbl, Och
Amb	August Wilhelm Ambros	1816–1876	A Wn
Awb	John Awbery	c.1721–?	Gb Ob
Ba	Thomas Barrow	C18	GB Lam
Bo	Henry Bowman	C17–C18	GB Lbl
Br	Sébastien de Brossard	1655–1730	F Pn
Ca	Ercole Capelloni	C19	I Rsc
Chi	Girolamo Chiti	1679–1759	I Rsg
cd1 cd2 cd3 cd4 cd5	Five unidentified scribes in I COd		I COd
Cft	William Croft	1678–1727	GB Lcm
Cch	William Crotch	1775–1847	GB Lbl
D	Gustav Düben	1624–1690	S Uu
etW	(see under W)		
Gei	Christian Geist	c.1640–1711	S Uu
Gev	François Auguste Gevaert	1828–1908	B Bc
G(i)	Richard Goodson, senior	1655–1718	GB Ob, Och
G(ii)	Richard Goodson, junior	c.1685–1741	GB Och
Gos	William Gostling	1696–1777	GB Lbl
H	Matthew Hutton	1639–1711	GB Y
Ja	Samuel Jacobi	1652–1721	D-ddr Dl(b)
Je	George Jeffreys	c.1610–1685	GB Lbl
jW	(see under W)		
K	Raphael Georg Kiesewetter	1773–1850	A Wn, D-brd MÜs, D-ddr Bds, F Pc
King	Charles King	1687–1748	GB Lbl
Lb	Thomas Laub	1852–1927	DK Kk
Lc	Joannes Lechler	1594–1659	A KR
Mal	Johann Baptist Malchair	c.1728–1812	GB T
Mor	Charles Morgan	fl.1682	GB Lbl
P	André Philidor	1647–1730	F Pc, GB T
Pog	Alessandro Poglietti	? –1683	A KR
Pur	Henry Purcell	1659–1695	GB LK (anon; in fact by Cazzati)
Re	Pietro Reggio	1632–1685	GB Lbl
Ro	Pancrace Royer	1705–1755	F Pn
S	Fortunato Santini	1778–1862	D-brd Mbs, MÜs, GB T, NL At
etW	Edmund Thomas Warren	c.1730–1794	GB Lbl, T
jW	Joseph Warren	1804–1881	GB T
X	Unidentified scribe		F Pc, GB Ckc, Lam, Lbl, Ob, Och, T
Y	Unidentified scribe		GB Lbl, Lcm, I COd
ym1 ym2 ym3 ym4	Four unidentified scribes in GB Y		GB Y
Z	Unidentified scribe		GB Lcm, Lk, Ob

Column 6: Comments

When it is known definitely that a copyist made a transcription from a printed source, the source is referred to in this column by its place and date of publication; full details may be obtained by reference to Appendix B. If a manuscript can be dated fairly precisely, this information is given. Also in column 6 the correct composers are given for motets wrongly ascribed to Carissimi; in this case full details may be obtained by reference to Appendix A.

TABLE I

A KR: BENEDIKTINER-STIFT, KREMSMÜNSTER

Manuscript number	Pages or folios	Title of motet	Voices and instruments	Hand	Comments
L 12	17(-16)-19	Confitemini Domino	BB	Lc	Before c. 1633
	20-25	Immensus coeli conditor	SS	Lc	Before c. 1633
L 13	8-15	Audivi vocem	SSS VV L Tb	Lc	Before c. 1633
	16-19	Sancta et individua Trinitas	SS VV L/Tb	Lc	Before c. 1633
L 146	84	Domine Deus meus...	B	Pog	
	84-85	Incipit Oratio Jeremiae Prophetae...	S	Pog	In C minor

TABLE II

A Wn: NATIONALBIBLIOTHEK, VIENNA

Manuscript number	Pages or folios	Title of motet	Voices and instruments	Hand	Comments
15621		? Beatus vir	SATB SATB		
17011		Exulta, gaude, filia Sion Cantabo Domino Turbabuntur impii Cum reverteretur David Domine quis habitabit Annunciate gentes	SS SS ATB SSS SST SSATB		Rome, 1675 (three motets in the publication are omitted in the transcription)
SA.67.C.18		The Sacri concerti musicali....		K	Rome, 1675 (the A Wn card index does not specify the contents)
SA.67.C.19		Laudate pueri	SSS	K	
SA.68.Aa.111		? Ipse praeibit Ardens est cor meum ? Lapides praetiosi ? O sacrum convivium	SSTB SATB SmSAT (no bc) SAT (no bc)	K K K K	
SA. 68.Aa.112		Turbabuntur impii	ATB	K	
S.m.1550	34-36^v	Ardens est cor meum	SATB	Amb	

151

TABLE III

B Bc: BIBLIOTHÈQUE DU CONSERVATOIRE ROYAL DE MUSIQUE DE BRUXELLES

Manuscript number	Pages or folios	Title of motet	Voices and instruments	Hand	Comments
1057		...O felix gloria	SSS	Gev	Final section of 'Exultabunt justi'
		O vulnera doloris	B	Gev	
		Domine, Deus meus	S	Gev	
		Hodie Simon Petrus	TT	Gev	
		Praevaluerunt in nos	ATB	Gev	
		Dicite nobis...	SSAT	Gev	

TABLE IV

D-brd Hs: STAATS- UND UNIVERSITÄTSBIBLIOTHEK, MUSIKABTEILUNG, HAMBURG

Manuscript number	Pages or folios	Title of motet	Voices and instruments	Hand	Comments
M B/1979	1-4	Suscitavit Dominus	ATB		
	5-9	Surgamus, eamus	ATB		
	10-13	Militia est vita	SSB		
M C/270	1-[40]	(Jonas)	SATB SATB		pp.39-40 missing.
	41-80	(Judicium extremum)	SSATB		
			ATB ATB		
	81-114	(Baltazar)	SSATB		
	115-46	(Jephte)	SSSATB		
	147-71	Felicitas beatorum (=Exultabunt justi)	SSS		
	173-254	(Dives malus (=Historia divitis))	SATB SATB		
	277-89	(Judicium Salomonis (=A solis ortu))	SSTB		
		Damnatorum lamentatio (=Turbabuntur impii)	ATB		
	293-308	Martyres (=Tollite sancti mei)	SST		
	309-26	(Ezechias)	SSATB		pp.327-28 missing.
	329-92	(Diluvium universale)	SSATB SSATB		pp.387-90 and 393-[400?] missing.

153

TABLE V

D-brd Mbs: BAYERISCHE STAATSBIBLIOTHEK, MUNICH

Manuscript number	Pages or folios	Title of motet	Voices and instruments	Hand	Comments
Cod.lat. 1512/3	63-66	Ardens est cor meum	SATB		
Mus.ms.89		? Beatus vir	SATB SATB		
Mus.ms.102		x Nisi Dominus aedificaverit	S VV		
Mus.ms.103		x Veritas mea	SA		
Mus.ms.104		x A Domino factum est	SAT		
Mus.ms.105		Alma Redemptoris Mater x Locus iste	SSB SA		
Mus.ms.565	30^v- 33^v 33^v-	Ardens est cor meum ? Lauda Sion ? Ipse praeibit Desiderata nobis	SATB SATB SATB SSTB ATB		
Mus.ms.719		? Lauda Sion	SATB SATB	S	Dated 1828
Mus.ms.720/1 /2 /3		Ardens est cor meum Desiderata nobis ? Ipse praeibit	SATB ATB SSTB	S S S	
Mus.ms.2944	40-41^v	? Lapides praetiosi	SmSAT (no bc)		Dated 1829

154

TABLE VI

D-brd MÜs: SANTINI-BIBLIOTHEK, MÜNSTER

Manuscript number (Sant.Hs.)	Pages or folios	Title of mctet	Voices and instruments	Hand	Comments
893		? Beatus vir	SATB SATB	S	
894		? Lauda Sion	SATB SATB	S	Lost.
895		Laudate pueri	SSS		
896		? Ipse praeibit	SSTB		
897		? Veni sancte spiritus	SSA		
899		x Veni sancte spiritus	SATB		
900		Ardens est cor meum	[SATB]		bc only
901		x In memoriam suorum mirabilium	SAT		
902		x Domine, Deus virtutum	SAT		
		x A Domino factum est	SAT		
903		? O sacrum convivium	SAT (no bc)		

155

TABLE VI continued

905		Exulta, gaude, filia Sion	SS	K	Rome, 1675 (three
		Cantabo Domino	SS	K	motets in the publication
		Turbabuntur impii	ATB	K	are omitted and one - 'O
		? O sacrum convivium	SAT (no bc)	S	sacrum convivium' - is
		Cum reverteretur David	SSS	K	added from another source).
		Domine, quis habitabit	SST	K	
		Annunciate gentes	SSATB	K	
1202	130-34	? Alma Redemptoris Mater	SATB	S	
1206	54^v-55^v	? Diffusa est gratia	SATB	S	
	55^v-57^v	? Mihi autem nimis honorati	SSB	S	
	85-90	Turbabuntur impii	ATB	S	
	143-43^v	? Christum regem adoremus	SATB (no bc)	S	
	145-45^v	? Regina caeli laetare	SAT	S	
	157^v-59^v	? Deus meus, ad te de luce	SST	S	
	159^v-60^v	? Ad te levavi animam meam	AT	S	
	160^v-62^v	? Tui sunt caeli	SS	S	
	162^v-63^v	? Tecum principium in die	ATB	S	
	255-58	? Peccavi super numerum	SA	S	
1525	221-24	? Lapides praetiosi	SmSAT (no bc)	S	Lost.
2333		? Nisi Dominus aedificaverit	SATB SATB	S	
2748	31^v-34^4	Alma Redemptoris Mater	SSB	S	Rome, 1647?
	37-	Benedictus Deus et Pater	SSS	S	Rome, 1668
2758	11-15	Ardens est cor meum	SATB	S	Rome, 1664
	15-22	Desiderata nobis	ATB	S	Rome, 1667
	22-24	..Veni consolator suspirantis	SS	SS	The latter part of 'O ignis sancte' (pr Rome, 1667; but '...Veni consolator' is not transcribed from the print).
2968		? Viam mandatorum tuorum	SATB		Lost.

156

TABLE VI continued

3298	16-22	O dulcissimum Mariae nomen	SS	Rome, 1647[1]
	42-50	Quis est hic vir	SSS	Rome, 1647[1]
	138-45	Salve amor noster	SS	Rome, 1665
	186-93	Suscitavit Dominus	ATB	Rome, 1665
3679	117-20	O dulcissime Jesu	SS	Rome, 1672
4222	90-98	? Serve bone et fidelis	SSAT	

TABLE VII

D-ddr Bds: DEUTSCHE STAATSBIBLIOTHEK, BERLIN

1. Deutsche Staatsbibliothek (East Berlin)

Manuscript number	Pages or folios	Title of motet	Voices and instruments	Hand	Comments
Mus.ms.30372		? O sacrum convivium	SAT (no bc)		
W.49		(Proposui in mente mea)	SSATB		
W.68		Surgamus, eamus Praevaluerunt in nos O dulcissimum Mariae nomen Nigra sum sed formosa	ATB ATB SS SS		
W.103		Quis est hic vir O dulcissimum Mariae nomen	SSS SS		

2. Staatsbibliothek Preussischer Kulturbesitz (West Berlin)

3100		? Lauda Sion	SATB SATB		
3101	no.1 no.2 no.3 no.4 no.5	? Ipse praeibit Ardens est cor meum Desiderata nobis ? Lapides praetiosi ? Viri Galilaei	SSTB SATB ATB SmSAT (no bc) SSB	K K K K K	
3102		Viderunt te Domine	SB		
3103		? In voce exultationis ? In voce exultationis			Score. Without text. Parts. Without text.
3110		Turbabuntur impii	ATB		

158

TABLE VIII

D-ddr D1(b): SÄCHSISCHE LANDESBIBLIOTHEK, DRESDEN

Manuscript number	Pages or folios	Title of motet	Voices and instruments	Hand	Comments
Mus.1706-E-500		Turbabuntur impii	ATB VV	Ja	Perf. 1682 & 1685
Mus.1706-E-501		Quid tandem sunt mundi deliciae	ATB	Ja	Perf. 1681
Mus.1706-E-502		x Obstupescite redemti	ATB	Ja	F. della Porta Perf. 1688 & 1690

TABLE IX

DK Kk: DET KONGELIGE BIBLIOTEK, COPENHAGEN

Manuscript number	Pages or folios	Title of motet	Voices and instruments	Hand	Comments
C I, 5		Dicite nobis	SSAT	Lb	
		Exulta, gaude, filia Sion	SS	Lb	
		Annunciate gentes	SSATB	Lb	
		Cum reverteretur David	SSS	Lb	
C I, 650		Ardens est cor meum	SATB		
		? O sacrum convivium	SAT (no bc)		
		Turbabuntur impii	ATB		
Rungs Musik Archiv Nr. 196		...Gaudeat ergo...	ATB (no bc)		Fragment of 'Desiderata nobis'

TABLE X

F LYm: BIBLIOTHÈQUE MUNICIPALE, LYON

Manuscript number	Pages or folios	Title of motet	Voices and instruments	Hand	Comments
28329	1-6	? Ad dapes salutis venite	ATB		
	7-14	? Anima mea in dolore	SSATB		
	23-24	? Audi Domine	S		
	25-28	x Benignissime Jesu	SST		B. Graziani
	32-38	? Vanitas vanitatum	SS		
	38-44	? O admirabile commercium	SSB		
	44-49	? Cantate Domino	SSB		
133721	29-35	x Peccavi Domine et miserere mei	SAB		G. Ferrari
	36-42	Surgamus, eamus	ATB		
133989	85-89	Lucifer	T[sic]		bc missing
134025 [part A]	1-6	Super flumina Babilonis	SSAT		Anon.
	7-11	x O bonitas, o amor	SSB		Anon.
	16-22	x Domine, Dominus noster	SSB VV		Anon.
	23-24	? Duo ex discipulis	SST		G. Tricarico (original for ATB a tone higher (in D major) than MS 134025).
		x Deus qui[s] similis erit tibi?	SSB [sic]		
	24-34	(Jephte)	SSSATB		
	34-37	? (Cain)	SSSATB		
	37-39	? Sedente Salomone	SSB		
	39-43	Turbabuntur impii	ATB		
	43-47	x Ecce in dolore	SSSATB		
	47-51	O quam dilecta sunt tabernacula	SSATB		Anon.

161

TABLE X continued

[part B]	1-11 11-12^v	(Dives malus) Turbabuntur impii		SATB SATB ATB
[part C]	[1-13] [2-13^v] [sic]	(Judicium extremum) (Ezechias)	[J	SSATB ATB ATB SSATB
[part D]	1-13 45-49 49-60	(Proposui in mente mea) Vidi impium ? Filiae Jerusalem (=Sponsa Canticorum)		SSATB VV ATB SSSB VV

TABLE XI

F Pc: BIBLIOTHÈQUE DU CONSERVATOIRE, PARIS

Manuscript number	Pages or folios	Title of motet	Voices and instruments	Hand	Comments
Rés.F.934[a]	117-43	Turbabuntur impii	ATB VV		
	145-56	Vidi impium	ATB		
	157-64	? Sub umbra noctis	SST		
	165-84	? Quare fremuerunt	ATB		
	189-204	Si linguis hominum	SSS		
	205-16	Insurrexerunt in nos	ATB		
	217-26	? Qui descendunt mare	BB		
	227-38	? Revertimini praevaricatores	ATB		F. Foggia
	239-45	x Iste sanctus pro lege Dei	ATB		
	246-50	O dulcissime Jesu	SS		
	251-61	Militia est vita	SSB		
Rés.F.934[b]	1-12	? Cernis panem	AB		F. Foggia
	13-24	? O vere et care Jesu	TB VV		
	25-35	x Adoremus Christum	SSB		A. Vermeren (there is also a ms attribution to F. Foggia in F Pn, Vm .1185).
	37-43	x O quam clemens	SS		
	44-50	? O piissime Jesu	ATB		
	51-66	? Errate per colles	SATB		
	67-74	Ecce sponsus venit	SA		
	75-85	? Tolle sponsa	SB		
	86-101	? Duo ex discipulis	SST		
	102-11	? Vanitas vanitatum	SS		
	112-20	Surgamus, eamus	ATB		
	121-25	x Gaudia felices	SS		B. Graziani
	126-34	? O admirabile commercium	SSB		
	135-47	? Sicut cervus	SSB		
	148-54	? Adeste mortales	S		
	155-63	x Deus quis similis erit tibi?	ATB		G. Tricarico

TABLE XI continued

	164-68	? Audi Domine	S	
	169-75	x Benignissime Jesu	SST	
	176-84	? Cantate Domino	SSB	
	185-97	? Notus in Judaea Deus	STB	
	198-210	? Qui non renunciat	TTB	
	211-22	x Domine, ne in furore tuo	SSB	
	223-33	x Vox turturis audita est	SA	
	234-46	? O miraculum miraculorum	SB	
	247-50	? Tu es Petrus	SSB	
	251-60	x Salve Jesu spes nostra	SAB	
Rés.F.934[c]	1-4	O vulnera doloris	B	x
	5-13	Domine, Deus meus	S	x
	13-17	Lucifer	B	x
	18-26	Sicut stella matutina	S	x
	27-32	Cantabo Domino	SS	x
	33-39	Exulta, gaude, filia Sion	SS	x
	39-47	Quo tam laetus	SS	x
	47-52	Laudemus virum gloriosum	SS	x
	53-56	Hodie Simon Petrus	TT	x
	56-63	Audite sancti	SSB	x
	64-69	Egredimini caelestes curiae	SSS	x
	70-79	Quis est hic vir	SSS	x
	80-88	Militia est vita	SSB	x
	88-102	Exultabunt justi	SSS	x
	103-10	Cum reverteretur David	SSS	x
	111-17	Suscitavit Dominus	ATB	x
	118-25	Praevaluerunt in nos	SAT	x	B. Graziani
	125-33	Domine, quis habitet [sic]	SST	x	B. Graziani
	134-40	Vidi impium	ATB	x	Alessandro Melani
	141-47	Surgamus, eamus	ATB	x
	148-50	(Amante che dite)	SSB	x	G. Carisio
	151-61	Turbabuntur impii	ATB	x
	162-72	Dicite nobis	SSAT	x
	172-85	(A solis ortu)	SSTB	x
	186-95	Annunciate gentes	SSATB	x

TABLE XI continued

Rés.2182(I)	no.10	Exulta, gaude, filia Sion	SS	K	Rome, 1675 (three motets in the publication are omitted in the transcription).
		Cantabo Domino	SS	K	
		Turbabuntur impii	ATB	K	
		Cum reverteretur David	SSS	K	
		Domine, quis habitabit	SST	K	
		Annunciate gentes	SSATB	K	
	no.12	? Ipse praeibit	SSTB	P	
		Ardens est cor meum	SATB	P	
		Desiderata nobis	ATB	P	
		? Lapides praetiosi	SmSAT (no bc)	P	
		? Viri Galilaei	SSB	P	
	no.13	? Lauda Sion	SATB SATB	P	F. Foggia
Rés.Vm^b.ms.6	2-3	x Quare suspiras	SSB	P	
	4-5	Emendemus in melius	mSAT	P	
	6-7	? Sub umbra noctis	SST	P	
	8-9	Surgamus, eamus	ATB	P	
	10-11	Insurrexerunt in nos	mSAT	P	
	12-13	Militia est vita	SSB	P	
	14-15	Vidi impium	ATB	P	
	16-17	Quomodo facti sunt impii	SSB	P	
	18-19	? Cantate Domino	SSB	P	
	20-21	Audite sancti	SSB	P	
	22-23	? Isti sunt triumphatores et amici Dei	ATB	P	
	24-25	x O ignis qui semper ardes	SST	P	F. Foggia
	26-27	x Peccavi Domine et miserere mei	SAB	P	G. Ferrari
	28-29	x Benignissime Jesu	SST	P	B. Graziani
	30-31	? Revertimini praevaricatores	ATB	P	
	32-33	Salve Regina	SSB	P	
	34-35	x Animae amantes	ATB	P	M. Cazzati

165

TABLE XI continued

	36-38	x Ecce sonuerunt inimici tui	ATB	P	G. Pagliardi
	40-41	? Sedente Salomone	SSB	P	
	50-51	O dulcissime Jesu	SS	P	
	52-53	Ecce sponsus venit	SA	P	
	54-55	? Benedictus Redemptor	SS	P	
	56-59	Quo abijt dilectus meus	SA	P	
	60-62	? In te Domine spes mea	SS	P	
	63-65	? O miraculum miraculorum	SB	P	
	66-67	Sicut mater consolatur	SS	P	
	68-69	Laudemus virum gloriosum	SS	P	
	70-71	x Fideles animae	SB	P	M. Cazzati
	80-81	Silentium tenebant	SST VV	P	
	82-83	Super flumina Babilonis	SSAT	P	
	84-88	? Laeta caelestibus	S VV	P	C. Cecchelli
	88-89	x Peccaverunt habitatores	SATB	P	
L.11.897(3)	100-07^v	? Nisi Dominus aedificaverit	SATB SATB		
D.16331		x Sunt breves mundi rosae	B VV vc		M. Cazzati

TABLE XII

F Pn: BIBLIOTHÈQUE NATIONALE, PARIS

Manuscript number	Pages or folios	Title of motet	Voices and instruments	Hand	Comments
Mss. Latin 16830	106ᵛ-10	Caro mea	SmSATB VV		
Vm¹.1174	no.2	Surgamus, eamus	ATB		
	no.3	Salve Regina	SSB		
	no.4	Quomodo facti sunt	SSB		
	no.5	Suscitavit Dominus	ATB		
	no.7	Exulta, gaude, filia Sion	SS	[J	
	no.8	Desiderata nobis	ATB	J]	
	no.16	Audite sancti	SSB		
	no.17	Salve amor noster	SS		
	no.23	Confitemini Domino	BB		
	no.24	Inclinavit coelos Dominus	TT		
	288-301	Salve amor noster	SS		
	365-78	x Quare suspiras	SSB		F. Foggia
	515-24	x O mortalis quid mundanas	ATB		S. Durante
Vm¹.1175bis	no.1	? Deus Dominus	BB		
	no.2	Emendemus in melius	mSAT		
	no.3	Insurrexerunt in nos	mSAT		
	no.4	? Revertimini praevaricatores	ATB		
	no.5	Vidi impium	ATB VV		Violin parts added by Brossard in 1691.
	no.6	Si linguis hominum	SST		
	no.7	Super flumina Babilonis	SSAT	[J	
	no.8	? Panem coelestem	SATB		
Vm¹.1267	no.9	x Peccaverunt habitatores	SATB		C. Cecchelli
	no.10	? Anima mea in dolore est	SSATB		
	no.11	Surgamus, eamus	ATB VV		

167

TABLE XII continued

Vm¹.1267bis	[no.11a]	x Ave verum corpus		SATB	Br
	no.12	In te, Domine, speravi		ATB VV fag	Br
Vm¹.1268		Salve puellule		S	
	no.1	Ecce sponsus venit		SA	
	no.2	Anima nostra sustinet Dominum		SS	
	no.3	Hymnum jucunditatis		SS	
	no.4	Nigra sum sed formosa		SS	
	no.5	Immensus coeli conditor		SS	
	no.6	Salve Regina		SSB	
	no.7	Audite sancti		SSB	
	no.8	Confitebor tibi		SSB	
	no.9	Quasi stella matutina		SSSA	
Vm¹.1306		Lucifer		S	
		? Cum audisset Gedeon	[J]	S	
		? Concinant linguae		A	
		Sicut stella matutina		S	
		Convertere ad me	[J]	S	
		Domine, Deus meus	[J]	S	Possibly by E. Bernabei.
Vm¹.1420-21		x Sunt breves mundi rosae		B 2 fl VV fag	Ro(?) M. Cazzati
Vm¹.1469		Turbabuntur impii		ATB VV	
Vm¹.1638-39		In te, Domine, speravi		ATB VV	
		? O impij mortales		ATB VV	
Vm¹.1641	5-6	Vidi impium		[ATB]	B only
	7-10	Turbabuntur impii		[ATB]	B only
Vm¹.1738		x In tribulationibus		SS	Br A. Antonelli

168

TABLE XII continued

Vm^1.3123	50-65	...Somne laborum dulce levamen	SSB (no bc)	Dated 1765. Fragment of 'Silentium tenebant'.
Vm^7.3	37-47	x O miracula, o prodigia	S	P. P. Vannini
Vm^9.ms.8 (i-ii)(=F Pc, Rés.Vm^7.673)	i: 160 -77	Salve mi Pupule (sic; but T begins 'Salve, salve Puellule')	T VV	F Pc, Rés.Vm^7.673 (the Manuscrit Rost) may not be seen; the F Pn ms is a modern transcription by A. Laffaille-Terrier.

TABLE XIII

F V: BIBLIOTHÈQUE DE VERSAILLES

Manuscript number	Pages or folios	Title of motet	Voices and instruments	Hand	Comments
58	1-22 51-72 73-86	(Jephte) (Jonas) x Vir frugi et pater familias	SSSATB SATB SATB TTB		Not Carissimi's style

TABLE XIV

GB Bu: BARBER INSTITUTE OF FINE ARTS, UNIVERSITY OF BIRMINGHAM

Manuscript number	Pages or folios	Title of motet	Voices and instruments	Hand	Comments
5002	191-97 252-55	Audite sancti Lucifer	SSB S		

TABLE XV

GB **Cfm**: FITZWILLIAM MUSEUM, CAMBRIDGE

Manuscript number	Pages or folios	Title of motet	Voices and instruments	Hand	Comments
2 F 22	1–3^v	Viderunt te Domine	SB		⎞ Rome, 1647[2]
	3^v–6^v	Alma Redemptoris Mater	SSB		⎟
	7–8^v	Salve amor noster...	SS		⎠ Incomplete
	9–12	Exulta, gaude, filia Sion	SS		⎞
	12–14^v	Laudemus virum gloriosum	SS		⎟ Rome, 1675
	14^v–16	Quo tam laetus...	SS		⎠ (incomplete)
24 F 4	82^v–84^v	Lucifer	B		
	84^v–86	O vulnera doloris	B		
32 F 24	2–6^v	Surgamus, eamus	ATB		
	8–12^v	? Beatus vir	S VV		
	12^v–16^v	? Veni sancte spiritus	SAB		
	17–24	? Lauda Sion	SAB		
	24^v–27	x O beatae caeli mentes	AA		M. Cazzati
32 G 30	1–6^v	? Sonent organa	SAB VV		
	7–8^v	? Alleluia. O beatae caeli mentes	SB		
	9–11^v	? Pange lingua	SAB		
	11^v–12^v	? Christus factus est	ATB		
	13–16^v	x Venite gentes	SB		M. Cazzati
	16^v–18^v	x Ad cantus, ad melos	AA		M. Cazzati
	19–22^v	x Crucior in hac flamma	AB		M. Cazzati
	22–24^v	x Audite gentes	ATB		M. Cazzati
	25–28	x Ad festum venite	SS		M. Cazzati
	28–31	x Fideles animae	SB		M. Cazzati
	31–33	x Haec dies quam fecit Dominus	SS		M. Cazzati

172

TABLE XV continued

33-36^v	x Venite fideles festinate	ST	
37-44	? Exultate colles	B VV vc	
44^v-48	Salve amor noster	SS	
49-55	? Eia plebs fidelium laetare	B VV vdg	
56-60^v	? Gaude, laetare, Sion	TB	
61-74^v	? Beatus vir	A VV	
75-83^v	? Dominator Domine	A VV	
84-90	? Ecce nunc benedicite Dominum	SSS	M. Cazzati
91-93^v	x Vivat laeta triumphalis	ATB	M. Cazzati
94-98	x Siccine te Domine	ATB	M. Cazzati
99-105^v	x Gaudeamus omnes	SATB	M. Cazzati
106-11	? Nisi Dominus aedificaverit	SSATB	
112-13^v	...dies felicitatis aeternae	SS	End of 'Exulta, gaude, filia Sion'
113^v-16	Laudemus virum gloriosum	SS	
116-20^v	Quo tam laetus	SS	
120^v-23^v	Cantabo Domino	SS	Rome, 1675
123^v-28^v	Turbabuntur impii	ATB	
129-32^v	Cum reverteretur David) Cum ingrederetur N.)	SSS	
132^v-36^v	Domine, quis habitabit	SST	
136^v-41	Dicite nobis	SSAT	
141-45^v	Annunciate gentes	SSATB	

TABLE XVI

GB Ckc: ROWE MUSIC LIBRARY, KING'S COLLEGE, CAMBRIDGE

Manuscript number	Pages or folios	Title of motet	Voices and instruments	Hand	Comments
206	188-95	Annunciate gentes	SSATB		p.198 dated December 27 1704
207	1-12	Dicite nobis	SSAT	X	

174

TABLE XVII

GB Cmc: PEPYS LIBRARY, MAGDALENE COLLEGE, CAMBRIDGE

Manuscript number	Pages or folios	Title of motet	Voices and instruments	Hand	Comments
2803	80^V-87^V	Lucifer	[J B		

TABLE XVIII

GB Lam: ROYAL ACADEMY OF MUSIC, LONDON

Manuscript Number	Pages or folios	Title of motet	Voices and instruments	Hand	Comments
40	151-61	Exultabunt justi	SSS		
	162-84	(Salamonis Judicium)	SSTB VV		
	184-97	Confitebor tibi	SSB		
	197-202	Anima nostra sustinet Dominum	SS		
	202-06	O quam mirabilia sunt	SS		
41	1-7	Exulta, gaude, filia Sion	SS	Ba	⎫
	8-13	Laudemus virum gloriosum	SS	Ba	⎪
	13-23	Quo tam laetus	SS	Ba	⎪
	24-29	Cantabo Domino	SS	Ba	⎪
	30-44	Turbabuntur impii	ATB	Ba	⎬ Rome, 1675
	44-53	Cum reverteretur David ⎫	SSS	Ba	⎪
		Cum ingrederetur N. ⎭			⎪
	53-64	Domine, quis habitabit	SST	Ba	⎪
	65-78	Dicite nobis	SSAT	Ba	⎭
	79-94	Annunciate gentes	SSATB	Ba	
	95-105	Vidi impium	ATB	Ba	
	105-14	Audite sancti	SSB	Ba	
	115-25	Insurrexerunt in nos	mSAT	Ba	
	125-33	Si qua est consolatio	SSB	Ba	
	133-37	Lucifer	S	Ba	
	138-43	O quam mirabilia	SS	Ba	
	143-53	Militia est vita	SSB	Ba	
	153-62	Surgamus, eamus	ATB	Ba	
	162-65	Nigra sum sed formosa	SS	Ba	
42	1-17	Exultabunt justi	SSS		
	18-37	(Salamonis Judicium)	SSTB VV		

176

TABLE XVIII continued

	38-69	(Jephte)	SSSATB	
	70-90	Confitebor tibi	SSB	
	90-142	(Missa)	ATTB	
	143-53	x Oleum effusum est	S	
	154-59	x Anima mea liquefacta est	SAB	
	159-69	Ecce nos reliquimus omnia	ATB	
	169-70	Euge serve bone [J]	AT	
	171-80	Anima nostra sustinet Dominum	SS	
	180-83	? O vita cui omnia	A	
	183-88	O quam mirabilia	SS	
43	91^v-87^v	Sicut stella matutina	S	X
	78-76^v	O vulnera doloris	B	X
50	46-55	O quam mirabilia	SS	Rome, 1675[3]
52	6-9^v	Surgamus, eamus [J]	ATB	
107	119-24	Quo tam laetus	SS	Dated 22 Nov. 1715
	124-26	Hodie Simon Petrus	TT	

F. Marini
In A minor

177

TABLE XIX

GB Lbl(bm): BRITISH LIBRARY (formerly British Museum), LONDON

Manuscript number	Pages or folios	Title of motet	Voices and instruments	Hand	Comments
Add.17835	2-5^v	Quo tam laetus	SS	X	
	5^v-7^v	Laudemus virum gloriosum	SS	X	
	7^v-8^v	Hodie Simon Petrus	TT	X	
	9-12^v	Domine, Deus meus	S	X	
	13-17^v	Dicite nobis	SSAT	X	
	18-22	Annunciate gentes	SSATB	X	
	30^v-33	Cantabo Domino	SS	X	
	33^v-36	Exulta, gaude, filia Sion	SS	X	
	87-88	x Anima mea in aeterna dulcedine	SB		E. Trabattone
Add.22099	57^v	Lucifer	B		
Add.22100	56^v-58^v	Lucifer	B		c.1682
Add.29292	16-25^v	Salve puellule	S	Y	
	46-57	O quam pulchra es	S	Y	
Add.29379	16-18^v	Cantabo Domino	SS	King	Before 1719
Add.30382	13^v-15^v	Audite sancti	SSB	Bo	1680-86
	62^v-64	x Anima mea in aeterna dulcedine	SB	Bo	
Add.31409	46^v-50^v	Annunciate gentes	SSATB	etW	
Add.31412	59^v-60^v	Hodie Simon Petrus	TT	Cch	c.1798
Add.31460	5-7^v	Lucifer	B.	Bo	

178

TABLE XIX continued

Add.31472

2–3^v	O vulnera doloris	B		
4–7^v	Domine, Deus meus	S		
8–12	Sicut stella matutina	S		
12^v–15	Cantabo Domino	SS	x	
15^v–18^v	Exulta, gaude, filia Sion	SS	x	
18^v–22	Quo tam laetus	SS	x	
22^v–25	Laudemus virum gloriosum	SS	x	
25^v–27	Hodie Simon Petrus	TT	x	
27–30	Audite sancti	SSB	x	
30^v–33^v	Egredimini caelestes curiae	SSS	x	
34–38^v	Quis est hic vir	SSS	x	
38^v–42	Militia est vita	SSB	x	
42^v–49	Exultabunt justi	SSS	x	
49^v–53^v	Cum reverteretur David	SSS	x	
53^v–56^v	Suscitavit Dominus	ATB	x	
56^v–60^v	Praevaluerunt in nos	SAT	x	
60^v–64	Domine, quis habitat [sic]	SST	x	Index: '...habitet'
65–68^v	Vidi impium	ATB	x	
68^v–71^v	Surgamus, eamus	ATB	x	
72^v–73^v	(Amante che dite)	SSB	x	
73^v–78^v	Turbabuntur impii	ATB	x	
79–84^v	Dicite nobis	SSAT	x	
84^v–90^v	(A solis ortu)	SSTB	x	
91–95	Annunciate gentes	SSATB	x	

Add.31475

1–5^v	x O quam pulchra et casta es	SS		M. Cazzati
5^v–8^v	x Dulcis amor, Jesu	SS		M. Cazzati
8^v–14	x O Regina coeli	SA		M. Cazzati
14^v–21	x O anima mea, suspira	SA		M. Cazzati
21^v–27	x Magnificat anima mea Mariam	SA		M. Cazzati
27^v–33^v	x Cantemus jubilemus	ST		M. Cazzati
33^v–38	x O crux nobilitata	AT		M. Cazzati
38^v	x Ave, dulcissima Maria...	AT		M. Cazzati. First 8½ bars only.

Add.31476

1–4^v	Surgamus, eamus	ATB		
4^v–8^v	x Salve Regina	ATB		N. Monferrato

179

TABLE XIX continued

Add.31477	18^v-21^v	? O quam suave	SSS	Gos
	21^v-26	Exultabunt justi	SSS	Gos
	54 -57	x Salve Regina	ATB	Gos
	57-62^v	Confitebor tibi	SSB	Gos N. Monferrato
	63-64^v	Anima nostra sustinet Dominum	SS	Gos
	65-66	O quam mirabilia	SS	Gos
Add.31479		Lucifer	B	Je
		x Anima mea in aeterna dulcedine	SB	Je E. Trabattone
		Insurrexerunt in nos	mSAT	Je
		Desiderata nobis	ATB	Je G. Rovetta (altered)
		x Quam pulchra es	SSB	Je
		Audite sancti	SSB	Je
Add.31818	20-21^v	...Glory be to the Father	SSB	The Gloria (translated and slightly modified) of 'Confitebor tibi' (SSB).
Add.33234	13-14^v	Lucifer	B	Mor Date of ms: 1680-82.
	70-72	x Anima mea in aeterna dulcedine	SB	Mor E. Trabattone
	112-15	Audite sancti	SSB	Mor
Add.33235	4-7	Militia est vita	SSB	
	30^v-32^v	Suscitavit Dominus	ATB	
	33-36	Surgamus, eamus	ATB	
	92-94	x Anima mea in aeterna dulcedine	SB	E. Trabattone
	103-04^v	Lucifer	[J B	
Add.37027	19-21	Cantabo Domino	SS	
	21^v-24	Exulta, gaude, filia Sion	SS	
Egerton 2960	2-4	Lucifer	B	
Harley 1501	48-52	Audite sancti	SSB	Re Dated 1681

180

TABLE XX

GB Lcm: ROYAL COLLEGE OF MUSIC, LONDON

Manuscript number	Pages or folios	Title of motet	Voices and instruments	Hand	Comments
791	1-15	(Jeptha)	SSSATB		
	15^v-25	(Salomonis Judicium)	SSTB		
	25-27^v	O vulnera doloris	B		
	27^v-29^v	(Amante che dite)	SSB		
	30-31	...Sicut erat in principio	SSB		The final section of 'Confitebor tibi'.
792	1-6^v	Turbabuntur impii	ATB		
793	1-3^v	Surgamus, eamus	ATB		
	5-6	O vulnera doloris	B		
1059	36^v-38^v	Surgamus, eamus	ATB		
1064	1^v-2	Suscitavit Dominus	⎡ATB⎤		Only the bass voice part survives. All except 'Audite' and 'Salve' probably with VV vdg also: Cologne, 1666.
	2-2^v	Surgamus, eamus	ATB		
	2^v-3^v	In te, Domine, speravi	ATB		
	4-4^v	Militia est vita	SSB		
	5	Audite sancti	SSB		
	6-6^v	Turbabuntur impii	ATB		
	8^v	x Salve Regina	⎣ATB⎦		
1076	6^v-7^v	Nigra sum sed formosa	SS	Z	N. Monferrato. Cf. GB Ob, Mus.c.57. The motet appears twice in GB Lcm, 1076.
1101	25-28^v	Exulta, gaude, filia Sion	SS	Cft	Dated 11 April 1711.
	28-30^v	Laudemus virum gloriosum	SS	Cft	All except 'Euge' and 'Exultabunt': Rome, 1675.
	31-35^v	Quo tam laetus	SS	Cft	
	36-39	Cantabo Domino	SS	Cft	

181

TABLE XX continued

39-45^v	Turbabuntur impii	ATB	Cft
45^v-49^v	Cum reverteretur David	SSS	Cft
50^v	Euge serve bone	[J] AT	Cft
68^v-73^v	Domine, quis habitabit	SST	Cft
73^v-79^v	Dicite nobis	SSAT	Cft
80-86^v	Annunciate gentes	SSATB	Cft
100-05^v	Exultabunt justi	[J] SSS	Cft
1178	Dixit Dominus	SATB SATB	Y
1179	Confitebor tibi	SSATB VV	Y
1180	O pretiosum et admirandum convivium	S V	Y
2038	O quam pulchra es	[J] S	
	Salve puellule	[J] S	
2074	25^v ...Nos quoque socii	s[ss]	
	24 ...in sonitu tubae	s[ss]	

One soprano part only of each fragment. The first is from 'Quis est hic vir', the second from 'Egredimini caelestes curiae'.

182

TABLE XXI

GB Lgc: MUSIC LIBRARY OF GRESHAM COLLEGE, LONDON
(DEPOSITED IN THE GUILDHALL LIBRARY)

Manuscript number	Pages or folios	Title of motet	Voices and instruments	Hand	Comments
455	9ᵛ -	Cantabo Domino	SS		

TABLE XXII

GB Lk: KING'S MUSIC LIBRARY, LONDON
(DEPOSITED IN THE BRITISH LIBRARY)

Manuscript number	Pages or folios	Title of motet	Voices and instruments	Hand	Comments
R.M.20.h.8	127-25^v [sic]	x Crucior in hac flamma	AB	Pur	M. Cazzati
R.M.22.c.2		Dixit Dominus	SSATB		
R.M.24.c.10 (2)	69-72	Nigra sum sed formosa	SS	Z	Cf. GB Ob, Mus.c.57

TABLE XXIII

GB Lwa: WESTMINSTER ABBEY, LONDON

Manuscript number	Pages or folios	Title of motet	Voices and instruments	Hand	Comments
CG 63	189-208 209-21	(Jephte) Confitebor tibi	SSSATB SSB		

TABLE XXIV

GB Ob: BODLEIAN LIBRARY, OXFORD

Manuscript number	Pages or folios	Title of motet	Voices and instruments	Hand	Comments
Mus.c.24	32-40^v	In te, Domine, speravi	ATB VV vdg/fag	Awb	
Mus.c.57	11-12^v	Nigra sum sed formosa	SS	Z	Complete transcription of R.Floridus...has alias sacras cantiones...(Rome, 1650).
	92^v-96^v	Militia est vita	SSB	Z	Complete transcription of R.Floridus...has sacras cantiones...(Rome, 1652).
	107-11^v	Surgamus, eamus	ATB	Z	
Mus.d.26	1-4	O dulcissimum Mariae nomen	SS	Awb	
	5-13	Anima nostra sustinet Dominum	SS	Awb	
	14-20	Sicut mater consolatur	SS	Awb	
	21-27	O quam mirabilia	SS	Awb	
	28-39	Praevaluerunt in nos	ATB	Awb	
	40-48	Suscitavit Dominus	ATB	Awb	
	49-59	Vidi impium	ATB	Awb	
	60-83	Confitebor tibi	SSB	Awb	
	84-100	Ecce nos reliquimus omnia (Jeptha)	TTB	Awb	
	101-43	Exultabunt justi	SSSATB	Awb	
	145-63	(Solomonis Judicium)	SSS	Awb	
	165-88		SSTB VV	Awb	
Mus.d.215		x Lamentationes	SA VV		
Mus.e.34		Turbabuntur impii	ATB VV fag		
Mus.Sch.c.9	25-30	Sicut mater consolatur	SS	X	
	31-37	O quam mirabilia	SS	X	

186

TABLE XXIV continued

	37-44	Anima nostra sustinet Dominum	SS	X	
	46-50	x Salve Regina	ATB	G(i)	N. Monferrato
	51-55	Audite sancti	SSB	G(i)	
	82-85	(Amante che dite)	SSB	G(i)	
	86	x Gloria Patri	SSTB no bc	G(i)	Matthew Locke
	95-118	(Jeptha)	SSSATB	X	
	119-26	(E pur volo)	SS	G(i)	
	128-36	Exultabunt justi	SSS	G(i)	
	137-47	(Judicium Salomonis)	SSTB	G(i)	
	148-55	Annunciate gentes	SSATB	G(i)	
	156-68	Confitebor tibi	SSB	G(i)	
	170-75	Exulta, gaude, filia Sion	SS	G(i)	
	175-79	Cantabo Domino	SS	G(i)	
	180-87	Quo tam laetus	SS	G(i)	
	187-91	Laudemus virum gloriosum	SS	G(i)	
	192-98	Cum reverteretur David	SSS	G(i)	
	198-203	Egredimini caelestes curiae	SSS	G(i)	
	203-11	(A pie d'un verde alloro)	SS	G(i)	
Mus.Sch.c.11	175-70 [sic]	x Anima mea in aeterna dulcedine	SB	G(i)	E. Trabattone
Mus.Sch.c. 12-19		Anima mea in aeterna dulcedine(12,16,19)	SB bc	G(i)	E. Trabattone
		Audite sancti(12,13,16,19)	SSB bc	G(i)	
		x O crux benedicta (14,15, 16,19)	ATB bc	G(i)	F. Sances
		Turbabuntur impii (14,15, 16, 19) [J]	ATB bc	G(i)	
		In te, Domine, speravi(17, 18,14)	VV vdg	G(i)	
		Suscitavit Dominus(17,18,14) [J]	VV vdg	G(i)	
		Surgamus, eamus(17,18,14)	VV vdg	G(i)	
		Militia est vita(17,18,14)	VV vdg	G(i)	
		x Annunciate gentes(17,18,19)	VV bc	G(i)	The original motet (SSATB) <u>is</u> by Carissimi; these violin parts are not.

187

TABLE XXIV continued

Mus.Sch.c. 20-23	In te, Domine, speravi	ATB bc	G(i)
	Suscitavit Dominus	ATB bc	G(i)
	Surgamus, eamus	ATB bc	G(i)
	Militia est vita	SSB bc	G(i)
Mus.Sch.c. 24-27	Audite sancti	SSB only	G(i) bc missing
Mus.Sch.d. 375a-j	x O felix anima	ATB	M. Cazzati (fragment)
	x Benedicite	SSATB	
	x Jubilate	SSATB	

188

TABLE XXV

GB Och: LIBRARY OF CHRIST CHURCH COLLEGE, OXFORD

Manuscript number	Pages or folios	Title of motet	Voices and instruments	Hand	Comments
4		In te, Domine, speravi	ATB VV	G(ii)	
9	7-10	Ecce nos reliquimus omnia ⌐	TTB	Ald	
	10-10ᵛ	Euge serve bone ⌐	AT	Ald	
	11-14	Si linguis hominum ⌐	SSS	Ald	
13	1-5	x Venite pastores	S	G(i)	B. Graziani
	5-11	x Pastores dum custodistis	S	G(i)	B. Graziani
	11-17	x Quid agis cor meum	S	G(i)	B. Graziani
	17-24	Domine, Deus meus	S	G(i)	⌐
	24-29	Exulta, gaude, filia Sion	SS	G(i)	⌐
	30-34	Laudemus virum gloriosum	SS	G(i)	⌐
	34-41	Quo tam laetus	SS	G(i)	⌐
	42-46	Cantabo Domino	SS	G(i)	⌐ Rome, 1675
	47-56	Turbabuntur impii	ATB	G(i)	⌐
	56-64	Domine, quis habitabit	SST	G(i)	⌐
	64-72	Dicite nobis	SSAT	G(i)	⌐
	73-79	Annunciate gentes	SSATB	G(i)	⌐
	80-86	Cum reverteretur David	SSS	G(i)	⌐
	87-96	(O me infelice)	S	G(i)	
	97	(Care selve beate....)	B	Ald	
	105-07	Sicut stella matutina...	S	Ald	
	117-18	O dulcissimum Mariae nomen	SS	Ald	
	119-20	(Plorate filiae Israel...)	SSSATB	Ald	
	121-23	Hodie Simon Petrus	TT	Ald	
	123	O vulnera doloris...	B	Ald	
	125-28	Egredimini caelestes curiae	SSS	Ald	
	129-34	Quis est hic vir	SSS	Ald	
	135-39	Praevaluerunt in nos	SAT	Ald	
	140-44	Suscitavit Dominus	ATB	Ald	

189

TABLE XXV continued

	145-48	Militia est vita	SSB	Ald
	149-52	Ave dulcissime angelorum panis	SST	Ald
	153-58	Vidi impium	ATB	Ald
	159-62	Surgamus, eamus	ATB	Ald
	163-64	? Gaudete exercitus	SSB	Ald
	165-88	(Missa)	ATTB VV	Ald
	195-202	Exultabunt justi	SSS	Ald
	203-15	(Judicium Salomonis)	SSTB VV	Ald
	215-20	O vulnera doloris	SSB	Ald
	221-25	? Benedicite omnes angeli	ATB	Ald
	226-29	Quomodo facti sunt impii	SSB	Ald
	229-41	Confitebor tibi	SSB	Ald
18	23-25	Lucifer	B	Ald
23	2^v-3^v	Lucifer	B	G(i)
43	10-11^v	x Anima mea in aeterna dulcedine	SB	Ald E. Trabattone
	12-14	Audite sancti	SSB	Ald
46	12^v-14	O vulnera doloris	B	
53	1-4	O vulnera doloris	B	X
	5-9	Lucifer	B	X
	9-17	Domine, Deus meus	S	X
	17-25	Sicut stella matutina	S	X
	25-28	Hodie Simon Petrus	TT	X
	29-36	Quo tam laetus	SS	X
	36-41	Laudemus virum gloriosum	SS	X
	42-46	Exulta, gaude, filia Sion	SS	X
	46-52	Cantabo Domino	SS	X
	52-58	Egredimini caelestes curiae	SSS	X
	58-64	Militia est vita	SSB	X
	65-70	Audite sancti	SSB	X
	71-79	Quis est hic vir	SSS	X
	80-94	Exultabunt justi	SSS	X

TABLE XXV continued

	94-102	Domine, quis habitabit	SST	x
	103-11	Cum ingrederetur N.	SSS	x
	111-18	Surgamus, eamus	ATB	x
	118-21	? Gaudete exercitus	SSB	x
	121-32	Turbabuntur impii	ATB	x
	132-42	Dicite nobis	SSAT	x
	143-55	(Judicium Salomonis)	SSTB	x
	156-66	Annunciate gentes	SSATB	x
	166-71	...Gloria Patri	ATB VV	Final section of 'In te Domine speravi'.
55	1-18	Dixit Dominus	SSATB	Ald
	25-29	Anima nostra sustinet Dominum	SS	Ald
	30-33	Sicut mater consolatur	SS	Ald
	34-37	O quam mirabilia sunt	SS	Ald
	39-65	(Missa)	TTB	Ald
75	11	...Sicut erat in principio	[SSB]	G(ii) Final section of 'Confitebor tibi'; bc only.
83	117-24	? O quam suave	SSS	
598	24-22	Lucifer	S	G(i) bc missing; half of f.22 torn out.
621	9ᵛ-11	x Anima mea in aeterna dulcedine	SB	G(i) E. Trabattone
623-26		Audite sancti	SSB	E. Trabattone
		x Anima mea in aeterna dulcedine	SB	
688		x Ego sum panis vivus	SSB	O. Benevoli
		x Non turbetur cor vestrum	S[B]	Bass voice missing.
1154,ms A	2-4ᵛ	x Crucior in hac flamma	AB	M. Cazzati

191

TABLE XXV continued

	3^v-4^v		SB	G(i)	E. Trabattone
1178		x Anima mea in aeterna dulcedine	[B?]	Ald	bc only.
1210		O vulnera doloris			

TABLE XXVI
GB T: LIBRARY OF ST MICHAEL'S COLLEGE, TENBURY

Manuscript number	Pages or folios	Title of motet	Voices and instruments	Hand	Comments
310	213-17	x Adoro te	ATB		
	222-28	Cum reverteretur David	SSS		
335	70-78	Audite sancti	SSB		
	97-99	(Amante che dite)	SSB	X	
	99-105	Surgamus, eamus	ATB VV	X	
	106-12	Quis est hic vir	SSS	X	
	113-18	Vidi impium	ATB	X	
	118-27	Turbabuntur impii	ATB VV	X	
	128-35	Militia est vita	SSB VV	X	
	136-43	Cum reverteretur David	SSS	X	
	144-49	Egredimini caelestes curiae	SSS	X	
	150-56	Praevaluerunt in nos	SAT	X	
	157-65	Domine, quis habitat [sic]	SST	X	Title: '...habitet'.
	166-72	Suscitavit Dominus	ATB VV	X	
	173-83	Exultabunt justi	SSS	X	
	184-94	(A solis ortu)	SSTB	X	
	195-209	Confitebor tibi	SSB	X	
	226-37	In te Domine speravi	ATB		
713	169-75	Alma Redemptoris Mater	SSB		
728	39ᵛ-44	Militia est vita	SSB	jW	Dated 1833.
739		Egredimini caelestes curiae	SSS		

193

TABLE XXVI continued

746	23-27	? Ipse praeibit	SSTB	S	
	27-30	Ardens est cor meum	SATB	S	
	30^v-36	Desiderata nobis	ATB	S	
	36^v-39	? Lapides pretiosi	SmSAT(no bc)	S	
	39^v-43	? Viri Galilaei	SSB	S	
	45-55	Turbabuntur impii	ATB	S	
900	6-9	Hodie Simon Petrus	TT	Mal	
926	38-45	Cantabo Domino	SS		
	46-52	Laudemus virum gloriosum	SS		
	126-37	? O quam suave	SSS		
	168-77	Vidi impium	ATB		
	178-90	Militia est vita	SSB		
935		? Beatus vir	SATB SATB		
936	1-13	x Amo te	ST VV vc		
	13-36	x Quando Jesus adest	SA VV vc		
	36-41	x Laetamini...	S VV vc		
	42-48	x ...O veneranda Aurora	SS VV vc		
	48-54	x Ah quid obdormis...	S VV vc		
	54-64	x ...Convertimini ad me	SB VV vc		
	64-66	x Quid gloriaris	ATB		
	67-71	x ...Per labores ad sudores...	T VV vc		
	72-90	x ...O sane stulta...	ATB VV vc		J.H. Wilderer
	91-105	x ...Vix homo nascitur	ATB VV vc		J.H. Wilderer
	106-32	x Ah Deus ego amo te	SSA VV vc		J.H. Wilderer
	133-48	x Audite peccatores	SSB VV vc		J.H. Wilderer
	149-78	x Ah vide Domine	SATB VV vc		J.H. Wilderer
	179-209	x Qui vult post me venire	SATB VV vc		J.H. Wilderer
	210-54	x O anima festina	SATB VV vc		J.H. Wilderer

TABLE XXVI continued

958	111–	Vidi impium	ATB	etW	The MS is lost
	120–	Surgamus, eamus	ATB	etW	
	128–	Militia est vita	SSB	etW	
	138–	Praevaluerunt in nos	SAT	etW	
	146–	? Stillate rores	[SSS]	etW	Probably a fragment of 'O quam suave'.
	149–[53]	Quomodo facti sunt impii	SSB	etW	
1031	134–36	Lucifer	B		
1225	1ᵛ–4	Sicut mater consolatur [J]	SS		
1226	125–28	Surgamus, eamus	ATB	X	
1245	20–39	Annunciate gentes	SSATB		
1260	no.5	Annunciate gentes	SSATB		
	no.6	Confitebor tibi	SSB		
1423	1ᵛ–16	Turbabuntur impii	ATB VV	P	MS now in F Pn.
	17–45ᵛ	Exultabunt justi	SSS VV	P	
	46–52	x Dilatatae sunt tribulationes	SS	P	A. Antonelli
	53–56	O dulcissimum Mariae nomen	SS	P	
	57–61	O dulcissime Jesu	SS	P	
1424	1ᵛ–12	Quo tam laetus	SS	P	MS now in F Pn.
	13–24	? Peccavi Domine, peccavi multum	SSB	P	
	25–37	x Vir frugi et pater familias	TTB	P	
	38–43	? Sub umbra mortis profundae	SST	P	
	44–51	Militia est vita	SSB	P	
	52–66	Super flumina Babilonis	SSAT	P	

TABLE XXVI continued

1425				
	1^v-9	Vidi impium	ATB	P
	10-17^v	? Sub umbra Jesu	ATB	P
	19-33	Quo abiit dilectus meus	SA	P
	34-42	Insurrexerunt in nos	mSAT	P
	43-48	? Congratulamini	S	P
	49-55	? Surge propera	S	P

MS now in F Pn.

TABLE XXVII

GB Y: LIBRARY OF YORK MINSTER

Manuscript number	Pages or folios	Title of motet	Voices and Instruments	Hand	Comments
M.35/1(S)		Annunciate gentes	SSA[TB]	ym1	TB missing; bc incomplete.
M.35/2(S)		? Beatus vir	SSATB	ym2	
M.35/3(S)		Dixit Dominus	SSATB	ym2	
M.35/4(S)		Ecce nos reliquimus omnia	TTB	ym1	
M.35/5(S)		Euge serve bone	AT	ym1	
M.35/6(S)		Hodie Simon Petrus	SS	ym1	
M.35/7(S)		? Laudate pueri	[SS]A[T]B	ym2	SST missing.
M.35/8(S)		? Laudate pueri	SSB	ym2	
M.35/9(S)		Quo tam laetus	SS	ym1	
M.35/10(S)		Si linguis hominum	SS[S or T] V[V]	ym1	Third voice, V2 and bc missing.
M.35/11(S)		Summi regis puerpera	SS Vv spinet or lute	ym1	
M.35/12(S)		Super flumina Babilonis	SSAT	ym3	
M.35/13(S)		Tollite sancti mei	SST VV lute	ym4 ym1	
M.36	1^v-3	Quo tam laetus	SS	H	
	3^v-5	Domine, quis habitabit	SST	H	
	13-16	(Judicium Salomonis)	SSTB	H	
	16^v-18	Sicut stella matutina	S	H	

197

TABLE XXVIII

I Ac: BIBLIOTECA COMUNALE, ASSISI

Manuscript number	Pages or folios	Title of motet	Voices and instruments	Hand	Comments
Vol.misc. n.5	65^v-66	Regina coeli [I]	SATB		
	76^v-77	Regina coeli [II]	SATB		

TABLE XXIX

I Ad: ARCHIVIO DELLA CATTEDRALE DI S. RUFINO, ASSISI

Manuscript number	Pages or folios	Title of motet	Voices and instruments	Hand	Comments
		O stupor			Written for the basilica of San Francesco.

TABLE XXX

I Bc: CIVICO MUSEO BIBLIOGRAFICO MUSICALE, BOLOGNA

Manuscript number	Pages or folios	Title of motet	Voices and instruments	Hand	Comments
Q 43		Lamentationes Jeremiae Prophetae (Feriae Quintae in Coena Domini):			
	1-4^v	Lectio Prima: 'Incipit lamentatio'	mS		
	5-6^v	Lectio Seconda: 'Vau. Et egressus est a filia Sion'	S		
Q 45	12-18^v	Super flumina Babilonis	SSAT		
	23-25^v	Egredimini filiae Sion	S		
	26-31^v	Quasi columba speciosa	SSS [J]		Printed in part in 1670; see above, Chapter Three, section XXX.
	95^v-99^v	Immensus caeli conditor	SS		
	124^v-32	Quasi stella matutina	SSSA VV vc		
X 233	6^v-7	x Pulchra et decora	SATB		G. Ghizzolo; lacks bc. Gaspari's catalogue implies that all ten anonymous pieces ff. 6^v and 14 are by Carissimi; but see above, Chapter Three, section XXX.
	16^v(-18) -17^v	Emendemus in melius	mSAT		
	24^v-26	Insurrexerunt in nos	mSAT [J]		Lacks final cadence.

200

TABLE XXXI

I COd: ARCHIVIO MUSICALE DEL DUOMO DI COMO

Manuscript number	Pages or folios	Title of motet	Voices and instruments	Hand	Comments
I-V-8		Domine, Deus meus	S	cd1	
I-V-9		Exultabunt justi	SSS VV	cd2	
I-V-10		O pretiosum et admirandum convivium	S	cd3	
I-V-12		Plaudite caelestes chori	S	cd1	
I-V-13		Quo abijt dilectus meus	SA	Y	
I-V-14		Timete Dominum	SSATB	cd4 cd5	
I-V-15		Vidi impium	ATB	cd2	

201

TABLE XXXII

I Ls: BIBLIOTECA DEL SEMINARIO, LUCCA

Manuscript number	Pages or folios	Title of motet	Voices and instruments	Hand	Comments
B.251		x Christus factus est	SATB		

TABLE XXXIII

I Mc: BIBLIOTECA DEL CONSERVATORIO DI MUSICA GIUSEPPE VERDI, MILAN

Manuscript number	Pages or folios	Title of motet	Voices and instruments	Hand	Comments
		Arde il cor nel petto	SATB		Italian text to the motet 'Ardens est cor meum'.
		Turbabuntur impii	ATB		

TABLE XXXIV

I PAc: BIBLIOTECA DEL CONSERVATORIO DI MUSICA A. BOITO, PARMA

Manuscript number	Pages or folios	Title of motet	Voices and instruments	Hand	Comments
		x Christus factus est	SATB		

TABLE XXXV

I PS: ARCHIVIO E BIBLIOTECA CAPITOLARE, PISTOIA

Manuscript number	Pages or folios	Title of motet	Voices and instruments	Hand	Comments
B 25 n.3	[1-1^v]	Si linguis hominum	$\begin{bmatrix}SSS\end{bmatrix}V[V]$		Music = 'Summi regis puerpera'.
	[2]	Omnes sancti	$\begin{bmatrix}SS\end{bmatrix}V[V]$		
	[2^v]	Si qua est consolatio	$\begin{bmatrix}SSB\end{bmatrix}V[V]$		Music = 'Ave dulcissime angelorum panis'.
	[3]	Ave dulcissime Jesu	$\begin{bmatrix}SST\end{bmatrix}V[V]$		
	[3^v-4]	Militia est vita	$\begin{bmatrix}SSB\end{bmatrix}V[V]$		
	[4^v]	Paratum cor meum	$\begin{bmatrix}S/B\end{bmatrix}V$		
	[5^v-6]	(? Magnificat)	SATB		
	[6^v-7]	Dixit Dominus	$S\begin{bmatrix}ATB\end{bmatrix}$ [J] $\begin{bmatrix}SATB\end{bmatrix}$ $\begin{bmatrix}SAT\end{bmatrix}B$		No attribution
	[15^v]	Veni sponsa Christi	$\begin{bmatrix}SS\end{bmatrix}A[TTB]$		

205

TABLE XXXVI

I Rc: BIBLIOTECA CASANATENSE, ROME

Manuscript number	Pages or folios	Title of motet	Voices and instruments	Hand	Comments
5394		Elevatis manibus benedixit eis	SAT		
5397		Si qua est consolatio	SSB		

TABLE XXXVII

I Rsc: BIBLIOTECA MUSICALE GOVERNATIVA DEL CONSERVATORIO DI SANTA CECILIA, ROME

Manuscript number	Pages or folios	Title of motet	Voices and instruments	Hand	Comments
2050		x Ave verum corpus	SATB	Ca	
3749	119-21	Praevaluerunt in nos	ATB		Rome, 1661.

TABLE XXXVIII

I Rsg: ARCHIVIO DI SAN GIOVANNI IN LATERANO, ROME

Manuscript number	Pages or folios	Title of motet	Voices and instruments	Hand	Comments
II Settimana Santa, N.15		Christus factus est	SSATB SATB	Chi	

TABLE XXXIX

I TLP: BIBLIOTECA DEL MUSEO DI CASA PUCCINI, TORRE DEL LAGO PUCCINI

Manuscript number	Pages or folios	Title of motet	Voices and instruments	Hand	Comments
40.M	51-	Alma Redemptoris Mater	SSB		

TABLE XL

NL At: TOONKUNST-BIBLIOTHEEK & OPENBARE MUZIEKBIBLIOTHEEK, AMSTERDAM

Manuscript number	Pages or folios	Title of motet	Voices and instruments	Hand	Comments
Ms-Cari-2	[76-81]	? Ipse praeibit	SSTB	S	Dated 1821; re-copied in 1855.

210

TABLE XLI

S Uu: UNIVERSITETSBIBLIOTEKET, UPPSALA

Manuscript number	Pages or folios	Title of motet	Voices and instruments	Hand	Comments
Bd.79 (Libro 3 di motetti e concerti)	no.1	Hodie Salvator mundi	SSATB VV vdg		Tablature score.
Bd.80 (Libro 4 di motetti e concerti)	no.59	x Deduxit illum Dominus	SSB	D	F. Foggia. Tablature score. The music, to the words 'Gaudete cum Maria', was published as Carissimi's in Arion Romanus... (Konstanz, 1670).
Tab.Caps.12:	no.2	Simile est regnum	SS	D	[c.1664]
Tab.Caps.77:	no.95	Audite justi	SSB	D	Music = 'Audite sancti'.
	no.101	Desiderata nobis	ATB	D	[1663] [1663]
Tab.Caps.78:	no.80	Super flumina Babylonis	SSAT	D	[1667]
	no.85	x Audite omnes quodquod estis	SSB	D	[1667]
Tab.Caps.79:	no.41	Suscitavit Dominus	ATB VV		[1664]
Tab.Caps.80:	no.115	Surrexit pastor bonus	SSS	D	[1665]
	no.116	...Omnes gentes gaudete...	SSS	D	[1665]. Fragment of 'Quasi columba'.
	no.117	Salve Regina/Salve Rex Christe	SSB	D	[1665]

211

TABLE XLI continued

Tab.Caps.83:	no.2	Cum reverteretur David	SSS	D
	no.2b	Si qua est consolatio	SSB	D
	no.3	x Audite omnes quodquod estis	SSB	D Music = 'Alma Redemptoris Mater'.
	no.5	Alleluia. Jesum nostrum laudate	SSB	D
	no.13	Insurrexerunt in nos	mSAT	D
	no.13a	Emendemus in melius	mSAT	D
	no.61	Caro factum facta parens	SS	
	no.62a	O mi chare Jesu Christe	SS	Music = 'O dulcissimum Mariae nomen'.
	no.64	Sacerdotes Dei	SS	
	no.67	Si linguis hominum	SSS VV	D
	no.68	(Vanitas vanitatum) [Proposui in mente mea]	SSATB VV vc	
Tab.Caps.85:	no.30	Parce, heu, parce jam	SSAB	D
Vok.mus. i hdskr. Caps. 11:	no.1	Alleluia. Jesum nostrum laudate	SSB	D Music = 'Alma Redemptoris Mater'.
	no.2	? Isti sunt triumphatores sancti	SSATB	Music = 'Audite sancti'.
	no.3	Audite justi	SSB	D
	no.4	x Audite omnes quodquod estis	SSB	D
	no.5	Caro factum facta parens	SS	
	no.6	Cum reverteretur David	SSS	D
	no.7	Desiderata nobis	ATB	D
	no.8	Dixit Dominus	SATB SATB	D
	no.10	Doleo et poenitet me	SSTB	D
	no.11	Emendemus in melius	3 viols	
	no.12	Gaudeat terra	SSB	D Transposed.
	no.13	Insurrexerunt in nos	SS	
	no.14	Jubilemus omnes	mSAT	Gei [c.1672]
	no.15	...Omnes gentes gaudete...	SSB	D [1664]. Fragment of 'Quasi columba'.
	no.16	x O quam terribilis est	SSS	D MS attributis to V. Albrici.
			SS	

212

TABLE XLI continued

	no.17	O vos populi	ATB VV	D
			vla vc	
	no.17a	O vos populi	ATB VV	D
			vla vc	
	no.18	Parce, heu, parce jam	SSAB	
	no.19	Salve Regina	SATB SATB	
	no.20	Salve Regina/Salve Rex Christe	SSB	D
Vok.mus. i hdskr. Caps. 12:	no.1	Si linguis hominum	SSS VV	
	no.3	Super flumina Babylonis	SSAT	
	no.4	Surrexit pastor bonus	SSS	
	no.5	Suscitavit Dominus	ATB VV	D
	no.6	Veni sponsa Christi	SSATTB	D
Vok.mus. i hdskr. Caps. 44:	no.3	Militia est vita [J	SSB	
			VV vdg	
Vok.mus. i hdskr. Caps. 45:	no.9	Sacerdotes Dei	SS	
Vok.mus. i hdskr. Caps. 53:	no.9	Quid tandem sunt mundi	ATB	
Vok.mus. i hdskr. Caps. 53:	no.10/1	...Omnes gentes gaudete...	SSS	D [1665]
	no.10/2	Surrexit pastor bonus	SSS	D [1665]
	no.10/3	Confitebor tibi	SSB	D [1664]
	no.10/6	Salve Regina/Salve Rex Christe	SSB	
	no.10/7	Alma Redemptoris Mater	SSB	
	no.10/11	Cum reverteretur David	SSS	
	no.10/12	Simile est regnum	SS	
	no.10/13	Viderunt te Domine	SB	
	no.10/14	Audite sancti	SSB	
	no.10/19	Emendemus im melius	mSAT	Fragment of 'Quasi columba'.

213

TABLE XLI continued

Vok.mus. i hdskr. Caps 70:	no.10/20	Insurrexerunt in nos	mSAT
	no.10/21	Veni sponsa Christi	SSATTB
	no.10/23	Paratum cor meum	S/B V
	no.10/25	Ecce nos reliquimus omnia	TTB
	no.10/26	Desiderata nobis	ATB
	no.16	(Vanitas vanitatum) [Proposui in mente mea]	SSATB VV vc	D

214

APPENDIX C: ADDENDA

The information in Table XLII (see over) is derived from Craig A. Otto, <u>Seventeenth-Century Music from Kromeríz, Czechoslovakia: A catalog of the Liechtenstein Music Collection on microfilm at Syracuse University</u> (Syracuse, N.Y., 1977).

TABLE XLII

CS KR: LIECHTENSTEIN MUSIC COLLECTION, ORIGINALLY IN THE ARCHIVES
OF THE COLLEGIATE CHURCH OF ST MAURICE, KROMĚŘÍŽ (KREMSIER), NOW
IN THE EPISCOPAL RESIDENCE

Manuscript number (from Craig Otto: see previous page)	Title of motet		Voices and instruments	Comments
II 2	Si linguis hominum	[J]	[SSS]	Missing; without attribution
II 130	(Interfecto Sisara)		SSSATB VV	Probably an oratorio
II 131	Quo tam laetus	[J]	[SS]	Missing; without attribution
II 132	Sicut stella matutina		S	Missing
II 133	Salve puellule	[J]	T VV	Anon.; attributed to Carissimi by Otto and Buff
II 134	Quasi aquila	[J]	T V vdg	Anon.; attributed to Carissimi by Otto and Buff
II 160	Quo abijt dilectus meus		SA	
II 161	(Dives malus)		SSTB SATB VV vlne	Oratorio
II 163	(Judicium Salomonis)		SSTB VV "3: Violae in Con:"	Oratorio
II 164	Sustinuimus in pacem		SSATTB	
II 165	(Jonas)		SATB SATB VV	Oratorio
II 166	Si linguis hominum		SSS VV	
II 167	(Proposui in mente mea)		[SSATB VV]	Missing; oratorio; attributed to Carissimi by Otto
II 168	(Diluvium universale)		SS SSATB SSATB VV	Oratorio
II 184	Laudemus virum gloriosum	[J]	[SS]	Missing; without attribution
II 188	Usquequo peccatores	[J]	[SSS SAT SATB VV L]	Missing; without attribution
II 287	Usquequo peccatores		SSS SAT SATB VV L	
II 288	(Stabunt adversus Israel)		?	Probably an oratorio
II 289	(Persarum Rex Maximus assuersus[?])		5 voices VV	Probably an oratorio
II 295	Sicut stella matutina	[J]	[S]	Missing; without attribution
II 298	Quasi aquila		T V "Viola"	"Viola" is probably vdg

216

TABLE XLII continued

II 300	Quo tam laetus	SS
II 301	Turbabuntur impii	ATB VV L
III 83	Dixit Dominus	SSATB
III 120	Laudate pueri	SSS VV

Appendix D

Transcriptions of Motets

General Editorial Practice

1 *General*

The following procedures are carried out without editorial comment: rectification of obvious mistakes and omissions; insertion of regular barring and of punctuation and capitalisation; the writing out in full of abbreviations such as "ij" and �, and of abbreviated spellings (e.g. "leonu" in "Audite sancti," bar 77, becomes "leonum"); the translation and/or modernisation of names of voices (e.g. canto/cantus becomes soprano).

Editorial additions and alterations are placed in square brackets. Square brackets without a corresponding editorial comment imply an omission.

Original slurs are retained because of the occasional clarification which they provide about underlay, even though in a performing edition they would be better omitted. Crossed ties and slurs (⌒) are editorial.

2 *Rhythm and Metre*

Original note values are retained throughout.

It is doubtful whether what appear to be subtle differences of metre as indicated by time signatures have any significance. (On the prevailing confusion in the sources, see chapter seven, section 3.) Thus no attempt is made to retain such distinctions in the transcriptions: C and ₵, for example, are both transcribed as $\frac{4}{4}$, and O_1^3 and ϕ_1^3 both become $\frac{3}{1}$.

When notes in triple time need to be perfected by the addition of a dot, the dot is placed in square brackets because occasionally it happens that not a dot but a rest is omitted. (This seems to be the case, for example, in "Si qua est consolatio" at bar 41 in S1: cf. bar 37, B, and 45, S2.)

Black notation in the source is indicated in the transcription by a horizontal square bracket.

3 *Basso Continuo*

Not all the implied figuring or accidentals are inserted; baroque scribes and printers were content to leave much to musical common sense, especially the insertion of a sharp against the 3 of a 43 cadential suspension, and of a 6 at obvious places.

A sharp cancelling a flat in the key signature is transcribed as a natural; a flat meaning that the third above the bass is natural (not sharp) is transcribed as a natural.

4 *Accidentals (Except in bc Figuring)*

(i) *All* accidentals which appear in the original are transcribed in the edition, even those which, because of the modern convention according to which an accidental retains its force until the next bar-line, are strictly unnecessary. All accidentals which are added in the edition are placed in square or round brackets (see below, (iii) and (iv)). The practice of including all the original accidentals looks superfluous to the modern eye, but it is perfectly intelligible. More important, however, is the fact that this practice is actually *essential* if the editor is to achieve the fundamental aim of giving the reader sufficient information to enable him to reconstruct the original: the radical differences between seventeenth-century and modern conventions make it impossible to show one set of conventions by means of the other.

(ii) A sharp in front of a note used to cancel a flat in the key signature is transcribed as a natural without editorial comment.

(iii) Accidentals in square brackets (in front of or above the note) are editorial additions. They are often justified not by the immediate melodic context but by a parallel phrase a few bars distant, or by the tonal, harmonic or contrapuntal context.

(iv) Accidentals in round brackets (in front of or above the note) are, it is believed, implied by the immediate context of the original notation and by seventeenth-century practice (cf. (v) below.

(v) Despite consistent inconsistency in seventeenth-century sources, certain practices ("principles" would be too strong a word) seem to have been a fairly common, and must be taken into account when making decisions about accidentals:

   (a) In a group of two or more notes of the same pitch, the first of which is prefixed by an accidental, the implication is almost always that the second note, and subsequent ones, if any, are also affected by the accidental. In such cases an accidental in round brackets has been inserted only when an intervening (modern) bar-line would, to the modern reader, appear to cancel the force of the accidental (e.g. "Desiderata nobis," bar 115, T; "Quis est hic vir" (SSS), bars 48-50, S2).
   (b) An accidental also retained its force *sometimes* when only one or a few notes intervened between the original note (with accidental) and its repetition (without accidental) (e.g. "Anima nostra sustinet Dominum," bar 14, S2; "O ignis sancte," bar 57, S1).
   (c) A rest had the effect of cancelling the force of an accidental (e.g. "Confitebor tibi" (SSB), bar 142, S2; "Sicut stella matutina," bar 210, S).
   (d) An accidental occasionally had a retrospective effect (e.g. "Quis est hic vir" (SSS), bar 32, S1 (cf. 33, S2), and Bar 52, S1).

5 *Editorial Commentaries*

The information given under "variants and comments" is arranged for each item as follows:

Bar. beat   Part (S1, V2, bc, etc.)   [Source:] comment

The source is specified only if more than one has been used for the edition.

ALMA REDEMPTORIS MATER (SSB bc)

BASIS OF THIS EDITION: <u>Floridus modulorum hortus...</u> (Rome: A. Fei, 1647). GB Lwa.

VARIANTS AND COMMENTS:

28.1	S2	♩.♪
82.4	bc	♭
106.2-3	bc	4 6
		2
109-10	B	Underlay: ♪ ♪ |♪ ♪
		mi sere re

Al - - -
Al - - -
Al - - -
6
- - - ma
Redempto - - - - -
- - - ma
Redempto - - - ris
Ma - - - -
- - - ma Redem - pto - - - ris
Ma - - - - - - - - - -
43
- ris Ma - - - - - - - - - - - - ter, Redempto - - - - ris Ma - - - - - - - - -
- - - - ter, Redem - ptoris Ma - - - ter, Redem - pto - - ris Ma - - - - - -
- - - ter, Redem - pto - - ris Ma - - - - - - - - - - - ter, Redem - pto-ris Ma - - -
43#
76
43
- ter, quae per - - - - - - vi-a cae - - - - - - - li por - - - - -
- ter, quae per - - - - - vi-a cae - - - - - - - - - - - - - - - - li
- ter, quae per - - - - - vi - a cae - - - li
56
76
76

19
- - - - - - ta ma - - nes, et stella ma - - - ris, et stella ma - - - - - -
por - - - ta ma - - - - - - - nes, por - - ta
por - - - - - - - - - - - - - ta ma - - nes, et stella ma - - ris, suc-cur-re ca-
6 6 76 76 43
24
- ris, suc-cur-re ca - den - - - - - -
ma - - nes, et stella, et stel-la ma - - ris, suc-cur-re ca-
- den - - - - - - - - - ti, por - - ta ma - - nes,
43 54 43 6 5 4 43
28
- ti, por - - ta ma - - nes et stel-la
- den - - - - - - - - - - - - ti, suc - cur-re caden - - -
et stella ma - - ris, suc - cur-re caden - - - - - - - ti, et
43 43
32
ma-ris, et stel-la ma - - - - ris, suc - - cur-re, suc - cur-re caden - - - - -
- - - - - ti, suc - cur-re caden - - - - - - - - - - - - - - - - - ti, succur-re ca-
stel-la ma - - - - ris, suc - cur-re ca-den - - - - - - - - - - - - -
43 6 5 4 3 76 43

224

tu quae genu-i-sti, na-tu-ra mi-ran-te
tu quae genu-i-sti, natu-ra mi-ran-te,
tu quae genu-i-sti, natu-ra mi-ran-te, tu-um
tu-um sanctum Ge-ni-to-rem, tu-um sanctum Ge-ni-to-rem: Vir-go
tu-um sanctum Ge-ni-to-rem, tu-um sanctum Ge-ni-to-rem:
sanctum Ge-ni-to-rem tu-um sanctum Ge-ni-to-rem: Vir-

74
pri - - - us ac po - ste - - - - ri - us, Vir - - - go pri - - - us, Vir -
Vir - - - go pri - - - us ac poste - - - - - - - - - - - - ri -
- - go pri - - - - us ac poste - - - - - - - - rius, Vir - - - go pri - - - us ac poste - - -
6 # 76 # 56 # 43
79
- - go pri - - - us ac poste - - - - - - rius, Ga - - - - brie - - lis ab o - -
- us, Vir - - - go pri - - - us ac po - ste - - rius, Ga - -
[#]
- - - - rius, Ga - - - brie - - - lis ab
43 56 [6]
83
- re, Ga - - brie - - lis ab o - - re, Ga - brie - - lis ab o - - re, Ga - - bri -
- - bri - e - - lis ab o - - - re, Ga - - brie - lis ab o - - re, Ga - - brie - -
o - - re, Gabri - - e - - lis ab o - - re, Gabri - e - - lis ab o - -
b b b 6 5
86
- e - - lis ab o - - - - - - - - re su - - - mens il - -
- lis ab o - - re, ab o - - re pec - - ca -
- re, ab o - - - - - - - - re su - - mens il - - lud A - - ve,
43 43 76 6 76 43

91
- - lud a - - - - ve, pec- - - ca-to-rum mi-se-re-re, pec - - ca-
-torum mi-se- re - - - - re, su- - - mens il - - - - lud a - - -
su - - - mens il - - - lud a - - ve,
43 43 76 65 43 43
96
-to-rum mi-se- - re - - - - - re, pec- - - ca-to-rum
-re, su- - - mens il - - - lud a - - - re, pec - - ca-
pecca - to-rum mi-se-re - - - re, pec - - ca- to - - - rum
6 6 6 6 76 4 2 6 76 6 5 4 3
101
mi-se-re - - - - - - re, mi - - - se- re - - - - - -
-torum mi-se- re - - - re, mi- - - se-re - - - - - - - - -
(♯) (♯)
mi-se-re - - - re, mi- - - se-re - - - - - - re, mi - se - re - -
43 43 76 43 43
106
-re, pec- - ca-torum mi-se-re - - re, mi - - - se-
-re, pec - - ca- - torum mi-se- - re - - - - - re, mi-
-re, pec-ca- torum mi-se- - re - - re — mi - - [se - - re - re,]
[6 4 2] 6 6 6 6 6 6 5 4 3 43 6

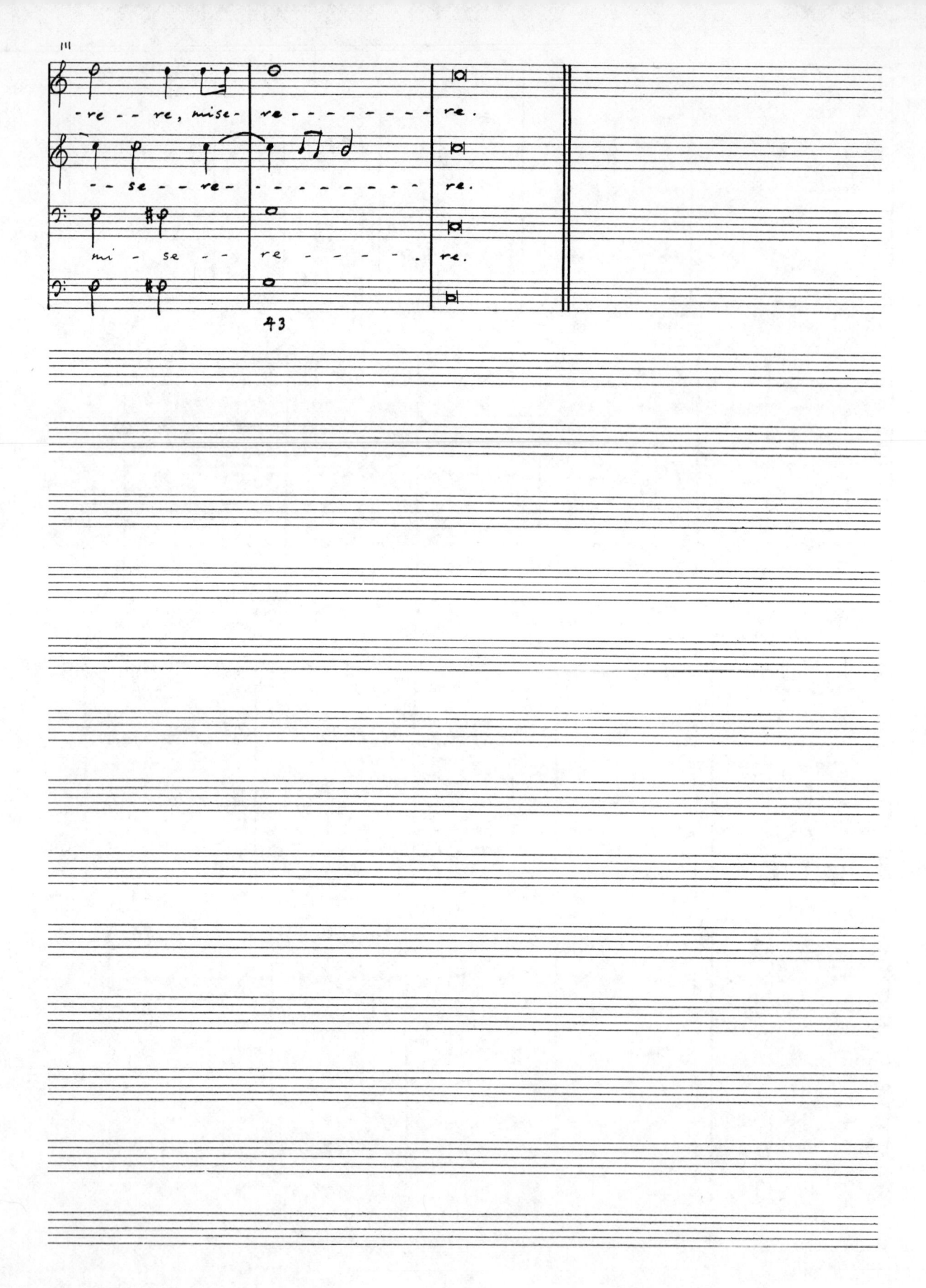
111
-re -- re, mise- re --------- re.
-- se -- re- --------- re.
mi - se -- re -----. re.
43

ANIMA NOSTRA SUSTINET DOMINUM (SS bc)

BASIS OF THIS EDITION: Arion Romanus... (Konstanz: D. Hautt jun., 1670). CH Zz.

VARIANTS AND COMMENTS:

4-7	S1	Underlay: ♩ ♩. ♪♩. ♫♩ ♫♫♩. ♩ o -stra su-stinet Do - - - - mi-num Cf. S2 bar 11.
47-53	SS	Underlay transcribed as printed. Each is consistent with itself.
55	S2	Black notation; but 62 and 67 white.
98	bc	Sic: white notation.

A - - - - nima no - - - - - - - - stra su - - stinet
5
Do - - - - - - - - - - - - mi - num
A - - - - nima no - - - - - - - - -
10
quo - niam ad -
- stra su - - stinet Do - - - - - - - - - - - - mi - - num quo - -
14
- jutor et pro - te - - - - - - - ctor no - - ster est, A - - nima no - - - - - - -
- niam ad - jutor et pro - te - - ctor no - - ster est,
18
- stra su - - stinet Do - - - - - - -
A - - nima no - - - - - - - - stra su - - stinet

- - - - - - - - - - mi - - num quo-
— Do - - - - - - - - - - - mi - - num quo - niam ad - jutor et prote - ctor no - ster est
- niam adjutor et pro - te - - ctor no - - ster est et
et Prote - ctor
prote - ctor no - - ster est, et pro - te - ctor no - - ster est.
et prote - ctor no - - ster est, et pro - te - ctor no - - ster est. In i - pso lae -
In i - pso re -
- ta - - - - - - - - - - - - - - - - bitur cor no - - - strum,
- flo - - - - - - - - - - - - - - - - - - ruit ca - ro no - - - - stra,
in

47
in i-pso lae-- --bitur cor no-- strum,
i-pso lae- ta-- --bitur cor no-- strum, in
52
in i-pso- re-- -- flo--ruit caro no-- stra,
i-pso re- flo-- --ruit caro no---- stra, re-
57
re- flo-- --ruit caro no--
-flo-- --ruit, re- flo-- --ruit caro no--
63
-stra, re-- flo-- --ruit caro no----
-stra, re- flo-- --ruit caro no----
68
-stra.
-stra. In De-- o, in De-- o spera--- -bimus, spera--

72
In De - - o, in De - - o spera - - - bimus, spera - -
- - - - bi - mus,
343
6
77
- - - - bi - mus,
in De - - o, in
in De - - o, in Deo exul - ta - - - - bimus,
343
6
6
43
3#
82
Deo exulta - - - - bi - mus, in Deo exulta - - - - bi - mus, in
in Deo exulta - - - - bi - mus, in Deo exulta - -
6
6
6
6
86
Deo exulta - - - - - bimus, in De - - o
- - bi - mus, in De - - o lau-
(b)
43
90
lau - dabimus tota die, tota di - - - - e. Et in no - mine san - cto
-dabimus tota di-e, tota die, to-ta di - - - e. Et in
98
6
43
6
6
7 [43]

234

127
sae - - cu - lum, in sae - - - - culum, in sae - - cu -
sae - - cu - lum, in sae - - - - culum, in sae - - cu -
6
4 3
133
- lum, in sae - - cu - lum.
- lum, in sae - - cu - lum.

ANNUNCIATE GENTES (SSATB bc)

BASIS OF THIS EDITION: <u>Sacri concerti musicali</u>... (Rome: V. Mascardi, 1675). GB Och.

VARIANTS AND COMMENTS

9.1-2	bc	A
10.1-2	bc	e
22.4	S2	a' Cf. 24, 26, 28
25.2	T	b natural
27.2	S1	b flat' a' quavers Cf. 23, 25
29.3	S2	b flat'
29.3	B	f
30-31	S2	(music example: - - vis)
37.4	S2	Last two semiquavers c'' b flat'' As indicated by the round brackets, there is <u>no</u> accidental in front of the last note.
48.2	A ⎫	It is possible that the two voices should
53.2	T ⎭	have the same (transposed) notes.
60.2	B	2nd and 4th notes d and e respectively
60.4	B	2nd note g
67.4	S2	b flat'
75.1	bc	6 4
81-82	bc	Semibreve
94.4	S1	Quaver g' Cf. 89 and 100
108.3	bc	65 printed under 108.4
110.1	bc	b
110.4	T	(rhythm)
110.4-111.1	T	Words should possibly be the same as those in the alto.
111.4	bc	65♯
111.4-112.1	S2	vitam nostram
114.1	bc	d
115.2	S2	2nd quaver e'
116.1-2	bc	56
118.2	S1	g'
119.3-4	bc	f
124.2	S2	c'
127.4	B	quaver

Annuncia - te gen - tes,
Annunciate gentes
Tacet
Annunciate gentes
Tacet
Annunciate gentes
Tacet
Annunciate gentes
Tacet
S'
bc
annuncia - te po - puli glo - - - riam Do - mi - ni; gentes et
po - puli annunci - a - - - - - - - - te, gentes et
po - puli annunci - a - - - - - - - - - te, annunci -

16
S¹
bc
-a
te.
65
743
21
S¹
S²
A
T
B
bc
O, O, O quam dulcis est Deus no - - ster,
O, O, O quam dulcis
O, O, O quam dulcis
O, O, O quam dulcis est Deus no - - ster,
98
76
43
76
6
43
25
O, O, O quam dulcis est Deus no - - ster,
O, O, O quam dulcis est Deus no - - ster,
est Deus no - - ster,
O, O, O quam dulcis
est Deus no - - ster,
O, O, O quam dulcis
O quam dul - cis
6
76
6
43
76
6
43

239

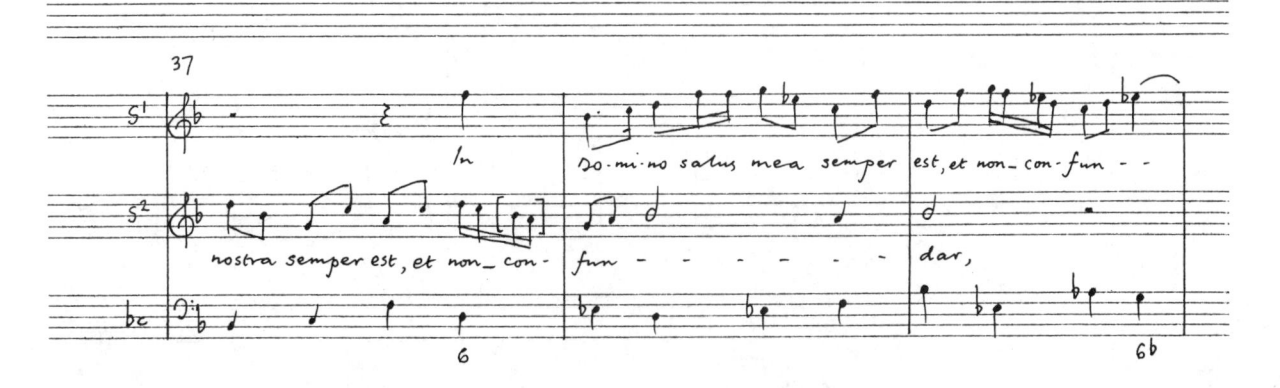

40
- - - dar, et non con- fundar, non, non, non con- fun- dar, et non—
et non confundar, non, non, non confundar, et non— confun- -
43
S¹
S²
A
T
bc
—confun- dar, non, non, non confun- - - dar.
-dar, et non con- fun- - - - - dar.
Memora- te om- - nes
48
A
T
bc
Memento- te om- - nes
quo- niam excel- sus est nomen e- - ius.
53
A
T
B
bc
quo- niam in cae- lis est Deus no- - ster.
Om- nes, omnes a- do-

57
-ra-te Do-mi-num quo- - - - - niam ex-cel- - - - - - -
76
34
61
- - - - sus est, et in caelo, et in caelo sedes e- - -
43
64
S1
Om-nes, omnes adora-te
S2
Om-nes, omnes a-dora-te
A
Om-nes, om-nes a-dora-te
T
Om-nes, om-nes
B
- - - - - - ius.
Omnes, omnes
bc
343
6 [6] 6
69
Do-minum, ado-ra-te Do-mi-num quo- - - - - - - - - -
Do-minum, ado-ra-te Do-mi-num quo- - - - - - - - -
Do-minum, ado-ra-te Do-mi-num
ado-ra-te Do-mi-num
ado-ra-te Do-mi-num
76
6 76

74
niam ex- cel - sus est,
niam ex- celsus est,
et in caelo sedes
et in caelo sedes e - ius,
et in caelo sedes e - ius,
et in
78
et in caelo sedes e - ius,
et in caelo se - des
e - ius, et in caelo sedes e - ius,
et in caelo sedes
et in caelo sedes e
et in caelo sedes e
caelo sedes e - ius,
se - des
e

243

91
Consolatio no - - stra Deus no - - - ster
Consolatio no - - - stra Deus no - - - - ster
-ni in deli-ci-is?
76
95
est.
Consolatio no - -
est.
Consolatio no - stra
Quid glo-ri- a - mini in vani- ta - te
76

99
- stra Deus no - - - ster est,
fortitu-do no - - - stra Deus no - - - - -
consolatio no - - - stra Deus no - - -
exultatio no - - stra Deus
♯ 4 3 [♯] [♮]
103
consolatio no - - - stra, consolatio no - - -
exultatio
- ster est, exultatio no - - - ster, exultatio
- - ster est, consolatio no - - stra, consolatio
no - ster est, exultatio no - - - stra, exultatio no - - -
4 3 ♮

106
-stra Deus no - - ster est. In Do-mino spes nostra semper, semper collae-
nostra Deus no - - ster est. In Do-mino spes nostra semper, semper collae-
nostra Deus no - - ster est.
nostra Deus no - - ster est.
-stra Deus no - - ster est.
43 65 [65]
109
-ta-bimur;
-ta-bimur; in Do-mino vita
in Do-mino cor nostrum semper, semper dele- cta-bitur;
in Do-mino cor nostrum semper, semper collae- ta-bitur;
in Do-mino cor
43 65 65 43 ♭ 65 [♯]

112
Quo-niam fortitu-do no- - - stra Deus
nostra semper, semper glori- a- bi-mur. Quo-niam exultatio
Quo-niam exultatio no-
nostrum semper, semper dele- cta- bitur.
4 3
115
no- - - - - - - - ster est, quo-niam consolatio no- -
no- - stra Deus no- - - ster est, quo-niam exultatio
-stra Deus no- - - - - - ster est, quo- niam
Quo- -niam fortitudo no- - - stra,
Quo-niam consolatio no-
[6 5] 4 3

119
- stra,
no - - - stra,
fortitu-do
fortitu-do no - - - stra Deus no - - - - - - - ster
consolatio no - - - stra Deus no - - - - ster
- stra,
consolatio no - - - stra Deus no - - ster
43
122
consola-tio no - - stra, consolatio no - - - stra Deus
no - - - stra, exultatio no - - - stra, exultatio nostra Deus
est, exultatio no - - - stra, exultatio nostra Deus
est, consolatio no - - - stra, exultatio nostra Deus
est, consolatio no - - - stra, consolatio no - - - stra Deus

125
no - ster est, Deus no - ster est, Deus no - - ster est.
no - - ster est, Deus no - ster est, Deus no - - ster est.
no - ster est, Deus no - ster est, Deus no - - ster est.
no - - ster est, Deus no - ster est, Deus no - - ster est.
no - ster est, Deus no - ster est, Deus no - - ster est.
43 43 43

ARDENS EST COR NOSTRUM (SATB bc)

BASIS OF THIS EDITION: R. Floridus...istas alias sacras cantiones... (Rome: I. de Lazzari, 1664). D-brd MÜs.

ALSO COLLATED: Arion Romanus... (Konstanz: D. Hautt, jun., 1670). CH Zz.

D-brd MÜs: Sant.Hs.2758, 11-15.

VARIANTS AND COMMENTS:

3 and passim	S(ATB)	1670: meum
4.3	bc	1670: 6♯
5 and passim	S(ATB)	1664: Iesu 1670: Jesu
6.3	bc	1670: 6
8-10	SATB	1670:

| 9 | bc | 1664: ♩   1670: o |

17-19	SATB bc	1670: [musical example]

| 18.4 | S | 1664: [musical example] "sua" |

Underlay is clear in T: [musical example] "su-a-"

| 18-19 | A | 1664: [musical example] "sua-vis-mo su-a-vis-si-mo" |

Sant.Hs. 2758 has underlay as in this edition.

19.1	bc	1664: 7 (<u>sic</u>; should be at 20.1?)
		1670: 65
		43
20.1	bc	1670: 7
22	T	1670: [musical example] (<u>sic</u>) "i - - gne su-a-"
24.3	bc	1664: 6 1670: blank
27.4-28.1	B	1670: extinqueris
31.4-32	S	1670: obfuscaris
39.3-40	T	1664: illuminans 1670: illuminas

41-45	SATB bc	1670:

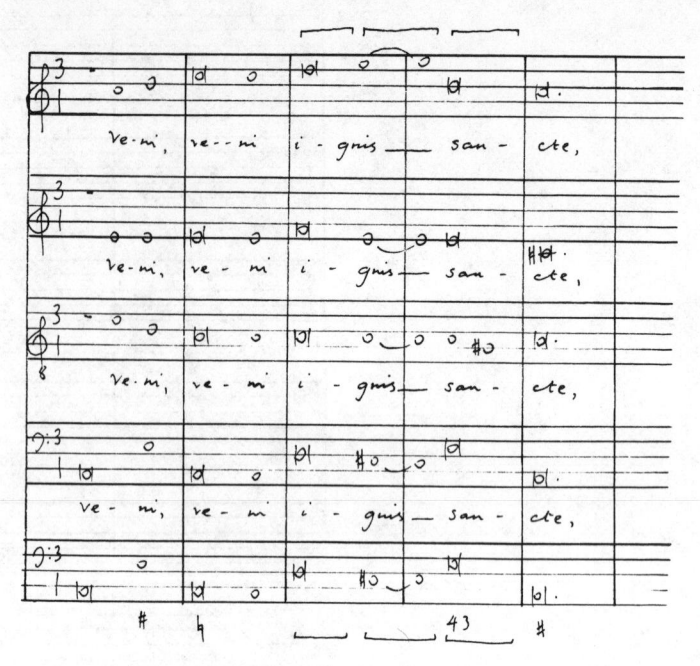

44.2-3	S	1664:
44.2	T	1664: 'san' is printed under 44.1
44.2-3	bc	1664: 64 1670: 43
46-50	SATB bc	1670:

48.3	A	1664: 'gnis' is printed under 49.1
51.1	A	1670: #
54.3	bc	1664: 44 1670: 43
59.4	A	1670: e' e' quavers
59.4	bc	1670: #
60.1	S	1670: no #
60.2	A	1670: d'
60.3	A	1670: e'
60.3	T	1670: g
61.4	S	1670: 'in', not 'pro'
63.4	B	1670: 'in', not 'pro'
65.4	A (only)	1670: 'in', not 'pro'
62.1-2	S	1670: 'totum', not 'solum'
64.1-2	B	1670: 'totum', not 'solum'
66.1-2	A and T	1670: 'totum', not 'solum'
62.3-63.1	S	) The subject of these verbs is plural: 'cor et
64.3-65.1	B	) anima'. 1664 does have a plural verb at 66.3-67.1: 'deficiant'. 1670 has all three verbs in the singular.
66-7	bc	1670: [musical notation]
68-9	bc	1670: octave higher
70	bc	1670: two minims on d
74	T	1670: [musical notation: a-nima]
74.3	B and bc	1670: no #

Ar - dens est cor no - strum, O bo - ne Je - su,
Ar - - dens est cor no - strum,
[sic]
Ar - - dens
[6#]
6
O bo - ne Je - su, O bo - ne
O bo - ne Je - su, O bo - ne Jesu, O bo - ne
est cor no - strum, O bo - ne Je - su, O bo - ne Jesu, O bone
Ar - dens est cor no - strum, O bo - ne
[6]
11
Je - su, tu - - i a -
Je - su, tu - - i a - mo - - ris
Je - su, tu - - i a - mo - ris i - gne sua - vis - - simo,
Je - su,
7 6

16
-mo - ris i - - gne sua- ris - - simo, su-a- vis - - - - si-
i - - gne sua- ris - - simo, suaris[- - - - - - - - - -] si-
sua- rissimo, sua- rissimo, su-a- ris - simo
tu - - i a-
20
-mo, i - - gne sua-ris - - - - si- mo.
-mo tu - - i a-mo - - ris i - - gne su-a- ris - - si- mo.
tu - - i a- mo - - - ris igne su-a-ris-simo, sua- ris - - - si- mo.
-mo - ris- i - - gne sua- ris - - - - - - si- mo.
25
i-gnis qui semper ar-des et numquam, et numquam es- tin - - queris,

29
i-gnis qui semper lu-ces et numquam, et numquam of-fu-sca--ris,
33
i-gnis qui semper ser-ves et numquam tepe------scis,
37
i-gnis qui non com-bu-ris sed, sed illu---mi-[nas]:

41
ve-ni, ve-ni i-gnis san-cte, ve-ni,
[san]
47
ve-ni i-gnis san-cte. A-mor et desi-
[gnis]
52
-de-rium cor-dis no-stri inflamma nos dilectione tu-
et desi-de-rium cor-dis no-stri in-
et desi-deri-um cordis no-stri
-de-rium cor-dis no-stri

56
- - - a, dilecti- o - - ne tu - - - a, inflamma nos dilecti- o-ne tu - - - - a, di-lectio- - ne
in - flamma nos dilectio-ne tu-
in-
4 3 ♯ 7 [♯] ♯
59
-flamma nos dilecti- o-ne tu - - - - a, ut pro te so-lum ar - - de-
tu - a, di-lecti- o - ne tu - - a,
- - - a, di-lecti- o - - ne tu - - a,
-flamma nos di-lecti- o - ne tu - - a,
7 [♯] ♯ [♯] 6 7 6 ♯ 7 6
63
-a[n]t, cor · et
et pro te so-lum defi - ci - ant cor et
et pro te so-lum defi-ci- ant
et pro te solum langue- a[n]t, cor et
♯ 7 6 ♯ 5 6[♯]

68
a- nima no - - - - stra, cor et a - nima no - - -
a - nima no - - - stra, cor et a - nima no - - -
cor et a - nima no - - -
a - nima no - - - stra, cor et a - nima no - - -
4 3 # 6 4 3
73
-stra, et a - - - nima no - - - - - - stra.
-stra, et a - - ni-ma no - - - stra.
-stra, et a-nima, et a-nima no - - - - stra.
-stra, et a - - ni-ma no - - - stra.
6 4 3

AUDITE SANCTI (SSB bc)

BASIS OF THIS EDITION: R. Floridus...has alteras sacras cantiones ... (Rome: L. Grignani, 1645). I Bc.

ALSO COLLATED: Scelta di motetti... (Rotterdam: J. Van Geertsom, 1656). GB DRc.

Carissimi, Arion Romanus... (Konstanz: D. Hautt jun., 1670). CH Zz.

VARIANTS AND COMMENTS:

42.2	B	Printed a crotchet. It is a quaver in both 1656 and 1670.
44.1	S2	'non' omitted. It is present in both 1656 and 1670.
51.2	S1	The rhythmic discrepancy between this beat and 55.4 (S2), 59.4 (S1) and 64.2 (S2) is almost certainly intentional: the melodic context in bar 51 is slightly different from the later phrases. The discrepancy appears consistently in the three printed sources (1645, 1656 and 1670).
53	S2	) The underlay has been made to agree with
57-8	S2	) 61-2 (S1) and 66 (S2) where the presence of a slur clarifies it.

S1
S2
B
bc
Au-di-- te, audi-te sancti, au- di-te ju-sti,
au-di-te fortes electo-rum a-nimae. Ec-ce vos tradet
Do-minus in manus impi- o--rum, ut cum pro- ba-verit vos
accipi-e-tis co- ro-nam vi--- -tae.
Si tradi-derit
Si tradi-derit

18
Dominus nos servos su-os in manus impi- o-rum,
Dominus nos servos su-os in manus impi- o-rum, sta--binus
21
sta--binus omnes in ma-gna constan-ti- a ad-versus an-
omnes in ma-gna con- stan- - - - - ti- a adversus an- gu- stias perse-
43 b
25
-gu-stias perse- quen-tium. Quis e-nim
-quen- - - - - - - - ti-um. Quis e-nim nos separa-bit,
b 6 [65] 43 76
29
nos separa-bit a charita--te Chri--sti?
nos separa-bit a charita-te Chri- - - - - - - - - sti?
76 # [♮] 76 ♮

33
Non, non, non separa - - - -
Non, non, non sepa - ra - - bit.
Tribula - tio?
an angustia?
37
- bit.
Non, non, non sepa - ra - bit.
Non, non, non separa - - - -
Persecu - tio
an fa - mes?
41
Non, non, non separa - - - -
- bit.
Non, non, [non] sepa - ra - - bit.
Nuditas, nuditas
an peri - culum?
45
- bit.
Non, non, non sepa - - ra - - bit.
Non, non, non separa - - - -
I - - - - - quis an gladius?

49
non time-bit cor
-bit.
non ti-
Si consistant castra adver---sum vos,
52
nostrum, non ti-me-bit cor no---strum.
-mebit, non ti-me-bit cor no--strum.
Si — exurgat praelium ad-
55
non ti-mebit, non ti- me-bit cor no-------
non ti- me-bit cor nostrum, non ti- me-bit cor no--strum.
-ver---sum vos,
58
-strum.
non ti- me-bit cor nostrum, non ti-
non ti-mebit, non ti-
Si male-di-xerint vo-bis ho-mines,

61
-me-bit cor no--strum.
non ti-
-me-bit cor no-----strum.
non time-bit cor
Si principes perse-cu-ti vos fu-e-rint,
65
-mebit, non ti-me-bit cor no---strum.
Scimus e-nim quod passio--nes
nostrum, non time-bit cor no--strum.
Scimus e-nim quod passio--nes
69
no-strae non sunt condignae ad fu-tu-ram glo---ri-
no-strae non sunt con-dignae ad fu-turam, ad fu-tu-ram glo--ri-
72
-am. non sunt con-di-gnae, non sunt con-
-am. non sunt condignae ad fu-
Saevien-tes tor-torum ma-nus

75
-dignae ad fu-tu-ram glo- - - ri-am.
-turam, ad fu- tu-ram glo- - ri - am.
Formi- da-biles le-o-num mo-
78
non sunt con- dignae ad fu-turam, ad fu- tu- ram glo- - - ri-
non sunt condi- gnae, non sunt condignae ad fu- tu- ram glo- - - ri-
-lae
81
-am. non, non sunt con- dignae,
-am. non, non sunt con- dignae, non,
Laniantes ungulae ignis can- den-tes laminae
85
non, non sunt con- dignae ad fu-turam, ad fu- tu-ram glo- - - ri-
non sunt condi- gnae, non sunt condignae ad fu- tu-ram glo- - - ri-

88
-am. Scimus e-nim quod passi- o- -nes no-strae non sunt condi- -gnae,
-am. Scimus e-nim quod passi- o- -nes no-strae non sunt con-
92
non sunt condignae ad fu- tu-ram glo- -ri- am,
-dignae ad fu-turam, ad fu- tu-ram glo- -ri- am,
non sunt condignae ad fu-
95
non sunt condignae ad fu- turam glo-riam, ad fu- tu-ram glo- -ri-
non sunt con- dignae ad fu-turam, ad fu- tu-ram glo- -ri-
-tu- -ram glo-riam, non sunt condignae ad fu- tu-ram glo- -ri-
98
-am, non sunt condignae ad fu- turam, ad fu-turam glo- - -ri- -am, non sunt con-
-am, non sunt con- dignae ad fu-tu- - -ram glo-ri-am,
-am, non sunt condignae ad fu- turam, ad fu-tu- -ram glo-ri-am, non,

101
-dignae, non, non sunt con- di- - - - gnae ad fu- turam glo- - - ri-
non, non sunt condignae ad fu- tu- - ram glo- - ri-
non sunt condignae ad fu- tu- - - - ram glo- - - ri-
6 76 76 [b] 4 2 6 43
105
-am.
-am.
-am.

BENEDICTUS DEUS ET PATER (SSS bc)

BASIS OF THIS EDITION: <u>R. Floridus...istas alias cantiones sacras...</u> (Rome: G. Fei (A. Poggioli), 1668). GB Lbl(bm).

VARIANTS AND COMMENTS:

Prefatory stave	bc	Key signature <u>sic</u>.
8.1	bc	4 2
25.1	bc	97
25–26	bc	Tie omitted; cf. 19–20.
26.1	bc	4 2
32.3–4	bc	97 65
33.1	bc	4 2
38–72	SSS bc	In the source the music is written out in full. There are only two discrepancies between bars 38–49 and 56–67:
56	S2	Flat omitted in front of a'' (present in 38)
65	bc	Figured 265 . (At bar 47 it is 765 .) 343 34 The 2 at bar 65 could signify 2[♭], but a more usual figuring would be 9[♭].
69	S2	𝅗𝅥
70–71	S2	𝅗𝅥.
71	bc	565 343
72	bc	𝅗𝅥

Benedi - ctus De - us et Pater Domini no - stri Je - su —
Chri - - - - - - - - - sti,
et Pater Domini
Benedi - ctus De - us et Pater Domini no - stri Je - su —
no - stri Je - su Chri - - sti, et Pater Domini no - stri Je - su —
Chri - - - - - - - - - - - sti,
et Pater Domini
Benedictus Deus et Pater Domini no - stri Je - su —
Chri - - sti, Jesu Chri - - - sti,
no - stri Je - su — Chri - - - sti, Pa - - ter
Chri - - - - sti, Pa - ter misericor - di -

17
Pa - - ter
mise- ri - cor - di - a - rum, et De-us to - ti - us consolati - o - - - - -
- a - rum, et Deus to - ti - us consolati - o - nis, consolati - o - - - -
21
misericor - di - a - - rum, et De - us to - ti - - us conso - la - ti -
- - - - nis,
- - - - nis, Pa - - ter misericor - - di - a - rum, et De - us to -
25
- o - nis, consolati - o - - - - nis, Pa - - ter misericor - di -
Pa - - ter misericor - di - arum, Pa - - ter
- ti - us consolati - o - - - - nis, Pa - - ter miseri - cor - di -
30
- a - rum, et De - us to - ti - us consolati - o - - - -
mi - seri - cor - di - a - rum, et Deus to - ti - us consolati - o - - - - - -
- a - - - rum, et De - us to - ti - us consolati - o - - - - - - -

34
38/56
-nis,
-nis,
qui con- - - - so-
-nis, qui con- - - - so- latur, consola- - - - tur nos
6
6
6
39/57
in omni tribulatio-ne nostra, tribulatio-ne
-latur, consola- - - - tur nos
in
in omni tribulati-o-ne
6
65
98
6
43/61
no-stra, in omni tribulati-o-ne no-stra, in
omni tribulatio-ne nostra, tribulati-o-ne no-stra, in omni tribulati-o-ne
no-stra, in omni tribulatio-ne nostra, tribulatio-ne
98
6
98
b
47/65
1
omni tribulati-o-ne no- - - - - - stra,
no- - - - stra,
no- - - - stra, qui con- - - so- latur, consola- - -
765
34 [3]

52
qui con - - - - so- latur, consola - - - - tur nos,
qui
- - tur nos,
67 2
-stra, in omni tribulatio-ne no - - - -
-stra, in omni tribulatio-ne no - - - -
-stra, in omni tribulatio-ne
71
- - stra.
- - stra.
- - stra.

CANTABO DOMINO (SS bc)

BASIS OF THIS EDITION: Carissimi, <u>Sacri concerti musicali...</u>
(Rome: V. Mascardi, 1675).   GB Och.

VARIANTS AND COMMENTS:

28	bc	Figured 6
42.3	S2	a'
53.3	S2	b flat'
63.1	bc	G
89.3	S2	g'
93.1	S2	Flat added because of the parallel with bar 94 (S1).
98-99	bc	Only bar 99 in black notation.
107.1	S1	(cf. 93.1) The case for adding a flat is even stronger here because of the preceding cadence in B flat major.
121.1	S2	a'
140.3	S2	e'
143.1	S1	b flat'
147-9	SS	Underlay:
153	bc	

Solo
Cantabo Domino tacet.
Solo
Can-ta-bo— Do-mino in vi-ta me-a;
S¹
bc
psal-- --lam De-o me-o quamdi-u sum.
In psalte-- --ri-o et ci-thara confi-te-bor-no--mini
san-cto e--ius, in psalte-- --ri-o et ci-thara confi-
S²
-te-bor-no--mini san-cto e--ius.
A-peri, a-peri
Do-- --mine o-- --ra ca-
-nen-tium in Lau-- --de tu--a, et om-nis_

lin-gua con-fi-te-a--tur no-- --mini
San-cto tu--o, et om-nis lin--gua con-fi-te-a--tur
no-- --mini San-cto tu--o.
S1 Flo-re---te flo-- --res, flo-re--
S2 Flo-re---te flo-- --res, flo-re--
bc
--te qua-
--te qua-
-si li--li-um, flo-re---te flo------res, flo-re----te
-si li--li-um, flo-re---te

67
- - res, flo- re - - - - te qua- si li - - li-
- - res, flo- re - - - - te qua- si li - - li-
43
73
-um, et da - te o - do - - - -
-um, et da - te o - do - - - -
43
43
79
-rem, et da - te o - do - - - rem. Fron -
-rem, et da - te o - do - - - rem.
84
-de - - - - - te, fron - de - - - - te, fron - de - -
Fronde - - - - te, fronde - - - - te,
89
- - - - te, fron - de - - - - te in gra - - ti - am,
fron - de - - - - te in gra - - ti - am,

93
et — col - lau - da - - - - te, et — col - lau - da - - - - -
et — col - lau - da - - - te, et — col - lau - da - - - - -
98
- - - te — Do - - mi - - num. Fron - - - - - - te in
- - - te — Do - - mi - - num. Fron - de - - - - - - te in
103
gra - tiam, fron - de - - - - - te in gra - tiam,
gra - tiam, fron - de - - - - - te in gra - tiam,
107
et — col - lau - da - - - te, et — col - lau - da - - - - -
et — col - lau - da - - - - te, et — col - lau - da - - - -
112
- - te — Do - - mi - num, et — col - lau - da - - - - -
- - te — Do - - mi - num, et — col - lau - da - - - - -

118
te Domi-
te Domi-
123
-num, et collanda- -te, et collanda-te
-num, et collanda- -te, et collanda- -te Do-
127
Do- mi- num.
mi- num.
Al-le-lu-ia, al-le-lu-
Al-le-lu-
43
132
-la, al-le-lu-ia, al-le-lu-ia,
-ia, al-le-lu-ia, al-le-lu-ia,
43
137
al-le-lu-ia, al-le-lu-ia,
al-le-lu-ia, al-le-lu-ia, al-le-lu-ia,

143
al- le- lu- ia, [al- le- - lu-
al- le- lu- ia, [al- le- - lu-
43
[56]
43
149
-ia,] al- le- - lu- ia.
-ia,] al- le- - lu- ia.
[43]

CONFITEBOR TIBI DOMINE (SSB bc)

BASIS OF THIS EDITION: R. Floridus... Psalmos istos...
(Rome: I. de Lazzari, 1662). I Md.

ALSO COLLATED: Motetti d'autori eccellentissimi...
(Loreto: P. & G. B. Serafini, 1646).
F Pc: bc part-book only, but it
contains also the solo vocal portions:
183-97 (S2) and 222-55 (B). All of
the pages are torn at the top.

VARIANTS AND COMMENTS:

2	bc	43 printed over the f in bar 1. 1646: in the F Pc copy of bc bars 1-3 are torn out.
14.2	bc	43 The figuring is absent in 1646.
21.1-3	S2	Each e'' must probably be flattened because of the parallel with bar 18; also e flat'' leads more naturally into the B flat major cadence in bars 22-23.
23.1-3	S1	Each e'' must be flattened because of the tonal context (B flat major), the parallels with bars 17 and 20, and the proximity of bar 21.
25.1-3	S2	Each e'' must be flattened in order to preserve exactness of imitation.
73.3	bc	33 1646: 43
85.3	bc	♯ 6 1646: the same
87.1	bc	♯ 76 1646: the same
109-10	B	Sic. Carissimi wanted the S2 entry in bar 109 in order to achieve a small climax by means of stretto; but to write the obvious in the bass voice –

- would give consecutive octaves with
S2. He therefore replaces the e with
a c, and prepares the ear for this lower
note by replacing the g (two notes earlier)
with a d.

142	S2	Donington notes (in <u>The Interpretation of Early Music</u> (London, 1974), p.617) a 'not unusual early convention' according to which a rest cancelled the force of an accidental. The convention would certainly apply in this bar.
150.3	bc	Figured 1 (<u>sic</u>). Absent in 1646.
150-51 153-54 158-59	B S1 S2	The second and third notes of the phrase 'Fidelia omnia' are printed as a ligature:
175.2	bc	43 printed over the B flat in bar 176. 1646: printed over the f.
180-82	SSB bc	1662:

ae - qui ta - te
ae - qui - ta - te
ae - qui - ta - te
43

180.1-2	bc	1646: b flat printed as
183.1-2	S2	1646: a' a' a'
184.4	S2	1646: a' g'. There is a trill (marked t) on the a'.
185.2	S2	1646: two quavers.
185.4	S2	1646: trill (t) on a'.
196	bc	1662: 5 43
197	bc	𝄐 (but none in S2).
199.2 200.2 201.2 202.2 203.2	S1 S1 and B B S1 and B S1	Cf. 201.2 (S2) and 203.2 (S2) where the ♪s are slurred in pairs.
206.4	bc	1662: ♮ is printed ♮ ; 1646: ♯

212.3–214	B	1662 printed thus: 'timor Domini'. But it is unlikely that Carissimi intended the Bass to sing these words before the point of imitation begins in bar 214; it is more likely that he repeated the word 'sapientiae' in B as in S2.
216.1	bc	1662: ♮ is printed ♮ ; 1646: ♯ .
219–20	bc	765 343
236	B	1646: [musical notation] But in bars 240 and 248 1646 = 1662.
241.1	bc	1662 and 1646: 6 5
244	bc	1646: [musical notation]
249	B	1662: all six notes slurred in pairs.
255	bc	1662: ⌢ omitted.
255	B	1662: [musical notation]
278	bc	1646: [musical notation]
286.3	bc	1662: discrepancy with bar 278 <u>sic</u>.
282.3–283.1	B	⎫
283.2–3	B	⎪
290.3–291.1	B	⎬ Ligature: [notation]
291.2–3	B	⎪
297.2–3	B	⎪
303.2–3	B	⎭
297.2–3	S2	⎫ Ligature: [notation]
303.2–3	S1	⎭
305	bc	1662: [musical notation] 1646: [musical notation]
307–08	bc	1662: [musical notation] 1646: [musical notation]
327.2	bc	6 in 1662. 1646, bars 326–7: [musical notation] 5
332	S1 and bc	⌢ omitted.
332	S2	[notation]

284

ne,
et con-gre-ga-ti-
ga-ti-o
-o
-ne, et congre-ga-ti-o
ne.
ne.
Ma-gna, ma-gna o
-pera Do-mi-ni,
exquisi-ta in omnes, exquisi-ta in
exquisi-ta in omnes, exquisi-ta in

43
omnes vo-lunta-tes e---ius, exqui- si-ta in omnes, exqui- si-ta in omnes volun-
omnes volunta-tes e---ius, exqui- si-ta in omnes volun-
exqui- si-ta in om--nes, exquisi-ta in
47
-tates, voluntates e----ius, exqui- si-ta in omnes volun- tates, volunta--tes
-tates, volun-ta--tes e--ius, exqui- si-ta in omnes volun- tates, voluntates e--
omnes volunta-tes e--ius, exqui- si-ta in omnes volun-ta--tes
51
e--ius. Confes-si-o et magnifi-centia o-pus e-- --
--ius.
e--ius.
56
-- --ius; et in-
et insti-tia eius ma--
et insti-tia eius, et in-

61
- sti - tia e - ius ma - - - - net, et in - - sti - tia e - ius manet in saeculum sae - -
- - - net, et insti - tia e - ius ma - - - - - - net, ma - net in saeculum
- sti - tia e - ius, et in - sti - tia e - ius, et in - stitia e - ius ma - - - net in
67
- - - - cu - li, ma - - - - net, manet in saeculum sae - cu -
sae - - - cu - li, manet in saeculum saecu - li, ma - net in saeculum
saeculum sae - - cu - li, manet in saeculum saecu - li, ma - - - - net
72
- li, in saeculum sae - - - - - - cu - li.
saecu - li, in saeculum sae - - cu - li.
in saeculum sae - cu - li. Me - mo - riam fe - - cit
77
mirabilium su - o - - - - - - rum, me - mo - riam fe - - - - - cit

82
mi- - - - sericors et mise- rator Do- mi-
mi- sericors et mise- ra - - - tor, et mise- ra- tor Do- mi-
mirabilium su- o- - - - - - - rum, mi-
43
6
[6#]
43
87
-nus, mi- - - sericors et mise- ra- - - - tor, et mise- ra- - - - - tor
-nus, mi- - - sericors et mise- ra- - - - - tor
-sericors et mise- ra- - tor et misera- - - - tor, et misera- tor
[76]
6
6
6
5
91
Do- minus. E- scam de- - - - dit, de-
Do- minus. E- scam de- - - dit, de- - - dit, de-
Do- minus.
43
6
6
97
-dit ti- men- tibus se, E- scam de- - -
-dit ti- men- tibus se,
E- scam de- - dit ti- men- tibus se,
987
765
43
43

104
-dit, de- - -dit, e-scam de- - -dit, de- -dit ti-
e-scam de- - -dit, de- - -dit, escam de- - -dit ti-
e-scam de- - -dit, de- - -dit ti- men- -
112
-men-tibus se.
-men-tibus se. Me- - -mor e- -rit, me- - -mor e-rit in sae- - -
- - -tibus se.
118
Virtutem operum suo-rum
- - - -culum testa- men-ti_ su- - i. vir-
vir-
123
annuntia- -bit annunti-a-bit po- -pulo su- - -
-tutem operum su- o- - - rum annunti- a- bit po- -pulo su- o annunti-
-tutem operum su- o- rum, vir-tu-tem operum suo- -rum,

127
-o, annunti-a - bit po - - pulo su - o, annunti-a - - bit,
-a - - bit, annunti - a - bit po - - pulo su - - - o, annunti-
vir - tutem operum su - o - rum
b 6 6 43
130
annunti-a - bit po - - pulo, po - pulo su - - - - o,
-a - bit, annunti-a-bit po - pulo su - - - - o,
annunti - a - bit po - pu - lo, po - pu - lo su - - o,
98 76 6 5 43
135
ut det il - lis hereditatem
ut det il - lis hereditatem
ut det il - lis he - reditatem gen - - - - ti - um.
65 43
139
gen - tium. ve - - - - ritas,
gen - tium. ve - - - - ritas, ve - - -
O - - - - pera ma - nuum e - ius
76

143
ve - - - ritas et in- di - - ci-um,
ve - -
- ritas, veritas et in-
- ritas, ve-ritas et in- di - - ci - um, ve - -
- ritas, veritas et in-
ve - - - - ritas,
ve - - ri - tas
et in - - -
147
- di - cium.
Fi - -
- -
- di - cium.
- di - cium.
Fi - -
- - de - -
- - li - a omnia mandata
153
- de - - -
- - li - a omnia mandata
e - -
- -
Fi - -
- -
e - - -
ius,
omnia mandata
e - - - - -
158
- - - -
ius,
omnia mandata e-ius, omni - a man-
- de - - -
- - - li - a omnia mandata
e - - ius,
omnia mandata
- - - -
ius,
omnia mandata
e - - - -

163
-data e- ius,
e- - - - ius,
-ius, confirma-ta in sae- - - -culum sae-culi,
343
45
168
fa- cta in ve-ri- ta-te et
fa- cta in ve- ri- ta-te et ae- qui- - ta- - te,
43
174
ae- qui- - ta- - te, fa- cta in ve- ri- ta-te et
fa- cta in ve- ri- ta-te et
fa- cta in ve-ri- ta-te et
[43]
180
ae- - qui- - ta- - te.
ae- - qui- - ta- - te. Re-dempti-o-nem
ae- - - - qui-ta- - - te.
43

184
S²
bc
misit po- - -
- - puto
188
Su- - - o;
mandavit in ae- ternum testa- men- -
193
S¹
S²
B
bc
- -
- - - tum su- um.
San- - -
199
-ctum et ter- ri- bile nomen eius, et ter- ri- bile nomen e- ius,
San- - - - -ctum et ter- ri- bile nomen
San- - - - - -ctum et ter- ri- bile nomen eius, et ter- ribile nomen
202
et ter- ri- bile nomen eius, et ter- ri- bile nomen e- - - - - - ius. I-
e- ius, et ter- ri- bile nomen e- - - - - - ius.
eius, et ter- ri- bile nomen e- - - - - - ius.

206
-ni-tium sapi- en- - - - - ti- ae,
i- ni-tium sapi- en- - - - ti- ae, i- ni-tium sapi-
i- ni-tium sapi- en- - - - -
211
i- ni- - ti-um sapi- en- - - - ti- ae ti- - - mor
-en- - - ti- ae, sapien- - - - - - - - ti- - ae ti- -
- - ti- - ae, [sa- - pi- en- - ti- - ae]
216
Do- - - - - mi- ni, ti- - - - mor Do- - mi- - ni;
- - mor Do- - - - - - - - - - - - mi- ni;
ti- - - mor Do- - - - - - mi- - ni; in- tel-
223
B
bc
-le- ctus bo- - - - nus omnibus fa- ci- en- tibus
230
e- - - - um. Lau- da- tio e- - ius ma- net in

237
sae - culum — sae - cu - li, ma - net — in sae - culum — sae - cu -
243
- li, lau - da - tio e - - - - - ius, ma - net in sae - - -
250
S¹
S²
B
bc
Glo - - - - -
- - - - culum — sae - cu - li.
258
- - ri - a Pa - -
Glo - - - - - - - ria Pa - -
264
- tri et Fi - li - o et — Spi - ri - tu - i san - - -
- tri et Fi - li - o et — Spi - ri - - tu - i san - -
268
- - - - cto, et — Spi -
- - - - cto, et — Spi - ri - tu -

272
S¹
S²
B
bc
- - tu - i San - - - - - cto, si - cut
- i San - - - - - cto, si - cut
si - cut
278
e - rat in prin - ci - pio, et nunc et sem - - - - per,
e - rat in prin - ci - pio, et nunc et sem - - - - per,
e - rat in prin - ci - pio, et nunc et sem - - - - per,
285
sicut e - rat in prin - ci - pio, et nunc et sem - - - - -
sicut e - rat in prin - ci - pio, et nunc et sem - - - - -
sicut e - rat in prin - ci - pio, et nunc et sem - - - - -
292
- per, et in sae - cula sae - culo - rum. A - -
- per, et in sae - cula et in sae - cula sae - culo - rum. A - - -
- per, et in sae - cula saeculo - rum. A - - - - -

298
-men, et in sae-cula sae-culo- rum A- -
-men, et in sae-cula sae-culo- rum, sae-cu- lo- - - rum A- - -
-men, et in sae-cula saeculo-rum A- - -
304
-men, et in sae-cula sae-culo- rum A- - - - men,
-men, et in sae-cula sae-culo- rum A- - - - men, Amen,
men, et in sae-cula saeculo-rum sae-culo- rum A- - - men,
310
A-men, A- -men, A- - - - men,
A- -men, A- - - - men, Amen, A- -men,
A-men, A- -men, A- - - men, Amen,
317
Amen, A-men, A- - - men, A-men, A- -men,
A- - - - men,
A- -men, A- - - men, A-men,

324
A - men, A - - men,
A - - men, A - - -
men, A - - -
men, A - - -
- - - men,
330
- - - men, A - - - -
men.
A - - men, A - - - -
men.
[6]
56
43

DESIDERATA NOBIS (ATB bc)

BASIS OF THIS EDITION: <u>Scelta de'motetti...</u> (Rome: A. Belmonte, 1667). D-brd MÜs (ATB) and I Bc (bc).

VARIANTS AND COMMENTS:

14.4	A	Last semiquaver d'.
40.1	A T bc	'piano' printed.
40.1	B	'for.' printed.
42.1	B	'pian.' printed.
42.3	T	Printed b. Not impossible; but probably tenor in 42 and alto in 46 should agree.
44.1	ATB bc	'forte' printed.
52	ATB bc	Original time signature 3 in AT, C_2^3 in B, and $O_1^{3/2}$ in bc. The change of time signature in ATB (from the previous O_1^3) is puzzling, as is the discrepancy in bc. Both O_1^3 and C_2^3 would sound the same in performance: according to the mensural practice of preceding centuries, the former goes three semibreves to the tactus and the latter three minims to the tactus (see Donington, <u>Interpretation of Early Music</u>, p.652). These peculiarities confirm the view that seventeenth-century practice was inconsistent and confused.
60.3	T	Printed b.
68-9	B	'nultus splendior'
90	T	'es'
121	B	Printed f d g.
123.3	A	Cf. 115.
124.2	T	Cf. 116 and 124.2 (bc).
129	bc	<u>Sic</u>; i.e. white notation.
134.4	T	Printed a.
142.1	bc	Printed B.
143.2	A	Printed ♪.
145.2-3	T	♯s added because of bar 136 (of which it is a decorated version).
148 and 149	A	'piano' omitted and 'forte' omitted.

147/148	bc	'piano' is printed at the beginning of 147 instead of 148, beat 3.
149/150	bc	'forte' is printed on the second beat of 149, instead of the first beat of 150.
150-51	T	Underlay and final note:

e no e no e

Desidera-ta no-bis et uni-ver-so opta-bilis mundo natalis
Desidera--ta no-bis et uni-ver-so o-
Deside-ra-ta no-bis et uni-ver-so opta-bilis
adest Salvato-ris di--es, de-sidera-ta no-bis et uni-ver-so opta-bilis
-pta--bilis mundo natalis adest Salva-toris, Salvatoris di------es,
mun---do natalis adest Salva-to--ris di---es,
mun---do natalis
na-talis adest Sal-va-toris di-es, Salva-to-ris di--es.
natalis adest Salva-toris, Salva-to--ris di--es.
adest Sal-va-toris di-- es, natalis adest Salva-to-ris di--es.

302

45
vi-deant Au-cto-rem sae-culi, Au-- cto-rem sae-cu-li.
vi-deant Aucto-rem saeculi, Au-- cto-rem sae-cu-li.
vi-deant Aucto-rem saeculi, Au-- cto-rem sae-cu-li.
43
52
Iam cur-rite pastores, cur-rite, natus est ho-die caelo-rum Rex
An- nun-ciant
43
60
laetantes An-geli quod nova sae-culi est a--tra lux.
En ru-tilent nascentis
67
O pu-pule, O pu-pule
O pu-pule, O
pu-eri [v]ultus splen-[di]-dior quam cla-ra fax. O pu-pule; O

74
O matris vir-ginis germen a-ma-bile, quam pul-cher est,
pu-pule, O matris vir-ginis germen a-ma-bile, quam pulcher est,
pu-pule, O matris vir-ginis germen a-ma-bile, quam pul-cher est,
81
O matris vir-ginis germen a-ma-bile, quam pul-cher est, germen a-
O matris vir-ginis germen a-ma-bile, quam pul-cher est, germen a-
O matris virginis germen a-ma-bile, quam pul-cher est, germen a-
88
-ma-bile, quam pulcher est. Con-gau-deant in terris ho-mines dum caelo
-ma-bile, quam pul-cher es[t].
-ma-bile, quam pul-cher est.
95
ca-nitur iu-cun-da pax
cum na-sceris tu caeli glo-ria orbis de-li-cia tu pu-er
Dif-

103
Nunc agite,
es.
Nunc
fugiunt horrentes tenebrae sole serenior est astra nox. Nunc
110
nunc agite caelestes spiritus plandite puero
agite, nunc agite caelestes spiritus plandite puero
agite, nunc agite caelestes spiritus plandite puero
117
qui natus est, nunc agite caelestes spiritus plandite
qui natus est, nunc agite caelestes spiritus plandite
qui natus est, nunc agite caelestes spiritus plandite
124
puero qui natus est, plandite puero qui natus est.
puero qui natus est, plandite puero qui natus est. No.è,
puero qui natus est, plandite puero qui natus est.

131
No - è, no-è, no-è,
no - è, no - è, no - è, no - è,
No - è, no - è, no - è, no - è, no-
136
no - è, no - è, no - è,
no - è, no - è, no - è, no - è,
è, no - è, no - è, no - è,
140
no - è, no - è, no - è,
no - è, no - è, no - e, no-
no - è, no - è, no - è, no - è,
144
no - è, no - è, no-
è, no - è, no - è, no-
no - è, no - è, no - è, no-

148
[piano]
[forte]
-è, no-è, no- è, noè, no- è, no- è.
piano
forte
-è, no-è, no- è, noè no- è, [no- - - è.]
piano
forte
-è, no-è, no- è, no-è, no- è, no-è, no- è.
[piano]
[forte]
43

DICITE NOBIS (SSAT bc)

BASIS OF THIS EDITION: Carissimi, *Sacri concerti musicali...*
(Rome: V. Mascardi, 1675). GB Och.

VARIANTS AND COMMENTS:

11.4	A	Quaver
12.2	bc	♭
13.4	T	) It is possible that the effect of the
15.4	A	) accidental on the second beat of each bar extends to the fourth beat.
15.3	bc	56
16.1	A	Cf. 14.1, tenor.
74.2	S1	The semiquaver in the S1 part-book is not quite clear, but it is probably a''. The bc part-book (in which the notes and the textual incipits of the voice-parts are given for bars 21-133) has g'', but a'' is preferable because of the harmonic context.
88.3-89.2	bc	Figured 34 only.
98	S2 bc	Original time signature C^6_4.
109.4	S2	a' in S2 part-book; b' in bc part-book (as transcribed).
116	S1	Original time signature C^6_4.
132	bc	Figured 65 / 743
156.1-2	S1	F sharps are probably implied because of the tonal context (G major, 154-63), the harmonic context (D major chord in bar 154), the accidentals in the same voice in bars 154 and 157, and the parallel with bar 146 (the B natural in 146 would correspond to F sharp in 156).
178.1	bc	4♯ / 2
178.3-4	T	f
183	bc	9♭8 / 76
208	bc	6♭5

308

205-11	SSAT bc)	These bars are written out in full
221-27	)	in the source. There are only two minor differences:
221	bc	♩· (♩ ○ as in 205 is more consistent).
227	bc	Lacks 43 figuring.
242.3-243.2	T	'trophea'
248	T	⌒

Dicite nobis.
O quam magna.
Dicite. Tacet. O vere
Dicite nobis.
Tacet.
O quam
Di - ci - te
Di - cite no - bis sancto - rum
no - - - bis sancto - rum ci - vium,
di - - ci - te,
ci - vium,
di - cite, dicite, faeli - ces a - - nimae,
A
T
bc
di - cite faeli - ces a - nimae, quantis exul - tat gau - diis caelestis illa
quantis exul - tat gau - diis caelestis illa
ci - vitas Ieru - salem,
in qua cum Chri - -
ci - vitas Ieru - salem, in qua cum Chri - - sto lae - ta - - - - - - mini sine fi - -
- sto laeta - - - mini sine fi - - - ne, lae - ta - - - - - mini, lae -
- ne, in qua cum Chri - - sto lae - ta - - - - - mini, lae -

311

50
S²
- - - - cu - la.
T
Di - cite, di - cite quam dilecta sunt taberna - cula
bc
43
76
56
S¹
O vere summa
T
Do - mini; di - cite, di - cite quam glorio - sa est domus De - i.
bc
76
6
63
S¹
gau - dia; O vere fe - lix glo - ri - a u - bi fa - cti su - mus dome - stici De - i, u -
bc
4
43
68
- bi fa - cti sumus cohe - re - des Chri - - sti. O ve - re sua - vis dul - cedo; O vere
73
requies beata; O vere merces co - pi - osa quam reddit nobis Do - - minus in per -
77
- pe - tuas, in per - pe - tuas ae - ter - nita - - tes, in perpe - tu -
82
- as, in perpe - tu - as, in perpe - tu - as aeter - ni - ta - - tes, ae - - -
43

87
- - - - - - terni - ta - - tes.
Di - cite, di - cite
92
quam felix est locus i - - - ste; di - cite, di - cite quam glori - o - sa est domus
97
Hi po - - - - - suit pa - - cem, hic po - - - - - suit pa - -
Do - mini.
102
- cem fons vitae, fons vitae peren - - nis Ali - gerum pennis sol tem - -
106
- - - - perat fa - - - cem, a - li - gerum pennis sol tem - - - -
110
- - perat fa - - - cem, sol tem - - - - perat fa - - -
114
Non lu - - ctus, non cla - - mor,
- - - - cem.

314

150
-tus, dant an-geli can- tus quo caeli ve- lo- - - -
-tus, dant an-ge-li can- - - tus, quo caeli ve- lo- - - -
157
- - ces dant an-geli can- - - tus, dant an-geli can- - - tus.
- - ces dant an-geli can- - - tus, dant an-geli can- - - tus.
165
S¹ O qui- - - es be- -
S² O qui- es be- -
A O qui- - - es be-
T O qui- es be- -
bc
173
-a- - - ta, O qui- - - es be- a- ta,
-a- - - - - ta, O qui- - - es be- a- - -
-a- ta, O qui- es be- a- - - -
-a- - - - ta, O qui- es be- a- - - -

180
pax ve- - - ra in- sto- - - rum, O
-ta, pax ve- - - ra in- sto- - - rum,
- ta, pax ve- - - ra in- sto- - - - - rum,
-ta, pax ve- ra in- - - sto- - - - - - rum, O
43 98 4 98 76 76 43
188
merces, O merces la- bo- - - rum, O sa- - - lus a- - ma- - - -
O merces la- bo- - - rum, O salus a- ma- - - -
O salus, O salus, O salus a- ma- - -
mer- - - - ces la- - bo- - rum, O sa- - - lus a- - ma- - - -
43
195
-ta. ve- ni- te, ve- ni- te, ve- ni- te, ve- ni- te,
-ta. ve- ni- te, ve- ni- te, ve- ni- te, ve- ni- te,
cur- ra- mus, cur- ra- mus cur-
cur- ra- mus, cur- ra- mus, cur-

202
205/221
ve- ni-te, et Re-gi cae- lo-rum in
ve- ni-te, et Re-gi cae- lo-rum in
-ra-mus, -cur- ra-mus, cur- ra-mus, et Regi cae- lorum in
-ra-mus, -cur- ra-mus, cur- ramus, et Re-gi cae- lorum in
208/224
au-la san- ctorum tro- phe-a ca- na- - - mus, ve- nite, ve- nite,
au-la san- ctorum tro- phe-a ca- na- - - mus, ve- ni-te, ve- ni-te,
au-la san- cto-rum tro- phe-a ca- na- - - mus, cur-
au-la san- cto-rum tro- phe-a ca- na- - - mus, cur-
215
ve- ni-te, ve- ni-te, -mus, ve-
ve- ni-te, ve- ni-te, mus,
-ramus, cur- ra - - - mus, cur- ramus, cur- mus,
-ramus, cur- ra - - - - mus, cur- ramus, cur- mus,

229
-ni-te, ve- ni- - - - te, et Re-gi cae-
-ni-te, ve- ni- - - - te et Re-gi cae-
cur-ramus, cur-ra- - - mus, et Re-gi cae-
cur-ramus, cur-ra- - - mus, et Re-gi cae-
43
43
236
-lorum in aula san-ctorum tro-phe-a ca-na- - - mus, tro-phe-a ca-
-lorum in aula san-ctorum tro-phea ca-na- - - mus, tro-phe-a ca-
-lorum in aula san-ctorum tro-phea ca-na- - - mus, tro-phea ca-
-lorum in aula san-ctorum tro-phea ca-na- - - mus, tro-phea [ca-
43
243
-namus, tro-phe-a ca-na- - - mus, ca-na- - - mus.
-namus, tro-phe-a ca-na- - - mus, ca-na- - - mus.
-namus, tro-phea ca-na- - - mus, ca-na- - - mus.
-namus,] tro-phea ca-na- - - mus, ca-na- - - mus.
43
43

DOMINE, DEUS MEUS (S bc)

BASIS OF THIS EDITION: <u>R.Floridus...has alteras sacras cantiones ...</u> (Rome: I. de Lazzari, 1663).   GB Och

VARIANTS AND COMMENTS:

7	S	The sign for a trill is printed as t in this bar; subsequently it is printed as tr.
9.4	S	tr. is printed closer to the d" than to the e".
18.1	bc	Figured 4♯ / 2
46.4	bc	Figured ♭
65.4	bc	The 3 is printed upside-down.
86.1	bc	Figured 4♯ / 2
107.1	bc	Figured ♭
126.4	bc	Figured ♭
142	bc	There is a change of line in the middle of the bar.
149.3	S	The fourth semiquaver of the group is printed d".
150.1 } 150.3 }	S	It is possible that the third notes of the semiquaver groups on the first and third beats of the bar should be flattened.
163 and 170	S	foelix

Do-mine, De-us me- - us, Do-mine,
De-us me- - us, te de-si- - - - - - - - derat, te semper
a- - - - - - mat, te ge-men-do et plo-rando requi-rit cor-
me- - - - - - - - - - - - - - - um.
Numquam, numquam e-rit in pa-ce lo- - cus e-jus, do-nec in
te, vera bo-ni-tas, re- - - - - - - - - - - qui-e- scat.
In hoc exi-lio lon-ge a te, Deus me- - us, lon-ge a te, Deus me-
-us, a-nima me-a renuit conso-la- - - - - - - ri.

Sine te, o sincera laetitia, sine te, o sincera laetitia, quid mihi est in coelo, et a te quid volui super terram? Te solum te quaero, o dignus, o dignus amari; te, te gaudio vero cor amat laetari, te, te, te gaudio vero cor amat laetari. Quis te non vocabit, quis te non vocabit, o risus, o

65
ri-sus ploran- - - - - - - - tum, voluptas a- man- - - tum, quis
69
te, quis te non_a- ma- - bit, voluptas aman- - -
72
- tum, quis te, quis te non_a- ma- - bit, quis te non a-
75
-ma - - - - - bit.
78
A- mo te Do- mine, Salva-tor me- - us, a- mo te Do- mine,
83
Salva-tor me- us, et- i-deo cla- - mo, ge- - mo, su-
88
-spi-ro, et ante o-culos tu-os effun-do planctum et_ ge-mitum et su-
92
-spi-ria cor- - - - - - dis_ me- - - -

96
-i, et ante o-culos tu-os effun-do plan-ctum et_ ge-mitum et su-
100
-spi-ria cor- - - - - - dis_ me- - -
104
-i. Si audis cla- mantem, si audis cla- mantem, videbis gau-
108
-den- - - - - tem; si fu- - - gis vo- cantem, relinques lan-
112
-guen- - - - - tem, si fu- - - gis vo- cantem, relinques lan-
117
-guen- - - - tem, re- linques lan- guen- - -
122
- - - tem. Te quando videbo, te quando videbo in
127
te de-lecta- - - - - bor, per-fe-cte_ lae- ta- - - - bor et

131
num-quam do-le- - bo, per-fe-cte lae-ta- - - - bor et
134
num-quam do-le- - bo, et numquam, et numquam, et num-quam do-
137
-le- - - bo. Gau-de- - - - - - bo,
141
lae-ta- - - - - - bor, et in aeter-num
145
tu-as misericor- - di- as, et in ae-ter-num tuas miseri-
148
-cor- - dias cele-bra- - - - - -
152
- - - bo. Te lauda-bit os me - um, te lau-da-bit os me-
156
-um, o, o cordis ve-ra spes, o, o delecta-tio, o, o ve- - ra, o

161
vera consola - - ti - o. Canta-bo fe - - lix in super-na pa-tria, et admi-
165
-rabile tu-um no-men per coele - stia re-gna lau-dum pe- renni reso-na- - -bo
169
can - tico, cantabo fe - - lix in super-na pa-tria, et admirabile tu-um
173
nomen per coele - stia re-gna lau-dum pe- renni resona - - bo can-tico, reso-
177
-na - - - - - - bo can-ti- co, lau - - - - - -
182
- dum perenni re-so- na - - - - - - - bo
186
can-tico, reso- na - - - - - - bo
190
can-tico, reso- na - - - - - -

- - bo can - - - - - ti - co.

DOMINE QUIS HABITABIT (SST bc)

BASIS OF THIS EDITION: Carissimi, *Sacri concerti musicali...*
(Rome: V. Mascardi, 1675).   GB Och.

VARIANTS AND COMMENTS:

3.2	S1	Semiquavers b' c''. These notes are not impossible, but c'' d'' are more likely because:

1. with b' c'' the c'' has the effect of an upper échappée; but this would normally fall by a third, not a fourth, as at 75.2-3 in this motet;

2. c'' d'' makes clearer the melodic relationship between bars 1-4.1 and 4.2-6, the latter being a modified version of the former: the c'' d'' semiquavers in bar 3 correspond to the d'' quaver in bar 5.

31.1	T	'tuo'. But, apart from the sense of the motet text itself, cf. Psalm 23 (Vulgate), verse 5.
33.3-4) 36.3-4)	S1	) 'ambulant'. 'habitant', as in S2,) makes rather better sense.
39.1 43.3 49.1	S2 S2 S1	) The rhythmic inconsistency in the imi-) tation (♪.♪ answered by ♪♪) is so) consistent as to suggest that it is probably intentional.
40	S2	Underlay: [musical notation] lo - rum lau - da -
43.4	S1	Despite the inconsistency with 39.2 (S1) and 49.2 (S2), ♪.♪ (as opposed to the expected ♪♪) may be intentional, in view of the fact that 44.2 (S2) is also altered from ♪♪ to ♪.♪ on the same two syllables (cf. 39.4 (S2) and 49.4 (S1)).
47	S1	[musical notation] -da - - bunt But cf. 42-3 (S2) and 53 (S1).
51.4	S1	The quaver rest on the third beat probably has the effect of cancelling the force of the sharp on the second beat; thus the resulting f' natural on the fourth beat corresponds to the g' natural at 45.4 (S1).

58.2	S1	Semiquavers e'' d''. Cf. above, 3.2.
70-71	T	'tua'
72.3	T	b
81	S1	'salus'. Cf. 81 (S2 and T) and 106 (SST).
90.3	bc	g
92.2	T	f
92.3 - 93.1	S1	Printed underlay:

It is printed with this underlay both here and at 117.4 - 118.1 (S2). But at 101.2-3 (S1), 126.4 - 127.1 (S2) and 136.4 - 137.1 (S2) the underlay is

(san) - - - - cti . On all five occasions the tenor is singing the same word, and in this voice the second syllable appears consistently under the third of the three crotchets.

113.4	S1	f''
116.3	S2	a'
117.4 - 118.1	S2	See 92.3 - 93.1.
119.4 - 120.1	S1	Printed underlay:

But cf. 94.4 - 95.1 (S2), 103.2-3 (S2) and 128.4 - 129.1 (S1).

130.3	T	d'
135.2	S1	d''
141	S2	𝄐
141	T	𝄐

Domine. Tacet.
Qui ingrederetur. Tacet.
Domine quis habitabit. Tacet.
Do- mine quis habitabit in taber-
-na- culo tu- - o? aut quis requi- escet in monte san- - cto tu- - o ?
Qui ingreditur sine macula, qui ingreditur sine ma- cula, et o- pe-
-ratur, o- pe- ra- tur iu- sti- - tia[m].
Quis ascendet, quis a- scen- det in mon- -

14
-- tem, in mon - - - tem Do - mini? aut quis stabit, aut quis sta - bit in lo - - - - - co, in
76
18
lo - - - co sancto e - - ius?
Qui non acce - pit in vano a - nimam suam, nec iu -
76
65
22
- ra - vit in dolo proximo su - - o. Hic ac - ci - piet benedictio - nem a
43
76
26
Do - mino, hic ac - ci - piet benedicti - o - nem a Do - mino, et mi - se - ri - cordiam a
76
7 5

Beati, be - a - ti qui [ha-bitant] in
Bea - ti, be - a - ti qui ha - bitant in
Deo saluta - ri [t]u - o.
domus tua Do - mi - ne, be - a - ti, be - a - ti qui [habitant] in domus tua Do - - mi -
domus tua Do - mi - ne, be - a - ti qui ha - bitant in domus tua Do - - mi -
- ne, quo - niam in saecula saecu - lo - - - - - rum lau - da - - - - - - -
- ne, quoni - am in saecula saecu - lo - - [- - - - rum lau]da - -
- - - - - bunt, laudabunt te, quoniam in saecula saecu -
- - - - - - bunt, lau - da - - - bunt te, quoni - am in
- lo - - - - - rum lauda - - - - - bunt, lauda - - - - bunt, lau -
saecula sae - cu - lo - - - - rum lauda - - - - bunt, lau -

47
-da- - -[bunt te,]
quoniam,
quo-niam in saecula saecu-
-dabunt te Do-mine,
quoniam in
saecula saeculo- - - - - -
50
-lo- - - - rum lauda- -
- - bunt, lauda-
- - - - bunt, lau-
-rum lauda- - - - - bunt,
lauda- -
- - bunt, lau-
53
-da- - - bunt te.
Do-mine,
Do-mine Deus
me-us, u-bi,
-da- - - bunt te.
57
ubi posuisti taber-
na- - culum tu- - -
um?
Taberna-culum
61
U-bi, ubi
meum cum homi- - ni-
bus, et habita-bo cum
e- - is.

333

84
domus be - - - a - - - ta,
domus be - - - a - - - ta, u - bi in
domus be - - a - - - ta, u - bi in Do - mino gau - de - bunt et exulta - -
89
u - bi in Do - mino gau - de - bunt et exulta - -
Do - mino gau - de - bunt et exulta - - - - bunt san - - - cti, et
- - - bunt san - - - - cti in conspe - - - ctu De - - i, et exul -
92
- bunt san - - - - [- - - cti] in conspe - - - - - ctu De - - - i,
exul - ta - - - bunt sancti in conspe - - - - - ctu De - i,
- ta - - - bunt san - - - cti, u - bi, u - bi in Domino, in
96
u - bi in
u - bi in Domino gau - de - bunt et exulta -
Do - mino gaude - bunt et exulta - - - - bunt san - - - - - - cti in con - -

99
Do - mino gau - de - bunt, et exulta - - - bunt san - - - - - cti in con -
- - - - - bunt san - - - - - cti, et exulta - - - - bunt sancti in con -
- spe - - - ctu De - - i, et exulta - - - bunt san - - cti in con -
102
- spe - - - - - ctu De - - - i. O, O sedes a - mata, O
- spe - - - - ctu De - - i. O, O sedes a - mata, O
- spe - ctu De - - - - - - - - i. O, O sedes a - mata, O
108
domus, O domus be - - a - - ta,
domus, O domus be - - - a - - ta, u - bi in Do - mino gau -
domus, O domus be - - a - - ta, u - bi in Do - mino gau -
113
u - bi in Do - mino gaude - - bunt et exulta - - - - bunt
- de - bunt, u - bi in Do - mino gau -
- de - bunt et exulta - - - - - bunt san - - - - cti in conspe - - - ctu

116
san - - - cti, et exul-ta - - - bunt sancti in con-spe - - - - ctu De - - [i, —
-de-bunt et exulta - - - bunt san - - [- - cti] in con-spe - - - - ctu De - - - -
De - i, et exul-ta - - - bunt san - - - cti, u - bi,
43 6 87 65 # # 43
120
—] u-bi in Domino, u-bi in
-i, u-bi in Do-mino gau - - - bunt,
u-bi in Do-mino, u-bi in Do-mino gau-de-bunt, et exulta - -
6 #
123
Do-mino gaude - - bunt et exulta - - - - - - bunt san - - - cti, et
u-bi in Do-mino gau-de-bunt et exulta - -
- - - - bunt san - - - cti in con-spe - - - ctu De - i et exul-
43 6 43 6
126
exulta - - - - bunt sancti in conspe - - - - - ctu De - - i
-bunt san - - - - cti in conspe - - - - - ctu De - - i, u - bi in
-ta - - bunt san - - cti, u - bi, u-bi in Do - mino
87 65 # ♮ 6 43

130
u- - bi in Do- mino gau- de - bunt, in Do - mino gau - de - bunt et exul-
Do- mino
u - - bi in Do- mino gau- de - bunt, in Do - mino gau - de - bunt et exulta - -
6 6 #
133
-ta- - bunt sancti in con- spe- ctu De - - - - i, et exul - ta - -
et exulta - - - bunt san - -
- bunt san - - cti in con- spe - - ctu De - i, et exul - ta - - - - -
43 6 87 65
136
- - - - bunt sancti in conspectu, in con- spe - ctu De - - -
- - - - - - cti in conspectu, in con- spe - ctu De - - -
- - bunt san - - cti in conspe - ctu De - - - - - -
87 65 # # # 43
139
- i, in conspe - - ctu De - - - - i.
- i, in conspectu De - - - - - - - - i.
- i, in conspe - ctu De - - - - - i.
43

EMENDEMUS IN MELIUS (mSAT bc)

BASIS OF THIS EDITION: <u>Scelta di motetti...</u> (Rome: L. Grignani, 1643). I COd.

VARIANTS AND COMMENTS:

Prefatory stave	A	Clef and first note <u>sic</u>. The clef should be C3, as it is on the second and subsequent lines of the source.
2.2	A	The a' is omitted.
21.1	bc	Flat printed under beat 3 (b flat).
43.3	A	♪.
58.4	T	b flat. Cf. 57.4 (mS), 60.4 (A) and 61.4 (mS).
68.4	bc	6 But this conflicts with the g' in mS.
82.2	A	f sharp'
92.2	A	f'
94	mS A	♮

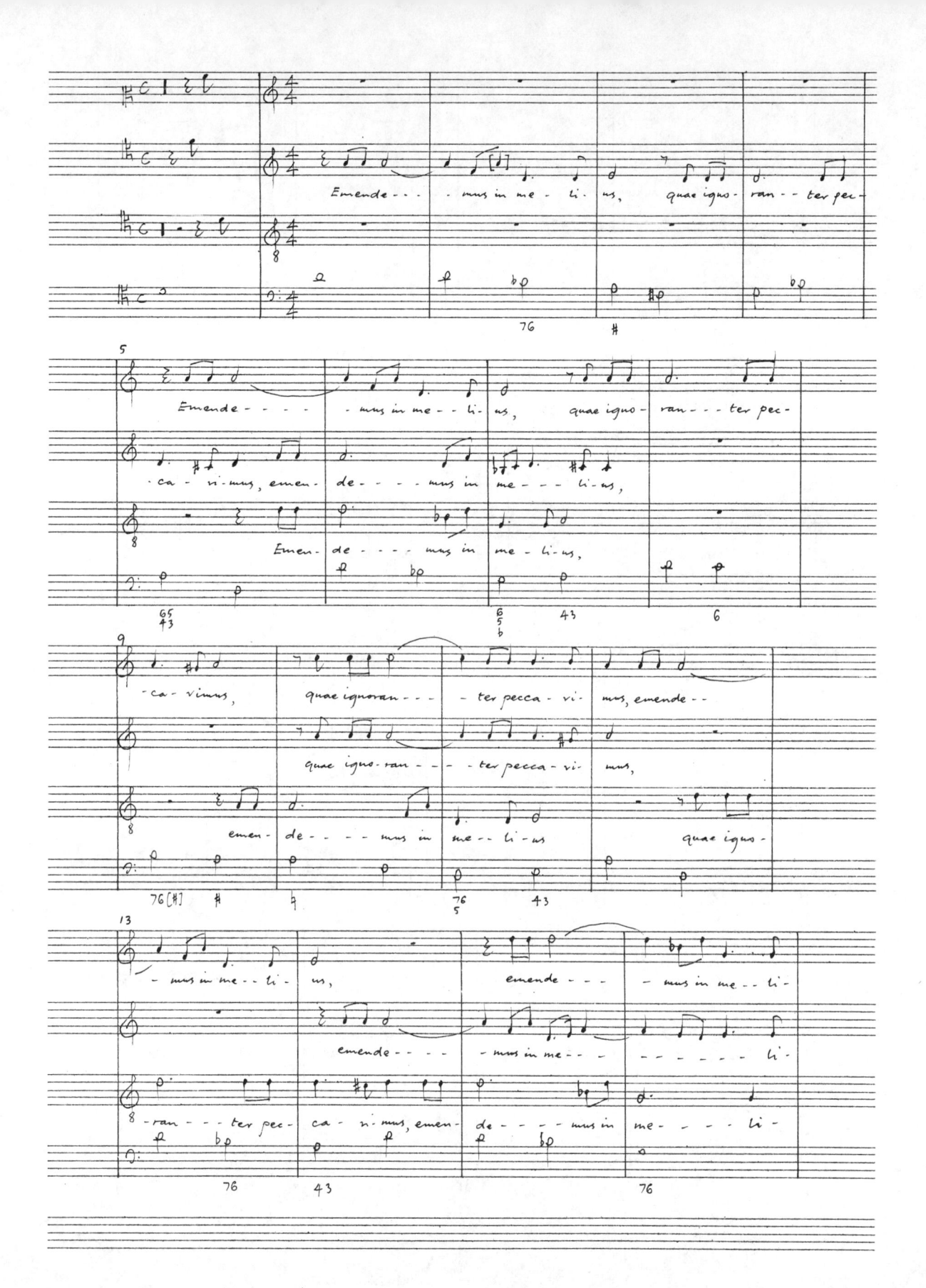

17
-us, quae igno- ran- - - ter pec- ca- vimus, quae igno-
-us, quae igno- ran- - - ter pec- ca- vimus, quae ignoran- - - -
-us, emende- - - - - - mus in me- li- us, quae igno- ran- ter, quae igno-
21
-ran- ter pec- ca- - - vi- mus:
- - ter pec- - ca- vi- mus:
-ran- ter pec- - ca- vi- mus: ne su- - bito, ne
25
quaeramus
quaeramus spa- - - ti-
su- - bito praeoc- cu- pa- ti di- e mor- - - tis,
28
spa- - tium paeni- ten- - ti- ae, et inveni- re non possimus, non pos-
-um paeniten- ti- ae, et inveni- re non possi- mus, non, non pos-

32
-si - mus, ne su - bi - to, ne su - - bi - to praeocu-
-si - - - mus, ne su - bi - to, ne su - - bi - to prae-
ne su - - bi - to, ne su - - bi - to
36
-pa - ti di - e mor - tis, praeoc - cu - pa - ti di - e mor - tis, di - - - e
-oc - cu - pa - ti di - e mor - tis, di - e mor - - - tis, praeoc - cu - pa - ti di - e
prae - oc - cu - pa - ti di - e mor - - - tis, di - - - e
39
mor - tis, quaeramus spa - ti - um paeni - ten - ti -
mor - - tis, quaeramus spa - - ti -
mor - - tis, quaeramus spa - - ti - um paeni - ten - - ti - ae, quaeramus
42
-ae, paeniten - - - - ti - ae, quaeramus spa - - - ti -
-um paeni - ten - ti - ae, quaeramus spa - ti - um paeni - ten - - ti -
spa - ti - um, quaeramus spa - - ti - um paeni - ten - - ti - - ae, quaeramus

45
-um paeni-ten-ti- - ae, et inveni- re
-ae, paeni-ten- - ti- ae, et inveni- re non possi- mus, non, non
spatium paeniten- - ti- ae, et inveni- re non possi- mus,
49
non possi- mus, et inveni- re, et invenire non pos- si- mus, et inve-
et inveni- re non possi- mus, non, non pos- si- - - mus,
non, non, et inveni- re non possi- mus, et inveni- - re
53
-ni- re, et inve- ni- re non pos- si- - - - - mus. At- - ten-de
et inveni- re non, non, non possi- - mus.
et inveni- re non possi- mus, non possi- - mus.
58
Do- mine, et misere- - - - - - re, at- - tende
At- - tende Do- mine, et
At- - tende Do- - mine, et misere- - - re,

62
Do - mine, et — misere - - - re: qui - a pec- ca - vimus, pec-
— miserere, et — mise - re - - re,
et mi - se - re - - re,
66
-ca - vimus ti - - - - - bi, at - tende
at - - tende Do - mine, et — misere - - - - -
at - - tende Do - - mine, et — misere -
71
Do - mine, et — misere - - - - - - - - - - re,
-re, at - - tende Do - mine, et — misere - - - re: qui - a pec- ca - vimus, pec-
-re, et mi - se - re - - re,
76
at - tende Do - mine, et — misere - - -
-ca - vimus ti - - - - - - bi,
at - - tende Do - - mine, et —

80
re, at - tende Do - mine, et — misere - -
at - tende Do - - mine, et — misere - - - -
— misere - - - re, et mi - se - re - -
84
-re: qui - - a pec - ca - vimus, pec-
-re: qui - - a pec - ca - vimus, pec - ca - vimus, pecca - - vimus, pecca-
-re: qui - - a pec - ca - vimus, pec - ca - - vimus, pec - ca - vimus, pec-
88
-ca - - vimus ti - - - - bi, pecca - - vimus, pecca - - vimus, pecca - vimus, pec-
- - vimus ti - - bi, pecca - ri - mus, pecca - ri - mus, peccavimus, pec-
-ca - vimus ti - - - bi, pecca - ri - mus, pecca - ri - mus, peccavimus, pec-
92
-ca - - - - vimus ti - - - bi.
-ca - vimus ti - - - - - - bi.
-ca - ri - mus ti - - - bi.

EXULTA, GAUDE, FILIA SION (SS bc)

BASIS OF THIS EDITION: Carissimi, *Sacri concerti musicali*...
(Rome: V. Mascardi, 1675). GB Och.

VARIANTS AND COMMENTS:

8.1	S2	A flat is printed in front of the first note in the bar (f'') and on the same line.
21.4	S2	Probably printed f'' (the print is rather faint).
24.1-2	S1	Both quavers.
28-32	SS	Differences in words ('princeps mundi' and 'princeps pacis') *sic*.
32	SS	It is not impossible that the different note-lengths are intentional: S1 needs a rest in which to breathe but S2 does not.
56	S1	The application (or omission) of editorial accidentals is problematical. It is felt that the leading-note function of the first f' and its proximity to the f sharp' in the previous bar imply the addition of a sharp; whereas the second f' is effectively a passing-note between g' and e flat'' (the latter displaced by an octave) and so should be natural. The second half of the bar sounds most convincing if it is an exact sequence of the first half, so the first b' is natural and the second flat. (At 56.4 - 57.1 the passing-note nature of the b flat' becomes explicit, since the a' at 57.1 is *not* displaced by an octave.)
66.2-3	S2	c' b flat'
81.3	bc	Figured flat. Possibly it is misplaced, and should be at 81.1.
86	S1	Printed: [musical notation] fae - li - ci - ta - -
89.2	S2	Flat in front of e''.
94.1	S2	Crotchets printed as minims.
105.3	S2	Admittedly there are no flats nearby in S2, but the parallel with bars 34 and 46 justifies ( ) rather than [ ].

109-38	SS	The underlay for most of this section is unclear or inconsistent.
117-21) 132-34)	SS	The ♪ melismas in these bars are very problematical. The principles followed in deciding which notes are printed wrongly are the following: 1. imitative phrases are likely to imitate exactly; 2. it is preferable to correct as few notes as possible; 3. despite the printed version of bar 132.3-4, the second passage (132-4) need not necessarily have the same notes as the first (120-2).
118.3	S1	d'' c''
119.1	S1	a'
120.3-4	bc	B flat, c, both crotchets, and the B flat is figured 6. This is not impossible, but it is more likely that the bc corresponds to the previous two bars (beats 3 and 4 in each case) and changes its pattern when the voice parts change theirs – i.e. in bar 121.3-4.
124.1	S2	Crotchet.
125	S2	Rest omitted.
126.2	S2	g'
132.4	S1	It is possible that the d' should be e'; but 133.4 (S2) is also printed d'.
132.3-4	S2	Printed:
133.3	S1	e''
138	SS	|o||o||o|
139		The heading 'Piva' (bagpipe) is found also in Graziani's motet 'Pastores dum custodistis'. The drone is suggested by the static harmony. Presumably the instrument had rural associations with shepherds, and hence with a Nativity text.

Exulta, gau-de, gau-de, fi-lia Si-on; tri-um-pha, ju-bi-la, fi-lia Jeru-sa-lem, triumpha, jubila, jubila, filia Jerusa-lem. In te natus est salvator mundi; in te natus est rex magnus, rex admira-... est rex pacificus;

Deus for- - - - - tis, prin - ceps mun- -
- - bilis, pater futuri sae- - - - culi, prin - ceps pa -
- di, prin - ceps mun - - di.
E - - xul - - ta,
- cis, prin - - ceps pa - - cis.
gau - - - de, gau - - de fi - - li - a Si - - - on;
E - - xul - - ta, gau - - de fi - li - a Si - - on; tri - um - pha,
tri - um - pha, in - - bi - la fi - li - a Ie - ru - - sa - lem,
in - - - bi - la, in - bi - la fi - li - a Ieru - - sa - lem,
tri - um - pha, in - - bi - la, in - bila fi - lia Ie - ru - - sa - lem.
tri - um - pha, in - bila fi - lia Ie - ru - - sa - lem.

Con- - - surge, se-de Ieru- - sa- lem, indu- - ere ve- - stibus iucundi-
-ta- - - - - tis et glo- - - - ri-ae.
Solve vin-cula colli
tui, solvi vin- cu- la colli tu- i captiva fi- - lia Si- - on.
Quo-niam il-lu-xit ti- - bi, il-lu-xit ti- - bi di-es redempti-
Quo-niam il-lu-xit ti- - bi
-o- - - - nis tu- - ae,
di-es gra- - - -

73
di-es feli-ci-ta- - - -tis ae-
- - - -tis-si-ma,
78
-ter- - - - - - nae,
di-es feli-ci-ta- - - -tis ae-
83
di- - es, [di-es feli-ci-ta] - - - -
-ter- - - - - - - - nae, di-es feli-ci-ta- - - - -
88
- -tis ae-ter- - - - - nae. E-xul-ta, gau- - de,
- -tis ae-ter- - - - - nae. E-xul-ta,
94
gau- - de fi- -li-a Si- - on;
gau- - de fi- -li-a Si- - on; tri-um-pha,

99
tri - um - pha, in - - - bila fi - li - a — lem - - sa - lem,
in - - - bila, in - - - bila fi - lia le - m - - sa - lem,
104
tri - um - pha, — in - - bi - la, in - bila fi - - li - a — lem - - sa -
tri - um - pha, — in - bila fi - - lia le - m - sa -
109
-lem. No - e, — no -
-lem. No - e, — no - e, no - e, — no - e,
112
-e, no - e, — no - e, no - e — no - e, no - e, no - e, no - e, — no -
no - e, — no - e, no - e, — no - e, no - e, — no -
116
-e, no - e, — no - e, no - e, — no -
-e, no - e, — no - e, no - e, — no - e, no - e, —

120
-e, no-e, no-e,
no-e, no-e, no-e, no-e, no-e, no-e, no-
124
no-e, no-e, no-e, no-e, no-e, no-e, no-e, no-
-e,
no-e, no-e, no-e, no-
128
-e, no-e, no-e, no-e, no-e, no-e,
-e, no-e, no-e, no-e, no-e, noe, no-
132
no-e, no-e, no-e, no-e, no-e,
-e, no-e, no-e, no-e, noe, no-
136
no-e, no-e, no-e, no-e, no-e.
-e, no-e, no-e, no-e, no-e, no-e, no-e.

Piva si placet

[Music: three-staff system with text underlay]

Dedere tandem caelites infantem, Dedere mundi
Dedere tandem caelites infantem, Dedere mundi

labilis Atlantem.
labilis Atlantem.

43

2 En terra nostra germinavit florem Calentem bruma protulit Amorem

3 Olympi clausi paruere sedes Sunt clause tandem a Cherontis Aedes

4 Cantemus ergo modulemur omnes Ducendo noctem hylares in somnes.

EXURGE COR MEUM (S VV vlne bc)

BASIS OF THIS EDITION: Carissimi, *Arion Romanus*... (Konstanz: David Hautt, jnr., 1670). CH Zz.

VARIANTS AND COMMENTS:

17.2	bc	The e is prefixed by a redundant flat.
18.1	S	The e' is prefixed by a redundant flat.
24.1-2	vlne and bc	Possibly the rhythm should be the same in both parts.
35.2	V2	Printed g'.
44.1	V1	The e' is prefixed by a redundant flat.
74.1	S	The e' is prefixed by a redundant flat.
75) 76)	S	Discrepancies with bars 86 and 96 sic.
77.2	vlne	Printed d.
66-107		Numerous discrepancies sic.
87.3) 97.3)	bc	Printed [music notation] (The figuring of the ground bass is inconsistent at each appearance.)
94.1	S	The e' is prefixed by a redundant flat.
108.1	bc	Printed 43 .

355

Care vir-gi-ni De-i-pa-rae, vir- -gini — De-i- - pa-rae.
Quid si- - -
-les? cur non au- -dis? Ma-riae semper re-sonent, Mariae semper

30
re - sonent mea la - - - bia lau - - - des.
35
Quid prodi - rit de o - re altis - - si - mi meo numquam ab
40
o - - - - - - re_re - ce - - - det.

44
Exur-ge, ex- ur-ge cor me-um, exur- - ge.
49
aria
So- noro gaude ju-bilo, dul-ci lae- tare can-tico, dul- ci laetare can-ti-
53
-co, Ma-ri-am ca- - ne Virginem. Quid si- - -

57
-les? cur non au- -dis? Ma- riae semper re- sonent, Mariae semper
61
re- sonent mea la- - -bia lau- - des, mea la- - - - -
66
- - bia lau- - - des.

Dei parens, naevo carens, puritate pu-ri-or, pro amicis inimicis adamante du-ri-or, adamante du-ri-or.

81
Salamone et sam- sone for- tior et sa- pi- ens, hinc averni tibi
[43]
6 4 ♮
7 4 3
85
sterni timet ira ru- gi- ens, timet ira ru- gi- ens.
89
Stella maris tu pro-

-baris caelo devianti- bus, caeli clavis tuta navis male fluctuanti-bus, male fluctuanti- bus.

Sine viro modo miro Virgo Dei mater

104
es; O sublimis alta nimis solo Deo di-gna es, solo Deo di-gna es, so-lo
43
108
De-o di---gna es.
[4 3] 6 5 43

HYMNUM JUCUNDITATIS (SS bc)

BASIS OF THIS EDITION: R. Floridus...has alteras sacras cantiones ... (Rome: L. Grignani, 1645).   I Bc.

ALSO COLLATED: Carissimi, Arion Romanus... (Konstanz: David Hautt, jnr., 1670).   CH Zz.

VARIANTS AND COMMENTS:

8.4	S2	A second flat is printed in front of the second e''.
16	S1	1670: the dot is printed.
18.3	bc	1645: figured ♭; 1670: blank.
19.1	bc	1670: figured ♭6.
19.3	bc	1670: figured 65♭.
20.1	S1	1670: flat is printed.
30.3	bc	1670: figured 65♭.
34.1	bc	Figured ♭. The cautionary flat (natural in this edition) is necessary because of bar 23.
36-7	S2	1670: black notation.
50.2 55.3	S2 S1	♮ sic in both 1645 and 1670.
54-55.1	bc	1645: [music example] 1670: [music example] The latter, avoiding a rhythmic hiatus, is preferable. (The hiatus is less objectionable at bar 42; at bar 47 it is again avoided.)
57	S1	1670: [music example] (but with the same bc figuring).
74.1	bc	Figured ♭ (unnecessarily).
74.2	bc	1670: ♭6.

75	bc		1670: ⌐♭⌐ ♮
76.2	bc	⎫	1670: figured 65.
78.2	bc	⎭	
77.1	S1		1670: a natural is printed in front of the first b'.
87–90	S1		Words are printed 'sit benedictum nomen tuum benedictum benedictum nomen tuum' in both 1645 and 1670. But cf. all the following phrases.

Hym-num ju-cun- - - di- ta-tis cante- - - - - mus, cante - -
[4]
2
4
- - - - - mus Deo no- - - stro,
Hymnum jucun- - - di-
Hym-num ju- cun- - di-ta-tis can- te- - - - mus Deo no- - -
8
-ta-tis cante- - - - - mus, cante- - - - mus Deo no- - - stro, can-
-stro, cante- - - - - mus,
Hymnum ju- cun- di-ta- - tis can-
12
-te- - - - - - mus, can- te- - - - - - mus, can- te- - - - mus Deo no- - - -
-te- - - - - mus, can- te- - - - - mus,
can-te- - - - mus Deo no- - -
16
-stro,
et in can- - - ticis et
-stro, et in can- - - ticis et cy- - - tharis

cy - - - tharis lan - de - - - - - - - - - - mus e - - - - - -
lan - de - - - - - - - - mus e - - -
um, et in can - - - ticis et cy - - - tharis
um, et in can - - - - ticis et
et in can - - - ticis et cy - - - tharis lan -
cy - - - - tharis lan - de - - - - - -
de - - - - - mus e - - - - um, lan -
- - - - - - mus e - - - um, lan - - -
de - - - - - mus e - - - um.
de - - - - - mus e - - - um.
Ma - - -

368

62
ma - - jesta - - - - - te,
excel - sus, excel - sus, excel - sus in sanctita - - -
65
excel - sus, excel - sus, excel - - sus in sanctita - - - -
- - - - - - - - te, excel - - sus, ex - cel - sus,
68
- - - - - - - te, excel - sus in sanctita - - - - - - - te,
excel - sus in sancti - ta - - - - - - - - - - - te,
72
to - tus desidera - - bilis, to - tus a -
to - tus a - ma - - bilis, to - tus a -
77
- ma - bilis, to - tus deside - - ra - - bilis et
- ma - bilis, to - tus desi - de - ra - - bilis et

81
dul - - cis, et dul - -
dul - - - - - cis, et
dul - - - -
98 43 98 98 43
85
- cis.
Sit bene-
- cis. Sit benedictum nomen tuum in aeternum, bene- dictum in aeter - - - -
6 43
88
- dictum nomen tuum [in ae- ternum,] benedictum [in ae- ter - - - - num,]
- num,
sit benedictum nomen
43
91
sit bene- dictum nomen tuum in ae-
tuum in aeternum, bene- dictum in aeter - - - - num, sit bene-
43 56
94
- ternum, in aeternum bene- dictum nomen tu - - um, bene-
- dictum nomen tuum, bene- dictum nomen tuum, bene- dictum nomen tuum, bene-

97
-dictum nomen tuum in ae- ter- - - num, bene- dictum nomen tuum in ae-
-dictum nomen tuum in ae- ter- - - num, bene- dictum nomen tuum in ae-
43
100
-ter- - - - num.
-ter- - - - num.
43

INSURREXERUNT IN NOS INIMICI NOSTRI (mSAT bc)

BASIS OF THIS EDITION: Sacrarum modulationum... (Rome: L. Grignani, 1642). I Bc.

ALSO COLLATED: R. Floridus...Florida verba... (Rome: G. B. Robletti, 1648). [to the words 'Praevaluerunt in nos'] GB Lwa.

Teatro musicale de concerti ecclesiastici... (Milan: G. Rolla, 1649). I Md.

Florida verba... (Antwerp: P. Phalèse, 1661). GB Och. ['Praevaluerunt']

VARIANTS AND COMMENTS:

19.1-2	T	1642:

The version with eight semiquavers appears in all three collated sources. Apart from the greater degree of word-painting (a semiquaver melisma on 'arcum'), it is more likely from a purely musical point of view, because of the parallels with bars 25 (A) and 29 (T).

25.3	bc	1642: 6 . 1649: 6

1648 has 56 over the g (a common misprint for 6) and 1661 has 6.
     5   5

35) 39) 43)		0^3_1 and 0^3_1 appear together and inconsistently.
35/39	bc	Discrepancy *sic* in all sources collated.
45	bc	*Sic*. (Not black notation.)
83	bc	Figured ♮.
100-01) 103-04) A 106.3-07) 104 S		The printed accidentals are the same in all collated sources. It is conceivable that every f' in these bars should be sharpened. But such wholesale sharpening cannot be said to be implied by the notation and by seventeenth-century conventions, and it is probably undesirable,

since it imposes 'modern', 'tonal' characteristics on an idiom which still retains a slight modal flavour.

102.4   bc   Figured ♭.

mS
A
T
bc
In - - - surre- xe - - - runt in nos inimici, ini-
In - - - - - - surre-
-mi - - ci no - - - stri, in - - - - surre-
-xe - - - - runt in nos inimici, ini- mi - - ci no - - - stri,
In - - - surre- xe - - - runt in nos inimici, ini-
-xe - - - runt in nos inimici, ini- mi - ci no - - - stri, in - - -
in - - - - surre- xe - - - runt in nos inimici, ini-
-mi - ci no - - - stri, in - - - surre-
- - surrexe - - - - - runt in nos inimici, ini- mi - - ci no - - -
-mi - - ci no - - - stri ini- mici no- stri, ini- mi - - ci no - - -
-xe - - - runt in nos inimici no - - stri ini- mici, ini- mi - ci - no - - -

16
-stri;
-stri; e-vagina- ve---runt gla-di- um,
-stri;
in-tenderunt ar--------
20
et si-cut gi- gantes steterunt contra nos,
et si-cut gi- gan-tes steterunt contra
-cum,
e-- ragina- re---runt gla-di-
24
e---vagina-
nos, in---tenderunt ar---------- cum, et si- cut gi-
-um, et si--cut gi- gan-tes ste-terunt contra nos,
27
-ve---runt gla----di- um, et si--cut gi- gan-tes steterunt contra
-gan-tes ste-terunt contra nos,
in--tenderunt ar-----

30
nos, et si - cut gi - gan - tes steterunt contra nos, ste - te - - -
et si - cut gi - gan - tes ste - terunt contra nos, ste - - - te - -
- cum, et si - cut gi - gan - tes ste - terunt contra nos, ste - te - - -
33
- runt con - - tra nos. E - xur - ge Do - mine in adiuto - rium
- - runt con - - tra nos.
- runt con - tra nos.
38
no - - strum,
e - xur - ge Do - mine in adiuto - - rium no - - strum,
e - xur - ge Do - mine in adiu - to - - rium no - - strum,
43
e - xur - ge Do - mine, exur - - - - ge, et dissipentur ini -
e - xur - ge Do - mine, e - xur - - - ge,
e - xur - ge Do - mine, e - xur - - - ge,

47
-mi--ci no---- stri, et dissi-
et dissipentur ini- mici no-----
et dissi- pentur ini-mici, ini- mi-ci no---
43 # 43
50
-pentur i-ni-mici, ini- mi--ci no--- stri, et dissi-
-stri, et dissipentur ini- mi-ci no---- stri, et dissipentur ini-
-stri, et dissi- pentur ini- mici, ini-
#
53
-pentur ini-mici no---- stri.
-mici, ini-mi--ci no---stri. E--ripe nos de manu fortio---
-mici, ini-mi-ci no---stri.
43
57
ex- pugna impugnan--- tes
-rum, ap-prehende
ap-prehende ar-ma et scu--tum,
76 # # 43

60
nos, ap-prehende ar-ma et scu- - - - - tum,
ar-ma et scu- tum, ap-prehende ar-ma et scu- tum,
ap-prehende ar- - ma et scu- tum, ex-pugna impug-
43
63
ap-prehende ar-ma et scu- tum,
ap-prehende ar- ma et scutum, ex- pugna impug-
-nan- - tes nos, ex-pugna impug- nan- tes nos,
76
76
66
ap-prehende ar- - ma et scu- tum, espugna impug- nan- tes nos, ex-
-nan- - tes nos, ex-pug- na
ap-prehende ar- - ma et scu- tum, ex-
76
43
69
-pug- na, ex- pug-na impug- nan- - - tes nos,
ex- pugna impug- nan- - tes nos, ap-prehende ar- - ma et
-pugna, expugna impug- nantes nos, ap-prehende
43
43

72
ap-prehende ar-ma et scutum, ap-prehende ar-ma et scu-tum,
scu-tum, ap-prehende ar-ma et scu-tum, ex-pug-na,
ar-ma et scu-tum, ap-prehende ar-ma et scutum, ex-
75
ex-pug-na, ex-pug-na, ex-pug-na
ex-pug-na, expugna impug-nantes nos, ex-
-pugna, ex-pugna impug-nantes nos, expug-
43
78
ex-pugna impug-nan--tes nos;
-pugna, expugna impug-nan-tes nos; ut ti-bi lan--dem,
-na, expug-na impug-nan--tes nos;
43
82
ti-bi vi-cto--riam,
ti-bi ca-na--- mus glo--ri-am,
43

88
ut ti-bi lau-dem, ti-bi vi- cto--riam,
ut ti-bi lau-dem, ti-bi vi- cto- riam, ti-bi ca- na----
ut ti-bi lau-dem, ti-bi ca- na---
94
ti-bi ca- na---- mus glo-ri- am,
-mus glo-ri- am, ti-bi ca- na-- mus glo- ri- am, cana---
-mus glo-ri- am, ti-bi ca- na--- mus glo--ri- am,
100
ca- na------ mus glo--ri- am, ca-
mus, ca- na---mus glo-ri- am, ca- na---
ca- na--------
103
-na------mus, ca- na--------mus glo--ri-am,
------mus, ca- na---------mus glo--ri-am, ca-
--mus, cana---- --mus, ca- na- mus glo- ri- am,

106
ca - na - - - - mus, ca-na - - - - mus, ca-na - mus
-na - - - - - - - - - mus, ca- na - - - - mus, ca- na - - mus
ca - na - - - - - - - mus, ca- na-mus, ca- na - mus
56 ♮ 5 [6] 5
109
glo - - ri - am.
glo - - ri - - am.
glo - - ri - am.
43

LAUDEMUS VIRUM GLORIOSUM (SS bc)

BASIS OF THIS EDITION: Carissimi, *Sacri concerti musicali...* (Rome: V. Mascardi, 1675). GB Och.

ALSO COLLATED: *Scelta di motetti...* (Rotterdam: J. Van Geertsom, 1656). GB DRc.

Carissimi, *Arion Romanus...* (Konstanz: David Hautt, jnr., 1670). CH Zz.

VARIANTS AND COMMENTS:

1-3	bc	1656 and 1670: F (not f), and two separate semibreves (no tie) in 1-2.
4.3	bc	1675: figured ♭.
5-6	bc	1656 and 1670: [music example], which is musically slightly preferable.
7) 13-15)	SS	1670: 'Parentem nostrum' instead of 'sanctorum decus'.
7.1	bc	1656 and 1670: flat is printed.
7	SS	Rhythmic discrepancy *sic* in all three collated sources.
10-11	SS	The use of the abbreviation 'N.' ('nomen') to stand for the name of a saint was quite common in the motets of Carissimi and his contemporaries. Usually, as here, sufficient rhythmic 'elbow-room' was given to permit the insertion of a variety of names.
16	S1	Because of the S2 imitative entry in the same bar and the presence of a flat in both 1656 and 1670, there can be no doubt that a flat is intended before the e'': hence the round, rather than square, brackets.
24.3	S1	1656: [music example] 1670 = 1675.
25.2	S1	1656 and 1670: e'' flat.
27.4	bc	1656 and 1670: figured 6♯.
28	bc	1656 and 1670: [music example] In 1670 the g is figured 6.

35.1	S1	1656: lacks first flat; 1670: lacks both flats.
34.4 35.4	S1 S2	Rhythmic discrepancy *sic* in all collated sources. But 1670 has b' flat instead of a' at 35.4 in S2.
37 40	S1	The printed slur makes the underlay clear in 1675. In 1656, even without a slur, the underlay is clearly different: *[music example]* e - - um____ . 1670 agrees with 1675; at 37 the slur is present, but at 40 it is absent.
37.1	bc	Figured ♭ in all three sources.
61.3	S1	Only in 1656 is the natural printed (as a sharp).
62.1	S1	1656 and 1670 both have the flat.
63.2	S2	1670: the sharp is present.
63	bc	1656: *[music example]* 1670 = 1675.
63-4	S1	1656: *[music example]* 1670 = 1675, except that the first e'' flat in 63 is replaced by an f''.
65	bc	1656: two c minims. 1670 = 1675.
68	S1	1670: both e''s are prefixed by a flat. (But 67.4 lacks a flat.)
69) 79)	S2	1670: underlay (without a slur) is *[music example]* e - - - - i
75 90-91 93 94-95	S1) S2) S1) S2)	1670: underlay is *[music example]* o - - - - ne At 93 and 94-5 a slur clarifies and confirms this underlay.

Lan - - de - - - mus, lan - - - de - - - mus, lande - - -
Lan - - de - - - mus, lan - - de - mus, lande - - -
- - mus virum glo - ri - o - - sum et sanctorum de - cus
- - mus vi - rum glo - ri - o - - sum et sancto - rum de - cus
be - a - - - - - - tum N., Lau -
be - a - - - - - - - tum N. Lau -
- de - - - - - - - - - mus sancto - - - rum de - - cus be -
- de - - - - - - - - - mus san - cto - - - rum de - cus
- a - - - - - - - - - - - tum N. Quem ho - die deduxit
be - a - - - - - - - - tum N.

21
Do - minus in vi - a mira - - - - - - -
76
25
- - - - - - bi - li,
quem ho - die deduxit Do - minus in vi - a mira - - -
♮ 43 76
30
et ad portas Para -
- - - - - - bi - li,
6 # 43
34
- di - si coro - na - - - - - vit e - - - -
et ad portas Para - di - si coro - na - - - - - - - vit e - - -
[♭] 43
38
- um, coro - na - - - - - - vit e - - - - um,
- um coro - na - - - - - - vit e - - um, et ad portas Para -
43

42
et ad portas Para- di- si coro- na- - - - - - rit e- - um, coro-
- di- si corona- - - - - - - - rit e- - - - - um,
46
- na- - - - - - - - - rit, corona- - - - - - rit e- -
coro- na- - - - - - - - - - - rit, corona- - - - - - - - - - - - rit
50
- - - um. E- - nar- r- nt_ po- - puli, e- - nar- rent_ po- - puli
e- - - um. E- - nar- rent_ po- - puli
55
glo- - - - - riam e- - ius, et_ lau- dem_
glo- - - - - riam e- - ius, et_ lau- dem_
60
e- - ius, et_ lau- dem_ e- - ius nun- tiet_ Eccle- - si-
e- - ius, et_ lau- dem_ e- - ius nun- tiet Ec- cle- - si-

65
-a. Can- te- - - - - - mus et exul- te- - - - - mus
-a. Can- te- - - - - - mus et exulte- - - - - - mus e- - -
69
e- - i in cytharis, in tympanis, in canticis et iubilati- o- - ne, in
- - i in
73
cytharis, in tympanis, in canticis et iubilati- o- - ne, Can- te- - -
cytharis, in tympanis, in canticis et iubilati- o- - - ne, can- te- - - - - mus
77
- - mus et exul- te- - - - mus e- - i
et exulte- - - - - mus e- - - - i in cytharis, in tympanis, in
81
in cytharis, in tympanis, in canticis et iubilati-
canticis et iubilati- o- - ne,

85
-o--ne, in tympanis, in canticis et in-bila-tio-ne, et
in tympanis, in canticis et in-bila-tio-ne, in tympanis, in canticis et
89
in-bila-tio--ne, in cythanis, in tympanis, in canticis, in canticis et inbilati-
in-bila-tio--ne, in cythanis, in tympanis, in canticis et inbilati-
93
-o--ne, et in-bila-tio---ne.
-o---ne, et in-bila-tio--ne.

MILITIA EST VITA HOMINIS (SSB VV vdg bc)

BASIS OF THIS EDITION: Carissimi, Missa a quinque et a novem, cum selectis quibusdam cantionibus... (Cologne: F. Friesser, 1666).   GB Lbl.

ALSO COLLATED: Floridus concentus sacras continens laudes... (Rome: A. Fei, 1643) [without VV vdg]   Manuscript copy in GB Ob.

Floridus...has sacras cantiones... (Rome: V. Mascardi, 1652) [without VV vdg] Manuscript copy in GB Ob.

Musica romana... (Bamberg: J. E. Höffling, 1665) [for SSB VV; the violin parts are not by Carissimi but 'Spiridio']   F Pn.

VARIANTS AND COMMENTS:

		The bass instrument, according to the 1666 publication, can be 'viola vel fagotto'.
6	bc	7 6 printed over the next note.
22.4	S1	1666: b' flat. 1643, 1652 and 1665: c''.
23.4	B	1643 and 1665: b flat instead of a for the last note. 1652 = 1666.
25.4	S2	1652: flat absent here too. 1643 and 1665: flat present.
28.1	B	1643, 1652 and 1665: all have a, which is musically preferable to the b flat in 1666.
36.1-2	bc	1666: 6 . 1643, 1652 and 1665: 43 . 43
46.1	vdg	1666: g
48.1	vdg	1666: e
56	vdg	1666: B flat
58	B	1643 and 1665: ♩.♪♩ — 1652 and 1666: ♩. ♪♩
61.1 - 67.1	S2	The printed notes for these bars in the 1666 version duplicate the notes of S1, except that the last note in bar 66 is an f', not a g'. The passage may be corrected by reference to the second appearance of the 'Non coronabitur'

		section at the end of the motet (123-47): the relevant bars are 138-44. In the S1 and B part-books this section is disposed of by the instruction 'Non coronabitur ut supra'; fortunately in the S2 part-book (and in the instrumental ones) the music is written out in full. All the collated sources agree with the corrected version of S2 in bars 61-67 as given in square brackets.
68.1 - 69	S2	The first note is an f' minim; thereafter the printed notes exactly duplicate those of S1. At the second appearance of the 'Non coronabitur' section these two bars are the same (145-46 = 68-69). But it is highly unlikely that Carissimi intended S2 to duplicate S1; more likely is that S2 should sing the notes which appear in 1643, 1652 and 1665 - as given in square brackets.
66.4	S1	Discrepancy between 59.4 and 66.4 sic in all four sources except 1643, in which the last note of 59.4 is a c''.
70	S1	1666 only: a'.
71-77		Only the bc's music is written out; for the other instruments the direction 'Ritornello ut supra' is given.
81.2	B	1666: a. All others: b flat.
86	bc	The figures refer to bars 86-7, these two tied notes being printed as a single breve. The sharp against the 3 is printed on the f line of the stave just above the note d.
88	S1	1666: bar's rest omitted. All other sources: rest present.
91	S2	1666: ♩·♪ All others: ♪♪ , thus agreeing with S1.
92	S1 and bc	1643: flat is present in S1, but absent in basso continuo. 1652 and 1665: both flats are present.
94.3-4	SS	All sources: rhythmic discrepancy sic, although there is no obvious reason for it. The effect in performance would be ♩ 𝄾 in both voices, since the singers would have to breathe.
95.3	bc	The flat is present only in 1643.
96	SSB	1643: slurs over pairs of semiquavers, thus clarifying the underlay of 'arma'.

97.4 – 98	S1	1666 and 1652: 'et pugnate et pugnate'. 1643 and 1665: 'et pugnate cum dracone', thus agreeing with S2 and B, and with the phrases in 99–102.
99.3	S1	1666: c''a'.　All others: e'' c''
100.1-2	S1	1666: ♩. ♪　All others: ♩ ♩
104.1-2	SS	Again the rhythmic discrepancy is present in all collated sources (cf. 94.3-4).
105.1	bc	See 95.3.
105-06	SSB	See 96.
110.3	S1	1666: ♩.♪　All others: ♫
114.3-4	S2	1666: e'　All others: g'
115	S2	1666: d'　All others: f'
116-22		See 71-77.
123-47		Only 1666 has the repetition of the 'Non coronabitur' section. S1 and B are headed 'Non coronabitur ut supra'; all other parts (including S2) are written out in full.
123.1	vdg	See 48.1.
133	V2	1666: minim.
133	vdg	See 56.
145-46	S2	See 68-69.
147	S1	See 70.

SYMPHONIA

12
Mili - tia est vita ho - - mi-
17
S1
S2
B
bc
Mi-li - - tia
Mi-
-nis super ter - - -
- - -
ram,
6 76
21
est vita ho - mi - nis, mi - li - tia est vita ho - - minis
-li - - tia est vita ho - minis, mi - li - - tia est vita ho - mi-
mili - - tia est, militia est, militia est vita

25
super ter- - - - - ram, mi-li-tia est, mi-li-tia est,
-nis super ter- - ram, mi- li-tia est, mi-li-tia
ho- - minis super ter- - ram, mi- li-tia est, mi-
43
6
28
mi- li- - - - tia est vi- - ta ho- - minis super ter- - ram, mili-tia
est, mi-li- - tia est vi- - ta ho- - minis super ter- - ram, mi-
-li-tia est, mi-li- - tia est vi- - ta ho- - minis super ter- - ram,
6 43 6 43
32
est, mi- li-tia est, mi- li-tia est, mi- li-tia est, mili-tia est vita
-li-tia est, mi-litia est, mi-litia est, mi-litia est vita
mi- li-tia est, mi- litia est, mi- litia est vi- - ta
56
35
ho- - minis super ter- - - ram, mi-li-tia est, mili-tia est, mili-tia
ho- - minis super ter- - - ram, mi-li-tia est, mi-li-tia est, mi-li-tia
ho- - minis super ter- - ram, mi-li-tia, est, mi-li-tia est, mi-li-tia
6 5 43 6

RITORNELLO

Non corona - - bi -

47
S1
S2
B
vdg
bc
Non corona - - - bi- tur
-tur
nisi qui legitime cer-
nisi qui legitime cer- ta- - - - ve- rit
50
nisi qui legitime cer- ta - - - - - - - - ve- rit, non corona - - - bi-
- ta - - - - - - - - - - ve - rit, non corona - - - bi-
non corona - - - bi- tur
343
53
- tur, non corona - - bi- tur,
- tur, non coro- na - bi- tur,
nisi qui legitime cer- ta - verit, nisi qui legitime cer-

56
non corona - - - bi- tur nisi qui legitime cer- ta - - - - - - ve-
non corona - - - bi- tur nisi qui legitime cer- ta - - - - - ve-
- ta-verit, nisi qui legitime cer- ta - - verit, non corona - - - bi-
60
- rit, nisi qui legitime cer- ta-verit,
- rit, nisi qui legitime cer- ta-verit,
- tur, non corona - - bi- tur, non corona - - - bi-
63
nisi qui legitime cer- ta-verit, nisi qui legitime cer- ta - - - - - ve-
nisi qui legitime cer- ta-verit, nisi qui legitime cer- ta - - - - - ve-
- tur nisi qui legitime cer- ta-verit, non corona - - - bi-
6
7 6 5
3 4 3

67
V¹
V²
S¹
-rit, non corona - - bi- tur, non coro- na - - - - bi -
S²
-rit, non corona - - bi- tur, non corona - - - bi- tur, non corona - - - bi-
B
-tur, non co - - ro - - na - - - bi-
vdg
bc
343
70
RITORNELLO
-tur.
-tur.
-tur.

State ergo dilectissimi succincti lumbos vestros in veritate, induimini loricam justitiae, et pugnate, et pugnate cum dracone. Induimini arma lucis. Induimini arma lucis.

400

102
et pu- gnate cum dra- co- - - - - - - ne. Su- mite scutum ju-
-co - ne, et pu- gnate cum draco - - ne. Su- mite scutum ju-
-gnate cum draco- - ne.
Sumite gladium Spi- ri- tus,
105
43
-sti- tiae, su- mite ar- ma lu- - cis,
-sti- ti- ae, su- mite ar- ma lu- - cis, et pu-
sumite galeam salu- - - tis, sumite ar- ma lu- - - -
107
[♭]
43
et pu- gnate cum dra- co- - ne, et pu- gnate cum draco- - ne,
-gnate cum draco- ne, et pu- gnate cum draco- - ne, et pugnate cum dra-
-cis, et pugnate cum dra- co- ne, et pu-
110
et pugnate cum dra- co- - ne, et pu- gnate cum dracone, et pu-
-co - - ne, et pu- gnate cum draco- - ne, et pugnate cum dra-
-gnate cum draco- - ne, et pugnate cum dra- co- - - ne,

RITORNELLO

-guate cum draco - - - ne.

-one, et pu-guate cum dra- co - - - ne.

cum dra - - co - - - ne.

403

130
-tur,
non corona - - bi- tur,
non corona - - - - bi-
-tur,
non corona - - bi- tur,
nisi qui legitime cer- ta - verit,
nisi qui legitime cer- ta - verit,
134
-tur
nisi qui legitime cer- ta - - - - - - ve - rit
-tur
nisi qui legitime cer- ta - - - ve - rit
nisi qui legitime cer- ta - - verit,
non corona - - bi- tur, non corona - - - bi-

138
nisi qui legitime cer- ta-verit, nisi qui legitime cer- ta-verit,
nisi qui legitime cer- ta-verit, nisi qui legitime cer- ta-verit,
-tur, non corona - - bi- tur nisi qui legitime cer-
142
nisi qui legitime cer- ta - - - - ve- rit, non corona - - bi-
nisi qui legitime cer- ta - - - - ve- rit, non corona - - bi-
-ta-verit, non corona - - bi- tur, non
6
765
343

145
-tur, non coro- na - - - - bi - tur.
-tur, non corona - - bi- tur, non corona - - bi- tur.
co - - ro - - na - - bi - tur.
343

MORTALIS HOMO QUID NON RECORDARIS (S bc)

BASIS OF THIS EDITION: Carissimi, <u>Arion Romanus</u>... (Konstanz: David Hautt, jnr., 1670). CH Zz.

ALSO COLLATED: GB Och: ms 51, pp.16-20: the cantata 'No, no, mio core', of which the motet is a contrafactum.

VARIANTS AND COMMENTS:

		The original barring of the cantus part is, unusually, quite regular enough to form the basis of 'modern' barring. In a motet of 119 bars, only 28 bar-lines have been added editorially. In the triple-time sections bar-lines are printed, for the most part, at a distance of six minims.
8	bc	G and d both figured ♭ (but not the c in bar 9).
10	S	At the end of this bar is printed :‖:
11	S bc	Original time signature C in soprano and ¢ in bc. (At 48 and 85 it is C in both.)
14.4) 19.4)	bc	Figured 3.
15.1	S	1670: e'' flat. ms 51: e'' natural.
27-8	bc	1670: tenor (C4) clef.
30.1) 32.1) 32.6)	bc	Figured ♭.
37.1	bc	Figured ♯.
38-47		In bc part-book all the music of the refrain is written out in full. In the Cantus part-book only bar 38 is written out, followed by the direction 'Comè soprà da Capo'.
50.1	bc	1670 and ms 51: e natural. This is not impossible in itself, but it is more likely that the pattern of bars 13 and 87 is retained.
50.4	S	The second semiquaver of the group has no leger line (it is misplaced, appearing slightly to the right of the note), but

		from the position of the note-head it is clearly an f''. In ms 51 the note is undoubtedly f''.
51.4 - 52.1	S bc	The bc figuring is 4♭; and the parallel 2 with bars 15 and 89 would suggest e'' flat in the soprano. But the melodic context at this point (an ascending phrase in contrast to 15 and 89) and the parallel with bar 56.4, where b' natural is specified, suggest that e'' natural is intended, and that the error is in the bc.
51.4) 56.4)	bc	Figured 3.
54.1	bc	Figured ♭.
64-65	bc	1670: tenor (C4) clef.
67.1) 69.1) 73.4)	bc	Figured ♭.
72.3	bc	The natural (sharp in the original), though present in bar 35, is lacking also in bar 109. But a sharp is present in each of the parallel phrases (30, 67 and 104), and in each of the f g a b c' phrases in ms 51 the sharp (= natural) is present. But it is not impossible that 35, 72 and 109 should all have b flat.
75-84		Cf. 38-47.
88.4) 93.4)	bc	Figured 3.
89.1	S	1670: e'' flat (as at bar 15). ms 51: e'' natural.
94.1	S	A sharp is printed in front of the first b'. But there is no reason why this bar should differ in this respect from bars 20 and 89.
101-02	bc	1670: tenor (C4) clef.
104.1) 106.1) 110.4) 117.1) 117.4) 118.4)	bc	Figured ♭.
109.3	bc	Cf. 72.3.
119.4	S	1670: a smudged (but recognisable) a'.

Mortalis homo quid, quid, quid — non recorda - -
- ris, mortalis homo quid, quid, quid — non re- corda - - ris, quid —
— non re- corda - - - - - ris.
Quis sit ille aqua
tantum diligaris, dili- garis qui te dum vi-det de-spe- ra - - - re, du-ram
mor - - - tem gra - - - vem sortem et tormen - - -
- - - - ta vult tole- ra - - re, duram mor - - - tem gra - - - vem
sortem et tormen - - - - ta vult tole- ra - - re.
Non las-sare — hum a- - ma- re — cui si dul- ce — te ser- va- re, —

29
ti-bi ri-tam- re-stau- ra-re, caeli glo- - - - riam
33
pa-ra- - re, tibi ri-tam- re-stau- ra-re, caeli glo- - -
37
- - riam para- - re. Morta-lis homo quid, quid, quid non recorda- -
41
-ris, mortalis homo quid, quid, quid non re- corda- - ris, quid
45
non re- corda- - - ris.
Salve Jesu O dulcis a-
49
-mator, coelo veniens a- ma- - - - tor, qui su
52
a- mas o-di- en- - tes, qui su ser- - - -
55
- - - vas fu-gi- en- - tes, qui su a- mas odien- tes, qui su ser- -

-vas fu-gien- - - tes. Jesu dul-cis
te a- - ma-bo, totamen-te hono-ra-bo, tibi lau-des,
tibi vi-cto-rias, tibi gra- - - - - - - tias canta-bo, ti-bi
lau-des, ti-bi vi-cto-rias, ti-bi gra- - - - - - - - - tias canta-
-bo. Mortalis homo quid, quid, quid non recorda- -ris, mortalis
homo quid, quid, quid non re-corda- - ris, quid
non re-corda- - -ris. Felix cor, be-a-tum
pectus, si est amor tibi re- - - -ctus, si te flam- - - ma exurit

ardens pi-eta- - - - -tis, pi-eta- - - - - - - - tis ve-ra pa- - reus, si te
flam- - - ma exu-rit ardens pi-eta- -
- -tis ve-ra pa- - reus.
Tunc in coe-lum e-vo- - la-bis,
aulam si-derum habi- - ta-bis; felix a-nima iam De-o ple-na
in qua ar- - - - - - - -det fax se-re- - na, felix a-nima iam De-o
ple-na in qua ar- - - - det fax se-re- -
-na. Mortalis homo quid, quid, quid non recorda- - ris, quid non re-
-corda-ris, quid, quid non re-corda- - ris.

O DULCISSIMUM MARIAE NOMEN (SS bc)

BASIS OF THIS EDITION: Scelta di motetti... (Rome: L. Grignani, 1647).   I Bc.

ALSO COLLATED: Delectus sacrarum cantionum... (Antwerp: P. Phalèse, 1652).   GB Och.

VARIANTS AND COMMENTS:

14.4	S2	1647: g' 1652: b'
15.3	S2	A sharp (present in neither source) preserves the imitation of bar 13, and may be implied by the retrospective effect of the sharp in bar 16.
27　　　　)		
28.3 - 29.2)	bc	Printed 765 in both sources.
30　　　　)		343

O dul- cis- simum Ma- ri- ae no- - - men,
O dul-
6
no- men ve- - re san- ctis- - - - - - si- -
-cis- simum Ma- ri- ae no- - - - - men, no- men ve- - re san- ctis- - - si-
12
-mum; O nomen gra- - - tiae,
sem- per cogi-
-mum;
O nomen gra- - - - tiae,
17
-tan- - - - dum, sem- per cogi- tan- - dum;
sem- per cogi- tan- - - - dum; O so- la- tium a- - - ni-
22
O so- la- tium a- - - ni- ma- rum, no- men vene- ran- dum;
-ma- rum, no- men vene- ran- dum; O, O

O, O nomen cae - li - cum, et ve - re ange - li -
— nomen cae - li - cum, et ve - re an - ge - licum, et
- cum, et ve - re, et ve - re an - ge - - licum: re - sonent
ve - re, et ve - re, et ve - re an - ge - licum: re - sonent er - go in
er - go in o - - - - - - re om - ni - um. O Maria ma - ter
o - - - - - - re om - ni - um.
pia nos defende in hac vi - - a; nos tu -
O Ma - ria ma - ter pia nos de - fende in hac vi - -
- ere, nos gu - berna, nos gu - berna, duc nos tecum ad su - per - - na,
- a; nos tu - ere, nos gu - berna, duc nos tecum ad su - per - - - na, duc nos

duc nos tecum ad super---na, ad super-----na, duc nos tecum ad su-tecum ad super-- ----na, ad su-per----

-per--na, duc nos tecum ad super------na.
---na, duc nos tecum ad super--- ---na.

O IGNIS SANCTE (SS bc)

BASIS OF THIS EDITION: Scelta de'motetti... (Rome: A. Belmonte, 1667).   D-brd MÜs (SS) and I Bc (SS bc).

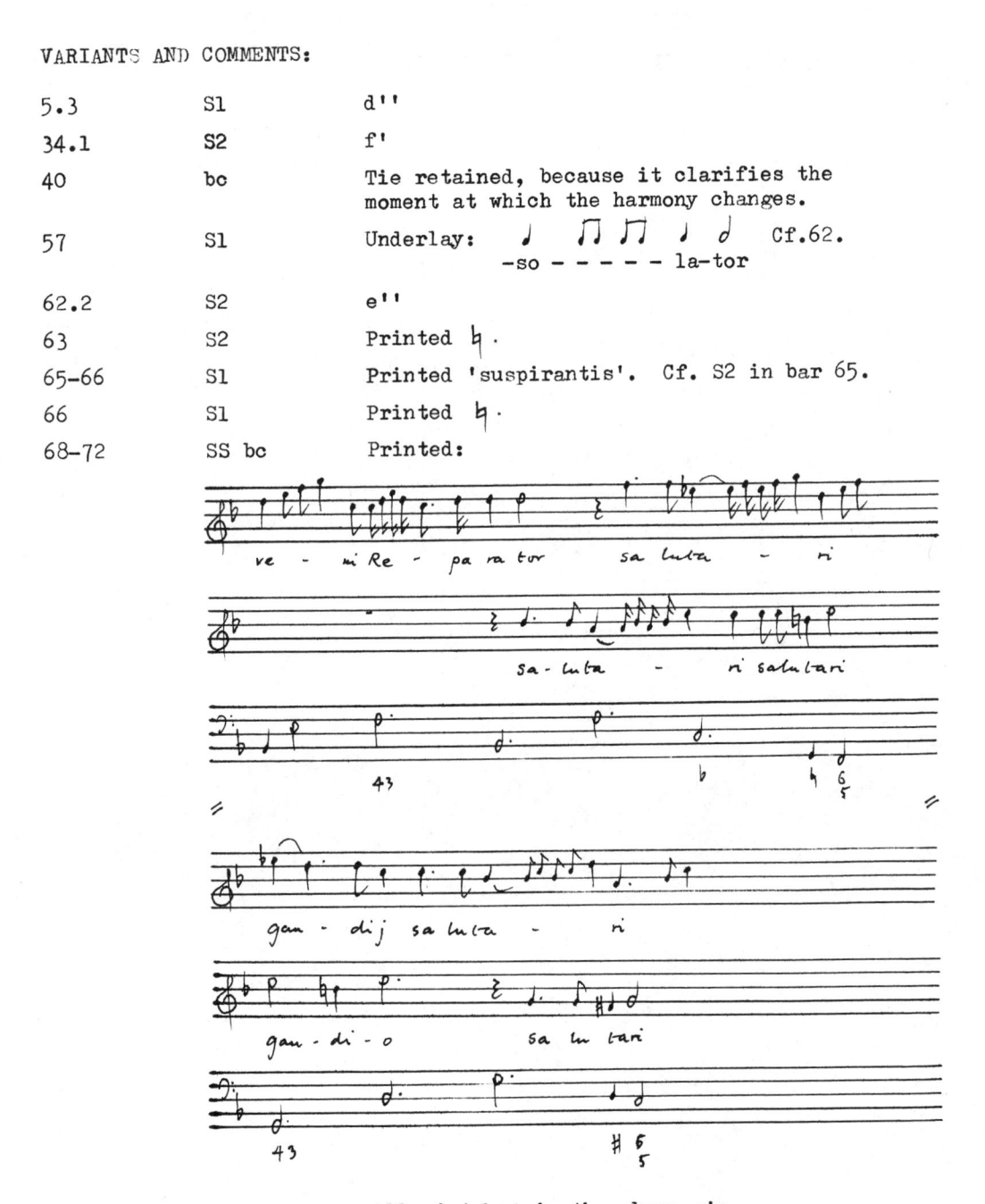

VARIANTS AND COMMENTS:

5.3	S1	d''
34.1	S2	f'
40	bc	Tie retained, because it clarifies the moment at which the harmony changes.
57	S1	Underlay: ♩ ♫ ♫ ♩ ♩ Cf.62. -so - - - - - la-tor
62.2	S2	e''
63	S2	Printed ♮.
65-66	S1	Printed 'suspirantis'. Cf. S2 in bar 65.
66	S1	Printed ♮.
68-72	SS bc	Printed:

All mistakes in the above sic.

76.1	S1	g'
79.6	bc	d Cf.103
80.5	S1	e'' natural Cf.104 (S2)
81.3	S1	f'' Cf.105 (S2)
81.4	S1	Printed ♮
84–86	SS bc	Printed:

89.4	S2	Must be flat, because of the bc at 89.5-6, and S1 at 88.1.
89.4	bc	c
92.4	S1	Dotted minim
96.1-3	S1	Underlay: mun-di
98.1-3	S1	Underlay: mun-di
100.1	bc	E
105.4	S2	Printed ♮
108.2	bc	b
110.4	S1	Dotted minim
115.1	bc	Pause sign omitted.

O ignis sancte, O ignis divine de caelo procedens a Patre lumine, qui beata Apostolorum pectora invisibiliter penetrasti, tuum in nos amorem inspirat ut de te semper, semper cogitemus, te optamus, te quaeramus, te diligamus, et charitate tua, et charitate tua semper, semper ardeat, et liquefiat anima nostra.

O quam bonus, O quam suavis est Domine spiritus tuus:

in-fir-ma_ ro-borans, a--speta explanans, cor-de pu-ri-ficans, men-tes vi-
-ri-ficans, pe-ctora in- flam-- -- mans. A-de-sto, a-
-desto sancte spi-ritus, a- de-sto, adesto sua- vissime para-cli- te, tu-a
nos reple gra-tia et saluta-- --ri
Ve-ni, ve-ni
gau-dio, et salu- ta-ri_ gau-di- o.
ve-ni, ve-ni con-- [- so--]- la-tor su-spirantis, su-spirantis
a-----ni- mae su-spirantis,
Ve-ni, veni, ve-ni, ve-ni con--- so-- lator su-spi-

64
su - spiran - tis a - - ni - mae; [ve - ni, ve - ni,] ve - ni,
- rantis, ve - ni, ve - ni, ve - ni, ve - - - ni re - - - parator
68
ve - - - - ni re - - - - pa - ra - tor sa - lu - ta - - - - ri
sa - lu - ta - - - - - - ri, saluta - ri
71
gau - - di - i, sa - lu - ta - - - - - ri gau - - di - i.
gau - di - [i], saluta - ri gau - di - [i]. O ve - ra mun - di
75
O ve - ra mun - di lux, sa - lus, salus et vi - - - ta,
lux, sa - - lus, sa - - lus et vi - - - ta,
79
ad cae - lestem amorem nos,
ad caelestem a - morem nos in - vi - - - - ta,

82
nos, nos ini - - - - ta, ad cae- lestem a-mo-rem
ad caelestem a- morem nos — ini- ni - - - - ta, nos, —
85
nos — nos ini - - - ta. Ve-ni, ve - - ni con - - - so-
— nos, — nos ini - - - ta. Ve-ni, veni,
89
-lator su- spi- ran - - - - - tis, suspi-
ve - ni, ve - - - ni con - - - solator su-spiran - - - -
92
-rantis a - - ni- mae, su- spi- rantis a - - ni-
- tis — a - - - ni- mae, su-spiran - - - - tis — a - - ni-
95
-mae. O ve-ra [mun - di] lux, o ve-ra [mun - di] lux,
-mae. O ve-ra mun - di lux, sa--

99
sa- - -lus et vi- - -ta, sa- - -lus, salus et vi- - -ta,
-lus, salus et vi- - -ta, sa-lus et vi- - -ta,
103
ad caelestem a-morem nos, nos in-vi- - -ta, ad caelestem a-
ad cae-lestem amorem nos, nos, nos invi- - -
107
-morem nos, nos in-vi- - - -ta, nos, nos,
-ta, ad cae-lestem amorem nos,
110
nos in-vi- - - - - -ta, nos
nos in-vi- - - ta, nos, nos
113
in- - vi- - - ta.
in- - vi- - - ta.

O QUAM PULCHRA ES (S bc)

BASIS OF THIS EDITION: GB Lbl: Add.29292, ff.46-57^v.

VARIANTS AND COMMENTS:

23-24	bc	The tie is inserted because of the parallel with 13-14.
24.4	S	The flat is inserted because of the parallel with 14.4.
30		The original rhythmic values <u>are</u> retained. The original time signature is 3.
49.3) 63.3)	S	In these bars the dynamic marking 'f' applies probably (bar 49) or definitely (bar 63) to the <u>last</u> semiquaver in the bar. But in the corresponding bars later in the motet (114, 128, 175 and 189) it is clearly written over the <u>penultimate</u> semiquaver in the bar.
136.1	bc	Figured 4 , perhaps meaning 6♭ ♭2 4 2
143.1	bc	Figured 4 , probably meaning 4♯ ♯2 2
153.4) 154.4)	S	The dynamic marking 'f' is written at the beginning of the fourth beat (over g'' and c'' respectively).
198.1	bc	Figured (slightly unclearly) 4 ♯2
202.1	bc	Figured ♯4 2
212.2	S	The 't.' is written over the e flat''.
216	S	The ornament <u>is</u> written as 'tr.' this time.
219-358		The three stanzas are written out in full in the manuscript. They are musically identical, except for the minor differences noted below.
225.3	bc	The 6 is missing.
290.3	bc	The 6 is missing.
296.1	bc	The sharp is missing.
318.3	bc	The 6 is missing.
337.3	bc	The 6 is missing.
356.2	bc	The sharp is missing.

O, O quam pulchra es, O, O quam pulchra es amica mea, quam dilecta, quam decora, quam formosa, O virgo beatissima, sine macula nata, virga Jesse, O castitatis lilium, sine macula nata, virga Jesse,

O ca-sti-ta - - - - - - - - - tis li - lium.
Bene-di-cta es, ma-ter Chri-sti, coeli ci-vium regi - - na,
mater fa-cta sed in-ta-cta genu-i-sti coeli so - - - -
- - - - - - - - mi-num, mater fa-cta sed in-
-ta-cta genu-i-sti coeli so - - - - - - - -
- - mi-num, coe - - - li so-mi-num.
O admi-
-ra - - - - - bi-lis mater, post partum virgo, post partum
virgo, O mater ca-stis-sima, portasti fi-lium, quem amplexa es

79
cum gandio, su- spi- ran- - tem,
82
su- spiran- - - tem et la- criman- - - tem, portasti
86
fi- lium, quem amplexa es cum
89
gandio, su- spi- ran- - tem, su- spi- ran- - tem et
93
la- criman- - - - tem.
Be- a- tis- sima ma- ter al- ma,
99
tu flos vir- ginum et pal- ma, cuius flo- re et de- co- re re- cre-
108
a- ri de- si- de- ra- - - - - - - - - - - -
116
mus, cuius flo- re et de- co- re- recre- a- ri desidera- ra-

125
mus, de- si- de- ra- mus.
135
O ma- ter veneran-da, O ma- ter vene- ran-da, quae nu-tri-
139
-vi-sti fi-lium De-i vi-vi vir-gi-neo la- cte. O felix
143
ma-ter, quae tribus re-gibus De- um ho- minem mon-
147
-stra-
150
sti, mon- stra-
154
sti. O for- mo-sa et ge-ne- ro-sa
160
David fi-li-a re-gis po- ten-tis, quam non fle-xit nec al-

-le-xit— dolus ve-teris ser-pen- - - - - - - - - - - -
- - - - - - tis, quam non fle-xit— nec al-[l]e-xit—
dolus ve-teris serpen- - - - - - - - - - - - - - -
-tis, ser- - -pen- - - tis.
O, O, O mater
gra- - - - - ti-ae, O, O, O fons a- mo- - - -
- - ris, lingua me-a, dic tro- phaea, lingua mea, dic tro-
-phae - - - - - a vir- - ginis pu- er- - perae, dic tro-
-phaea, dic trophae- - - - - - - a vir- ginis pu- er- - pe-

-rae, vir - - - - - - ginis puer - - - -
- - - pe - rae.
vir-go be-ni-gna, coe-lo-rum re-gi-na et por-ta san-cto-rum, O
mater Ma-ri-a, o dul-cis et pi-a, ad-e-sto po-ten-ti, ad-
pulchra ut lu-na, stel-la-rum co-ro-na, O mundi pa-tro-na, quam
do-mina an-gelo- - - - rum, te coe-li a-do-rant stel-lae-que ap-
e-sto ca-den- - - - ti, ut praedicent lau-dem et fu-gi-ant
mi-tis et bo- - - - na, O sa-lus re-o-rum et ter-ror pra-
-plau-dant, te prae-di-cat ter- - - - ra, te coe-li a-do-rant stel-
frau-dem ser-pen- - - - - - tis, ut praedicent lau-dem et
-vo-rum, re-gi-na coe-lo- - - - rum, O sa-lus re-o-rum et

240
287
334
-lae-que ap-plau-dant, te prae-dicat ter - - - - ra, tibi an-geli
fu-giant fraudem ser-pen - - - - - - - tis, tibi dicant vi-
ter-ror pra-vo-rum, re-gi-na coe-lo - - - - rum, tibi an-geli
247
294
341
ser- - - - - vi-unt cum gau-di-o, tibi an-geli ser- -
-cto - - - - - ri-am et glo-ri-am, tibi di-cant vi-cto - -
ser - - - - - ri-unt cum gau-di-o, tibi an-geli ser- -
254
301
348
- - - - viunt cum gau-di-o, ser-
- - - - ri-am et glo-ri-am, et glo-
- - - - viunt cum gau-di-o, ser-
261
308
355
264
311
- - viunt cum gau-di-o.
- - riam, et glo-ri- am.
- - viunt cum gau-di-

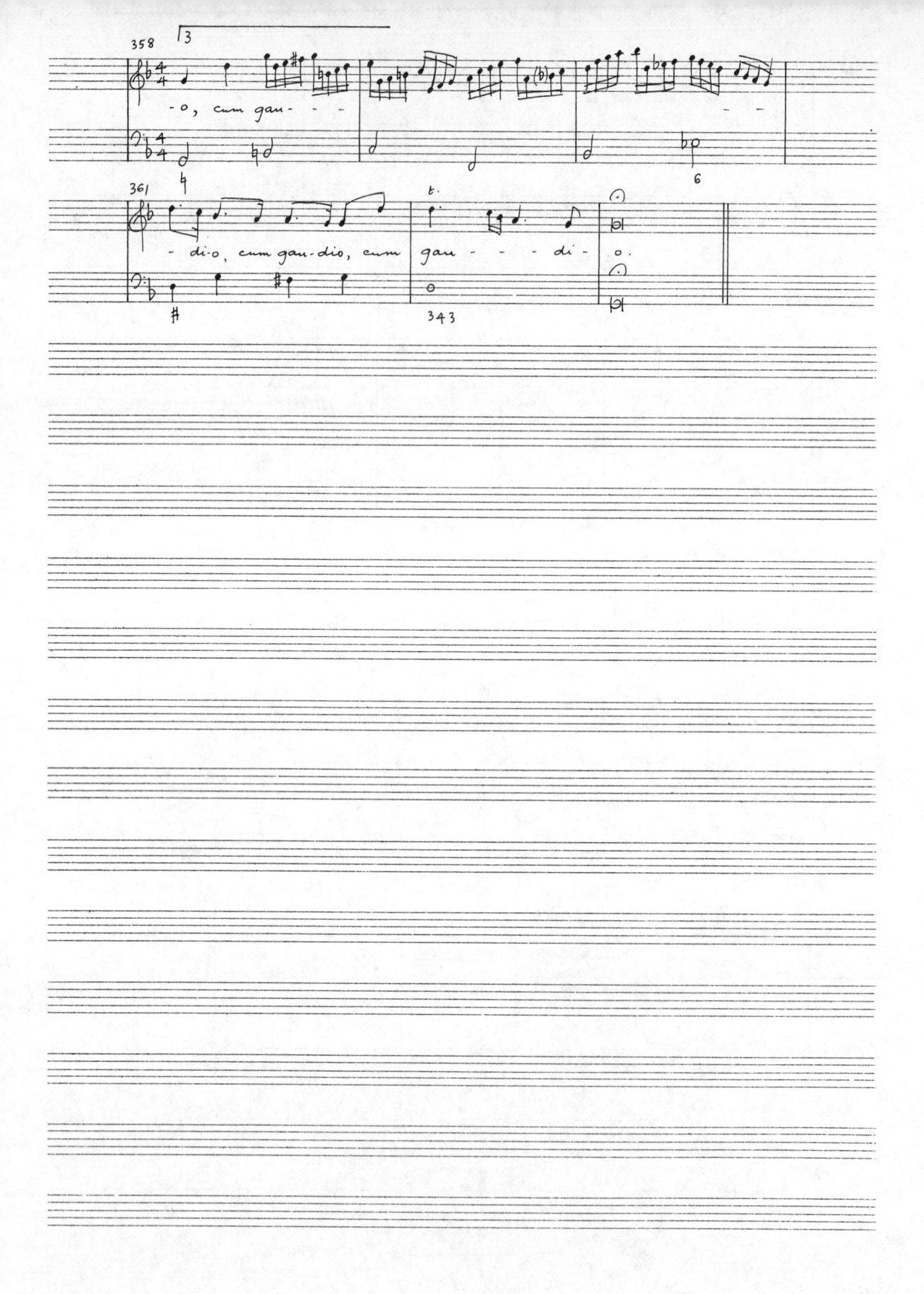
358
3
-o, cum gau- - -
6
361
-di-o, cum gau-dio, cum gau- - - -di- o.
343

PLAUDITE CAELESTES CHORI (S bc)

BASIS OF THIS EDITION: I COd: ms I-V-12

VARIANTS AND COMMENTS:

2-3	S		Each f' could well remain natural; but if they do, the effect of the subdominant sequence in bars 6-10 is lessened.
11.3	S	b' c'	Cf. bars 13, 20 and 94.
29.1	bc	B	Cf. 112.1.
44.3	bc		The figures 24 (sic) are written under the d. Throughout the motet, almost without exception, the scribe has written bc figuring above the notes. The figures 24 are in any case meaningless as bc figuring.
57.1	S	c'	
64.3-4	S	b'	
112.3	bc	d	Cf. 29.3.
113.2	S	a'	Cf. 30.2.

Plan - - dite, plan - dite cae - le - - -
- - - stes cho - - ri,
plan - dite, plan - dite cae - le - - -
- - - - - stes cho - - - ri; gau - de - - - - - te, gau -
- de - - - - - - te et exul - ta - - te, et exul - ta - - - te modu - lan - - tes Deo
Lau - - dem, gau - de - - - - - - - te, gau - de - - - - - - te et exul -
- ta - - te, et exul - ta - - - te modu - lan - - tes Deo Lau - - - dem, et exul -
- ta - - te, et exul - ta - - te, et exul - ta - - - te modu - lan - - tes Deo Lau - - -
Cur - - rite, cur - rite, cur - rite, currite ad re - gales, ad rega - - - les

38 nu- - ptias, cur- - rite, cur- rite, cur- rite, cur- rite ad re- gales, ad rega- - -
42 - - - les nu- - pti- as, qui- a u- xor Agni praepara- - - - - - - - - vit
46 se, qui- a u- xor Agni, qui- a u- xor Agni praepara- - - -
49 - - - - vit se. Jubila- te er- go Deo, jubila- te ergo Deo in voce e- xul-
53 - ta- tio- - - - - nis, jubi- la- te er- go Deo, jubi- la- te er- go
57 Deo in vo- ce e- xul- tatio- - - - - nis, e- - - - - -
61 - - - - - xultati- o- - nis. Mundi pom- pas
65 mundi pom- pas et omne ornatum sae- culi: haec contempsit

propter amorem Domini Iesu, haec contempsit propter amorem
Domini Iesu, quem vidit, quem amavit, in quem credidit, quem di-
-lexit, quem vidit, quem amavit, in quem credidit, quem dile-
-xit, in quem credidit, quem dilexit, quem dile-
-xit. Ac-
-currite ergo caelestes chori, accurrite ergo caelestes
chori, gaudete, gaudete et exul-
-tate, et exultate modulantes Deo laudem, gau-

103
-de - - - - - - - te, gau- de - - - - - - te, et exul- ta - - te, et exul-
108
-ta - - - te modu- lan - - tes Deo lau - - - dem, et exul- ta - - te, et exul-
43
113
-ta - - te, et exul- ta - - te modu- lan - tes Deo lau - -
43
117
-dem, modulantes Deo laudem, modulantes Deo lau - - -
120
- - - - - - dem.
56
765
343

QUIS EST HIC VIR (SSS bc)

BASIS OF THIS EDITION: Scelta di motetti... (Rome: L. Grignani, 1647).   I Bc.

ALSO COLLATED: Delectus sacrarum cantionum... (Antwerp: P. Phalèse, 1652).   GB Och.

VARIANTS AND COMMENTS:

30.2	bc	Figured ♭.
32	S1	Underlay: ha ben tes Bar 33 (S2) makes the intention clear.
53.3	S1	Possibly the a' should have a flat: cf. 62.3 (S2). It is absent in both 1647 and 1652.
55.2	S1	1647 and 1652: d' b' flat
74.3 - 75	S1	Underlay in 1647: ta tri-um - phat Underlay in 1652: ta tri-um - phat Cf. 72-3 (S2).
91	bc	Tie retained, because it clarifies the figuring.
98.3-4	S1	Because of the e''flat in bar 100, the e''s in 99 sound odd unless they are flattened; and then because of these and because of the sequential phrase in 97, the e''s in 98 must be flattened also.
101.3) 115.1)	bc	Figured ♭.
107.3-4	S3	Cf. 98.3-4
118.4	S3	1647 and 1652: a crotchet, without the quaver rest; but there is no reason why it should differ from S2 and S3 at 105 and S2 at 118.
119.4	S1	1647 and 1652: a crotchet; but cf. 117.4 (S2) and 118.2 (S1).
120.4	S1	1647 and 1652: a crotchet; but cf. 105.2 (S3). The fact that a crotchet is printed

		three times in bars 118-20 as the anacrusis raises the possibility that these three notes may not be misprints after all. But rhythmic discrepancies of this sort are not characteristic of the composer, and nor is the rhythmically weighty underlay of the first syllable of the word 'beato'.
132	bc	1647 and 1652: the e flat is split into two tied minims (but the f in 133 is not). In 1652 the figuring is (correctly) 5 over the first and 6 over the second; in 1647 both figures appear over the second.
142.2	bc	1647 and 1652: e

Quis est hic vir —— be-atis-si-mus
Quis est
hic vir —— be-a-tis-si-mus
cu-ius en-nar-rant caeli glo-riam,
cuius
laudibus terrarum orbis re-sonat?
Be-a-tus, bea-tus N.
Quis exulta-bi-lem hanc nobis red-di-dit celebrita---tis di-em?
Bea-tus, be-
5
10
14
6
76
43

18
Quis est cuius me-ritis et vir-tu-tibus uni-
-a-tus N.
43
76
22
-ver-sa fu-get Ec-cle-sia?
Be-a-tus, bea-tus N.
76
43
26
A-gite er-go, a-gite er-go cae-le-stes
A-gite er-go, a-gite er-go cae-le-stes
31
spi-ritus ha-ben-tes — sin-gu-li cy-tharas
spi-ritus
ha-ben-tes — sin-guli

S1
S2
bc
cy - tharas au - re - as. Iubila - - - te,
cy - tharas au - re - as. canta - - -
et modula - - - - mini et in so - - - - - - nitu laeti - tiae,
- - te, in voce lau - - - - dis, et in so - - - - - -
et in so - - - - nitu laeti - tiae, et in so - - - -
- nitu laeti - tiae, et in so - - - - - nitu, et in so - -
- - - - - - - nitu laeti - tiae novae car - men har - mo - -
- - - - - - - nitu laeti - tiae novae car - men har - mo - -
- ni - - ae be - - - - - - - a - - to N.
- ni - - ae be - - - a - - to N.

57
no-vae car--men harmo-- ni--ae be--
no-vae car--men harmo-- ni--ae be-------
63
-a--- -to N., cu-ius illu-stris
-a--- -to N., cuius in-clita virtus,
68
glo-ria, in cae-lis ho-die
cuius fe-lix vi-ctoria in cae-lis ho-die coro-na-----
72
coro-na- ---[ta tri-um--]phat, coro-
-ta trium--phat, coro-na-----
76
-na------ -ta, coro-na--- -
---ta, coro- na------- -

80
S¹
- - - - - ta tri- um - - phat.
S²
- - - - - ta tri- um - - phat.
S³
Nos quoque so-cii laetos et ca-
Bc
56
43
56
-no - ros dul - ce so - nantes an-gelo - rum cho - ros alter - nan - tibus prose -
88
Nos quoque so-cii laetos et ca-
Nos quoque so-cii laetos et ca-
-qua - - - mur vo - - cibus. Nos quoque so-cii laetos et ca-
43
56
92
-no - ros dul - ce so - nantes angelo - rum cho-ros alter - nan - tibus prose-
-no - ros dul - ce so - nantes angelo - rum cho-ros alter - nan - tibus prose-
-no - ros dul - ce so - nantes angelo - rum cho-ros alter - nan - tibus prose-

96
-qua-mur vo-ci-bus. can-te - - - - - mus
-qua-mur vo-ci-bus. Iubile - - - - mus, et module - - - -
-qua-mur vo-ci-bus. et module - - -
100
et module - - - - - mur triumphale, trium-phale, triumphale, trium-phale — can - - ti-
- - mur triumphale, trium-phale can-ti-
- mur triumphale, trium-phale, triumphale, trium-pha-le be-
104
-cum be-a-to, iubile - - - - - mus,
-cum bea-to, bea-to N.
-a-to, bea-to N. cante - - -
108
et module - - - - - - - mur
et module - - - - mur triumphale, trium-phale, triumphale, trium-
- - mus et modu-le - - - - mur triumphale, trium-

111
et modu- le - - - - - - mur, et modu-
-pha - - - le can - ti - cum, et modu - le - - - - - mur
-pha - - - le can - ti - cum, et modu - le - - - - - mur trium -
43 6
114
- le - - - - mur, trium - phale, triumphale, trium - phale, triumphale
triumphale, trium - phale, triumphale, trium - phale, triumpha - le
- phale, triumphale, trium - phale, triumphale, trium - phale, trium - pha - le
117
can - ticum be - a - to, be - a - to, be -
can - ticum be - a - to, be - a - to N. be - a - to, be -
can - ticum be - a - to N. be -
43 56 43 56
121
- a - to N.,
corona - - -
- a - to N.,
coro - na - - - ta, corona - - -
- a - to N.,
cuius in - clita vir - tus
43 76 56

125
- - ta_ tri- um - - phat,
corona - - -
- - ta tri- um - - phat,
corona - - - - ta, corona - - -
cu- ius illu - - stris glo- ria
343 76 56
129
- - ta trium - - phat,
corona - - - - ta, corona - - -
- - ta trium - - phat,
coro- na - - - - ta, coro- na - - -
cuius fe- lix vi- ctoria
♯ 43 ♮ 6 6 [5 6]
133
- ta, corona - - - - - ta tri- um - - phat,
- ta, coro- na - - - - - ta tri- um - - phat, cu- ius illu - stris
cuius in - clita vir- tus,
56 43 76 76
137
cuius fe- lix vi- cto- ria in cae- lis ho - die coro- na - - - - -
glo- ria, in cae- lis ho - die coro- na - -
in cae- lis ho- die
76 ♮ ♭

141
- ta trium - - phat, coro- na - - - - - -
- ta trium - - phat, corona - - - - - - - - ta, coro-
corona - - - - - - ta, coro- na - -
144
- - - - - - - - - ta tri-um - - - phat, co-rona - - -
- - - - - - - - - ta tri- um - - phat, coro- na- ta tri-
- - ta trium- phat, tri- um- phat, trium - - - phat, co- ro- na - - -
147
- - ta tri- um - - phat, coronata, coro- na- ta trium - - - phat.
- um- phat, tri- um - - phat, coronata, coro- na- ta tri- um - - - phat.
- - ta tri- um - - phat, coro- nata, coro- na- ta tri- um - - - phat.

QUOMODO FACTI SUNT IMPII (SSB bc)

BASIS OF THIS EDITION: R. Floridus... Has alias cantiones
sacras... (Rome: V. Mascardi, 1654).
I Bc.

VARIANTS AND COMMENTS:

| 37.1 | bc | Figured ♭. |
| 63.1 | bc | Figured ♭. |

Quomodo
tacet
Quomodo
tacet
Quo - modo fa - cti sunt impii in de - sola - tio - - -
- ne? Su - bito defe - ce - runt, su - bito peri - e - runt, su - bito aru - erunt sicut fae - num,
su - bito declinave - runt, su - bito declinaverunt sicut umbra, sicut um - bra.
Quo - - mo - do fa - - cti sunt im - pi - i
Quo - modo fa - cti sunt im - pi - i in de - so - la - - - ti -
Quo - - modo fa - cti sunt im - pi - i in de - so -

14
in deso-la- - - -ti- o - - ne?
-o - - - - - - - - - - - - ne? Su-bito defe-ce- - runt,
-la- - ti-o - - - - - - - ne? Su-bito peri-
6 76
17
Su-bito peri-e - - runt, su-bito aru- erunt sicut fae-num,
su-bito peri-e - - runt, su-bi-to aru- erunt sicut fae- num,
-e - runt, su-bito aru- e- - runt, aru- erunt sicut fae-num, su-bito declina-
6 43
20
su-bito declina- verunt sicut um- bra.
su-bito declina- verunt sicut um- bra. Le- va-sti,
-verunt sicut um- bra, si- cut um- bra.
43
24
Do- - - mi- ne, levasti manum tuam in super-bias e- o - - - - - -
6 6 6 ♮ 6

rum;
misisti iram tu-am, misisti iram tu-am quae devoravit
eos sicut sti-pu-lam, quae devoravit eos sicut sti-pu-lam,
et — dedisti
il-lis oppro-brium, op-probrium sem-pi-ter-num, et — dedisti
il-lis oppro-brium, op-probrium sem-pi-ter-num.
Propter

43
Propter hoc lan-da-bimus te, lan-da-bimus
hoc lan-da-bimus te, propter hoc lan-da- - - - - - bimus
Propter hoc lan-da-bimus te, propter hoc lan-da-bimus
49
te, et ma-gnifi-cabimus nomen tu-um, nomen
te, et magnificabimus nomen
te, et magnifi-cabimus nomen tuum Do- - - - - - - -
52
tu-um Do-mi-ne, quo-niam in multi-
tu-um Do-mi-ne, quo-ni-am in multitudine gloriae tu-ae
- - - - mi-ne,
56
-tudine gloriae tu-ae deposui-sti adver-sarios nostros, adversarios no-
deposuisti adversarios nostros, adver-sa- - - rios no- - -
deposu-isti adver-sarios nostros, adver-sarios no- - -

59
-stros, deposu- i-sti adver-sarios nostros, adversarios no - stros.
-stros, deposuisti adver- sarios nostros adver- sa - - rios no - - - stros.
-stros, deposuisti adver-sarios nostros adver- sarios no - - - stros.
43
62
Su-bito peri-e - - runt, su-bito aruerunt sicut
Su-bito defece - - runt, su-bito peri-e - - runt, su-bito aru-erunt sicut
Su-bito peri- e - runt, su-bito aru- e - - runt, aru-erunt sicut
65
fae- num, su-bito declina- verunt sicut um - bra,
fae- num, su-bito declina- verunt sicut um - - bra,
fae- num, su-bito declina- verunt sicut um - bra, si- cut um - bra,
43 6 43
68
subito, subito, su-bito de-clinaverunt sicut umbra, sicut um - bra.
subito, subito, su-bito declinaverunt sicut, sicut um - bra.
subito, subito, su-bito declinaverunt si - - - cut, sicut um - bra.
6 43

SALVE REGINA (SSB bc)

BASIS OF THIS EDITION: F Pn: ms Vm^1. 1268, no.6.

VARIANTS AND COMMENTS:

22.3	S1	Crotchet rest omitted.
34.3	bc	Figured ♯.
53, 55, 67 and 69		The dynamic marks are in the source.
55-6) 69-70)	S2	The words 'advocata nostra' are indicated by the sign ⁄⁄. Unfortunately in this case the underlay is not entirely self-evident: the syllable '-ta' could begin on the first, third or fifth note of the short crotchet melisma.
58.1	bc	Figured ♯, underneath the 5 of the 56 figuring. Probably the sharp should apply to the following e.
83.3	bc	Figured ♭.
85.1	B	Written ♩. ♪ Cf. 83.1 and 89.1.
117.1) 123.1)	bc	Figured ♭.
132.4	B	Written e. Cf. 141.4.
141.2	B	Written ♫ Cf. 132.2, and all other entries.

456

24
-mus e- -xules fi- -lii E- -vae. Ad
e- xules fi- -lii E- -vae, e- -xules fi- -lii E- -vae.
Ad te clama- -mus e- -xules fi- -lii E- -vae.
29
te suspira- -mus ge- -men- -tes et flen- -tes, ge- -men- -tes et
Ad te suspi- ra- -mus ge- -men- -tes et
Ad te suspira- -mus ad te suspira-
34
flen- -tes in hac la-cri- ma- -rum
flen- -tes, ge- men- -tes et flen- -tes in hac la-cri-
-mus ge- -men- -tes et flen- -tes
39
val- -le, in hac la-cri- ma- -rum, la-crima-rum
-ma- -rum val- -le, in hac la-cri- ma- -rum
in hac la-cri- ma- -rum val- -le, in

44
val - le, in — hac la - cri - ma - - rum - val - - - le.
val - - - - - - - - - - - - le.
— hac la - cri - ma - rum val - - - - - le.
49
piano
E - - ia — er - - go, e - - ia — er - - go, ad - voca - -
piano
E - - ia — er - - go, ad - voca -
piano
54
forte
- ta no - - stra, advoca - - - ta no - - - stra,
forte
- ta no - - stra, [advo-ca-ta —] no - - - stra, il - - los — tu - -
forte
59
- os misericor - des o - culos ad — nos conver - - - - te.
[98]

63
piano
E - - ia — er - - go, e - - ia — er - - go, ad - voca - -
E - - ia — er - - go, ad - voca -
E - - ia — er - - go, e - - - - ia er - - go, ad - voca -
68
forte
- ta no - - stra, advoca - - ta no - - - - stra, il - - los — tu - -
- ta — no - - - stra, [advo - ca - ta —] no - - - - stra,
- ta no - - stra, advoca - - ta no - - - - stra,
73
- os misericor - des o - culos ad — nos conver - - -
il - los — tu - - os misericor - - des o - culos ad —
il - los — tu - - os ad nos, ad
77
- - - - - - - - te, ad nos con - ver - - te. Et Je - -
— nos conver - - - - - te, ad — nos conver - - - - - te.
nos con - - ver - - te, ad nos, ad nos con - ver - - te.

82
-sum be-nedi-ctum fructum ventris tu - - - - - - - - - i,
Et Je - -
Et Je - - sum be-nedi-ctum fructum ventris tu - - -
43
7
86
et Je - - sum be-nedictum
sum be-nedi-ctum fructum ventris tu - - - - - - - -
- - - - - - - - i,
43
43
89
fructum ventris tu - - - - - - - - - - - i no - - bis,
- i be-nedi-ctum fructum ventris tu - - - i no - - bis,
be- nedi - ctum fructum ventris tu - i, ventris tu - - i
43
93
no - - bis post hoc e - xi - lium, post hoc e - xi - lium o - sten - -
no - - bis post hoc e - xi - lium, post hoc e - xi - lium o - sten - -
6
43

99
-de, no- -bis post hoc e- xi- lium, post hoc e- xi- lium
-de, no- -bis post hoc e- xi- lium, post hoc e- xi- lium
no- -bis post hoc e- xi- - lium post hoc e- xi- lium
105
o- sten- - de. O clemens, o pi- - a,
o- sten- - de.
o dulcis
o- sten- - de
O clemens, o pi- -
111
o dulcis virgo, dulcis virgo Ma- ri- - a,
vir- go, dulcis vir- go, dulcis virgo Ma- - ri- - a,
o dulcis
-a,
o clemens, o pi- -
117
o dul- cis virgo Ma- - ri- - a,
o dulcis virgo, dulcis
vir- go, dulcis vir- go Ma- - ri- - a,
o dul- cis
-a,
o clemens, o pi- - a,

123
virgo Ma - ri - - - a,
virgo Ma - ri - - - a,
o clemens, o
o clemens, o pi-a.
129
o clemens, o pi-a,
o
pi-a, o clemens, o pi-a,
o dulcis virgo Ma-
o clemens, o pi-a, o dulcis vir-go Ma-ri - - - - -
134
dulcis vir-go Ma-ri - - - - a,
o clemens, o
-ri - - - - - - - - a, o clemens, o pi-a, o clemens, o
a, o clemens, o pi-a, o clemens, o
140
pi-a,
o dulcis vir-go Ma-ri - - - - -
pi-a,
o dulcis vir-go Ma-
pi-a, o dulcis vir-go Ma-ri - - - - - - - - - - -

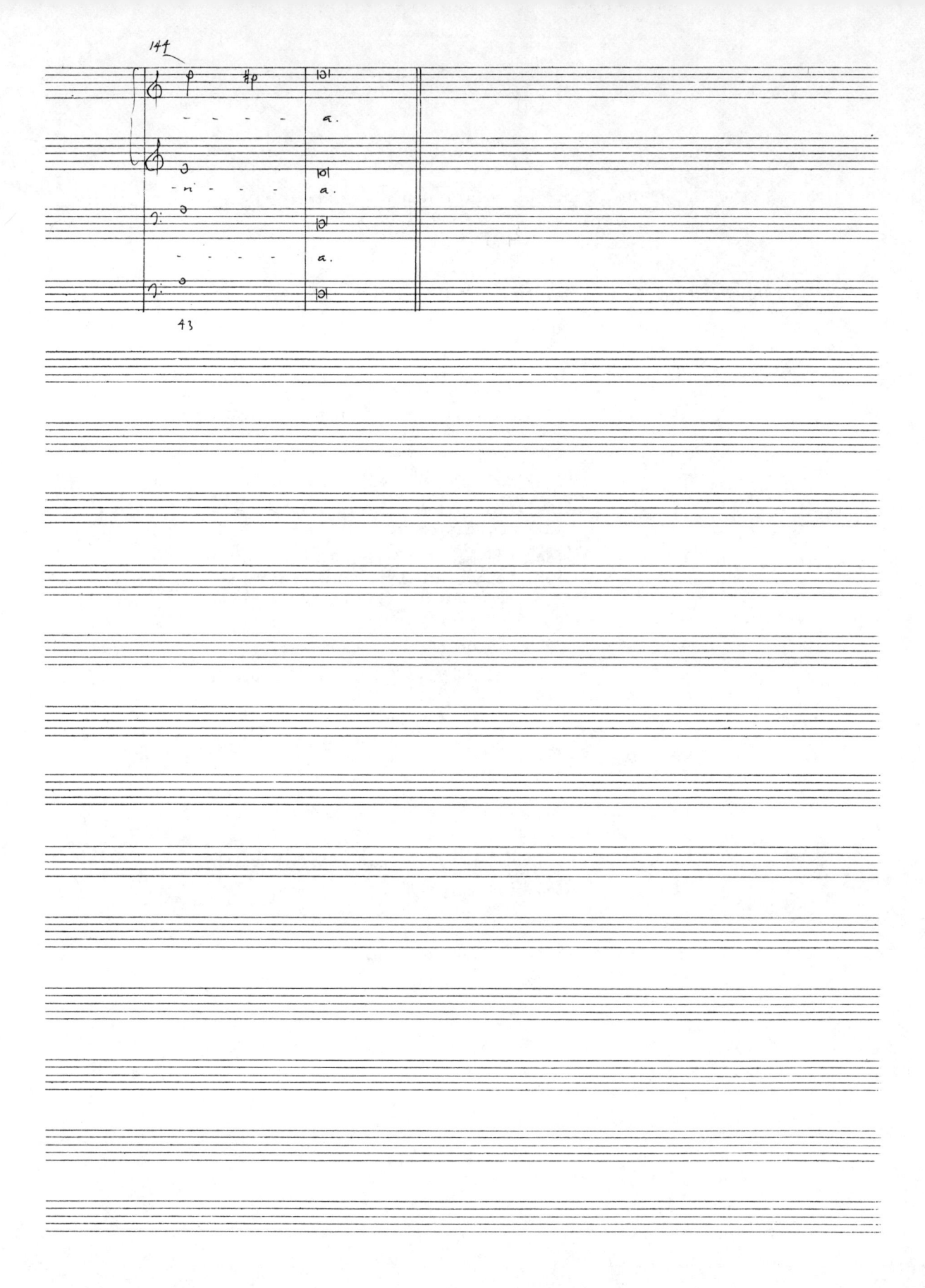
144
a.
- ri -
a.
a.
43

SI QUA EST CONSOLATIO (SSB bc)

BASIS OF THIS EDITION: Sacrarum modulationum... (Rome: L. Grignani, 1642).   I Bc.

ALSO COLLATED: I Rc: ms 5397.

VARIANTS AND COMMENTS:

6-7	S1	1642 (but not ms 5397): IESU is capitalised, a fairly common practice in seventeenth-century sources.
24.4	S2	1642 and ms 5397: c''
31	S1	1642 (but not ms 5397): DEI is capitalised, but only in S1.
41	S1	1642 and ms 5397: bars 37 (B) and 45 (S2) suggest that it is a semibreve rest, and not the dot of perfection, which is missing.
49	B/bc	Cf. note on bar 41. Cf. also 54 (S1).
55	S2/B	1642 and ms 5397: S2 is not in black notation.
86.1) 92.1) 94.1) 102.3)	bc	Figured ♭.
110.3	bc	1642: the 6 is printed above the a. ms 5397: it is written above the g.
116	S2	1642 and ms 5397: not black notation.
118.3	S1	1642 and ms 5397: g'
120.3	bc	1642: ♯. ms 5397: 6♯.
130	B	1642 and ms 5397: |◊|·
138	B	1642 and ms 5397: **not** black notation.

Si qua est con- so- la- - ti- o in Chri- sto
Je- - su,
si quod est so- la- - ti- um ca- - - - - ri- ta- - -
- tis,
si qua est so- ci- etas spi- ritus,
si qua sunt vi- scera mi- sera- ti-
- o - nis
im- plete gaudium meum ut si- tis imita- to- res

24
im - ple - te, im - plete gau-dium me-um, ut
im - ple - te, im - plete gau-dium me-um,
De - - - - i, im - plete gau-dium me-um, ut si - tis imita -
29
si - tis imita - to - - res De - - i.
ut si - tis imitato-res De - - i.
- to - res De - - - - - - i. A - gite
34
A - gite sem - per quae
sem - per quae sunt in - - sta.
40
sunt san - - cta.
A - gite semper quae sunt pu-di - - ca.
A - gite

46
A - gite semper quae sunt, —— quae sunt
A - gite semper quae sunt ——
Semper quae sunt —— amabi - li - a,
quae sunt ——
53
amabi - li - a, a - gite semper quae
amabi - li - a, a - gite semper, a - gite semper quae sunt, ——
ama - bi - li - a, a - gite semper, quae
59
sunt —— amabi - li - a. Si qua
— quae sunt amabi - li - a. Si qua vir - tus, si qua
Sunt —— amabi - li - a.
65
La - us,
La - us,
haec —— a - - gi - te, haec —— cogita - - -

haec cogita - - te, si qua la - us
haec cogita - - te, si qua la - us
- te, si qua la - us haec
haec cogita - - te, haec
haec cogita - - te, haec
- a - - gi - te,
haec
cogita - - te.
cogita - - te.
Psal - len - tes Do - mino in hym - nis et can - ticis,
cogita - - te.
Psal - len - tes Do - mino in
Psal - len - tes Do - mino in hym - nis et can - ticis,
psal - len - tes Do - mino in hym - nis et
hym - nis et can - ticis,
psal - len - tes

93
in hym-nis et can-ticis,
can-ticis, psal-len-tes Do-mino in
Do-mino, psal-len-tes do-mino in hym-nis et can-ticis, in
6
98
psal-len-tes Do-mino in hym-nis et can-ticis,
hym-nis et can-ticis, in hym-nis et can-ticis, can-
hym-nis et can-ticis, can- tantes in cor-dibus
6 6 #
104
can-
-tantes in cor-dibus vestris De-o no- - - - stro lau- -
vestris, in cor-dibus vestris De-o no-stro, De-o no- - - - stro lau- -
6 6# # 43
110
-tantes in cor-dibus vestris, in cor-dibus vestris, in cor-dibus
-dem, can- tantes in cor-dibus
-dem, can- tantes in cor-dibus vestris, in cor-dibus
[6] 6

116
vestris De-o no-stro, De-o no - - - stro lau - - dem,
vestris De-o no - - - stro lau - - dem, can-
vestris, can- tantes in cor- dibus
122
can- tantes in cor- dibus vestris De-o no- stro,
-tantes in cor- dibus vestris, in cor- dibus vestris De-o no-stro De-o
vestris, in cor- dibus vestris, in cor- dibus re- stris De-o
128
can- tantes in cor- dibus vestris, in cor- dibus
no - - - stro lau - - dem, can-
no - - - stro lau - - dem, can- tantes in cor- dibus
134
vestris, in cor- dibus vestris De-o no - - - stro lau - - dem, De-o
-tantes in cor- dibus vestris De-o no - - stro — lau - - dem, De-o
vestris, in cor- dibus vestris De-o no - - - stro lau - - dem, De-o

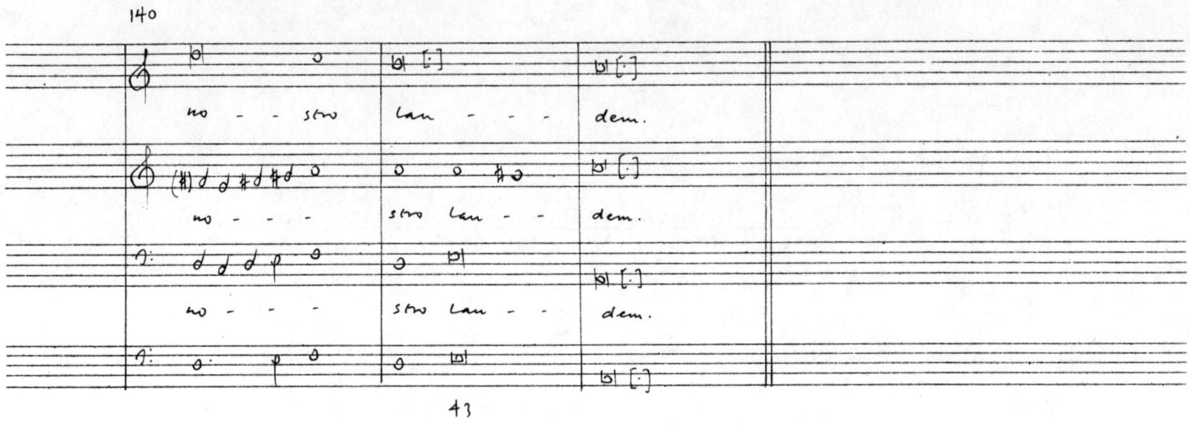
140
no - - stro lau - - - dem.
no - - - - stro lau - - dem.
no - - - stro lau - - dem.
43

SICUT STELLA MATUTINA (S bc)

BASIS OF THIS EDITION: <u>R. Floridus...has alias sacras cantiones ...</u> (Rome: F. Moneta, 1659).   GB Och.

VARIANTS AND COMMENTS:

4 and 6	bc	There is a change of line in the middle of each bar; it is likely that a single semibreve was intended in each case. Cf. bar 23, which is also divided by a change of line, but in which a tie between the two notes is printed. (This comparison, in fact, could support or weaken the editorial decision.)
11.1) 22.1) 33.1)	bc	Figured ♯4 2
51	S	The type is badly set in this bar. The first note could be g'' or e'', and the underlay of 'civem' is unclear. Comparison with bars 62 and 79 makes the intention clear.
50) 61) 68) 78)	S	Rhythmic discrepancy <u>sic</u>.
140.4	S	The last note in the bar is unclearly printed: it could be e'', g'' or a''. In view of bar 145, the last is the most likely.
170	bc	The two notes are slurred.
177.1	bc	Figured 6.
184.2-3	S	Rhythmic discrepancy with bar 175 <u>sic</u>.
215.1	bc	Figured 43.
227.2	S	Discrepancy with 213.3-4 <u>sic</u>.
228.4	S	Discrepancy with 215.2 <u>sic</u>.
231.4	S	f'' Cf. 218.2.
250) 261) 266)	S	Rhythm <u>sic</u>, despite discrepancy with 50, 61 and 68. (But 276 = 78!)
260.2-3	S	The printed underlay is unclear: the syllable '-res' could be under the e'' or the d'', but it is not under the f''. It thus differs from all

		previous appearances of the phrase (bars 49, 60 and 249); but such misplacement of a syllable is a common printing error.
265	bc	The brief bc solo (originally 66-67) is omitted.
272.2	S	Rhythmic discrepancy with 74.2 (and 75.3 and 273.3) <u>sic</u>; possibly ♫ is intended.
284.1	bc	Figured 4♯ / 2

Si - cut stel - la matu - ti - na in me - - dio
ne - - - - - - bu - lae, i - ta, i - ta re - ful - sit in do - mo
Do - mini bea - tis - simus, be - a - tis - simus N. N.
Si - cut rosa in die - bus ver - - - - - -
- nis, ita, ita florvit ante Do - minum bea - tis - simus, bea - tis - simus N.
N.
Si - cut
ros aurorae can - - - - - - didas, i - ta De - i Ec -
- cle - siam ir - roravit, ir - ro - ravit bea - tissimus, bea - tissimus N. N.

475

co-ro-na- - - te. Ver, ver fit
ae- - ter-num;
in- - - gis,
in- - - gis se- - re-mi- tas
dul-cis_a-
-me- - nitas spar-gat_in_ ter- - ris gau- - dium_ super- - num,
dul-cis_a- me- - nitas spar-gat_ in_ ter- - ris
gau- - di-um_ super- - - num, spar- - gat, spar-gat_in_
ter- - ris gau- - dium_ super- - num, gau- - dium,
gau- - dium su-per- - num. O,_ o_ di-es

133
Lae - ta, O, O fausta di - - es in qua N.
138
in qua N. bea - tis - - simam animam De - o red - - didit, in
142
qua N. in qua N. bea - tis - - simam animam De - o
146
red - - didit, et caelitum, et caelitum in choris su - - - i re - ce - - pit
150
prae - - - - mium la - bo - - ris, O, O fausta dies, O, O dies lae - - -
154
- ta, O, O fausta dies, O, O dies lae - - ta, O
158
dies lae - ta. In hac val - le,
164
in hac val - le la - cri - ma - rum cae - li gau - - - - - -

170
--dium su-spi-ra--vit; ser-vum me-ritis — praecla-- rum nunc super
176
a-- --stra De-us e-xalta--vit, ser-vum
182
me-ritis — praecla-- rum nunc super a--- ---stra
188
De-us e-xalta--vit, e---
194
--xal--ta--vit.
202
Mil--le fon-tes, mil---le fon-tes
206
la--cte cur--- rant, flu--ant mel---le; nunc coro-nent
210
fron-tem di-vi mil-le flo---res, mille, mil-le stel-lae.

nunc co- ro- - nent- fron- tem- divi mille flo- - - -
- - res, mille, mil- le stel- lae, mil- le flo- - res-
- res, mille, mil- le stel- - lae, mil- le fon- tes, mil- le
ri- vi la- cte cur- rant, flu- ant mel- le, nunc co- ro- nent fron- tem
divi mil- le flo- - - - - res, mille, mil- le stel- - lae, nunc coro- nent
fron- tem- divi mil- le flo- - - - res, mille, mil- le stel- lae,
mil- le flo- - - - - - res, mille, mil- le stel- lae, mil- le,
mil- le, mil- le flores, mil- le, mil- le, mil- le stel- - - - - lae.

238
Stil- la- te — ro- - res,
stel- lae — mi- ca- - te,
244
flo- re- te — flo- - - - - - res, —
250
et — cae- li — ci- - vem — om- nes co- ro- na- - te,
256
flo- re- te — flo- - - - - [res, —] et — cae- li —
262
ci- - vem — om- nes co- ro- na- - te, et — cae- li —
267
ci- vem — om- nes co- ro- na- - te, corona- te, co- ro-
273
- na- te, coronate, co- rona- - - te, — et cae- li — ci- - vem —
278
om- - - nes co- ro- na- - te, co- ro- nate, co- ro-

283
- na - - -
- - te, et caeli civem omnes,
287
omnes, omnes, omnes co - ro - na - - te, co- nate, co - ronate, co - ro - na - - -
291
- - - te, co - - - - - - - - - - ro - na - - te.

SUSCITAVIT DOMINUS (ATB VV vdg bc)

BASIS OF THIS EDITION: Carissimi, *Missa a quinque et a novem, cum selectis quibusdam cantionibus...* (Cologne: F. Friesser, 1666). GB Lbl.

ALSO COLLATED: *Scelta de'motetti...* (Rome: G. Fei, 1665) [ATB bc only] I Bc.

VARIANTS AND COMMENTS:

18.2	A	1665: f' f', both quavers.
19.4	A	1666: a' 1665: g'
25.3	bc	1666 only: figured ♭.
28.2	A	1665: a quaver rest followed by semi-quavers g' f'; this version has a practical advantage for the singer.
32.1-2	bc	1666: printed half-way between the f and d. 1665: it is under the d.
36.3-4	bc	1666: ♩. ♪ 1665: ♩ ♩ Cf. 1666 bars 33 and 146.
37.3-4	A	1666: [music example] 1665: [music example] Cf. 147.1-2, where both versions have the same rhythm and melody.
45.3-4	T	1665: only the first sharp is present (but the second is obviously implied); this would be more normal practice.
46.1	B	1665: the flat is present (and bc has the flat in 1666).
46.4	T	1665: the sharp is present.
47.4	T	1665: the sharp is present, and is more likely because of the D major chord which precedes it (figured ♯ in bc).
52.4	vdg	1666: d

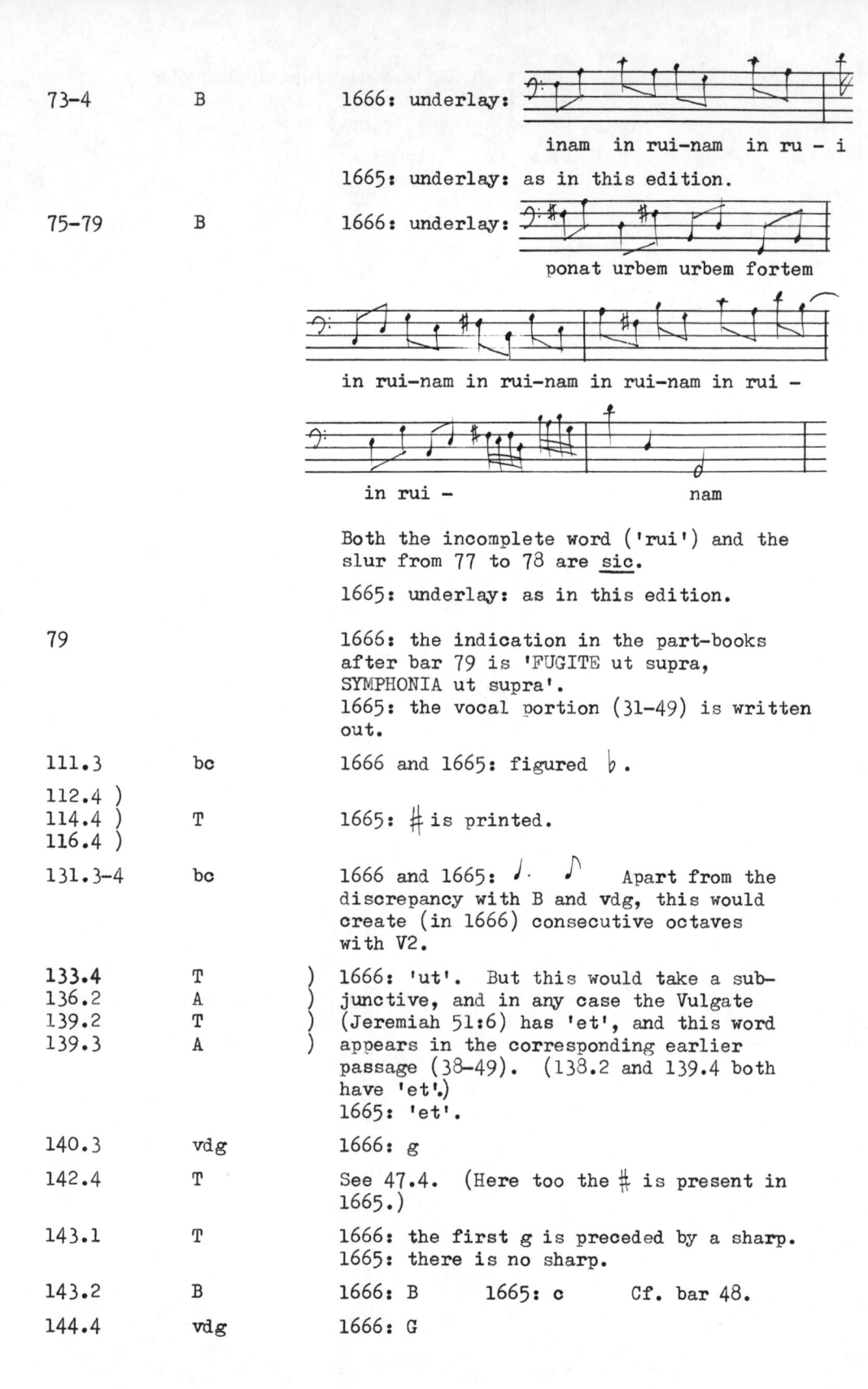

73-4	B	1666: underlay: [music: inam in rui-nam in ru-i]
		1665: underlay: as in this edition.
75-79	B	1666: underlay: [music: ponat urbem urbem fortem / in rui-nam in rui-nam in rui-nam in rui- / in rui- nam]

Both the incomplete word ('rui') and the slur from 77 to 78 are <u>sic</u>.

1665: underlay: as in this edition.

79		1666: the indication in the part-books after bar 79 is 'FUGITE ut supra, SYMPHONIA ut supra'.
		1665: the vocal portion (31-49) is written out.
111.3	bc	1666 and 1665: figured ♭.
112.4)		
114.4)	T	1665: ♯ is printed.
116.4)		
131.3-4	bc	1666 and 1665: ♩. ♪ Apart from the discrepancy with B and vdg, this would create (in 1666) consecutive octaves with V2.
133.4	T)	1666: 'ut'. But this would take a sub-
136.2	A)	junctive, and in any case the Vulgate
139.2	T)	(Jeremiah 51:6) has 'et', and this word
139.3	A)	appears in the corresponding earlier passage (38-49). (138.2 and 139.4 both have 'et'.)
		1665: 'et'.
140.3	vdg	1666: g
142.4	T	See 47.4. (Here too the ♯ is present in 1665.)
143.1	T	1666: the first g is preceded by a sharp.
		1665: there is no sharp.
143.2	B	1666: B 1665: c Cf. bar 48.
144.4	vdg	1666: G

146	T/bc	1665 also has the discrepancy between bc (figured ♯) and T (no ♯); but at 145 both T and bc have a ♯.
148.4	T	1666: f 1665: g

Symphonia

16
A
T
B
bc
Do-minus super Ba-by-lo-nem et super habitato--res e-ins quasi
20
ven---tum pesti-len--tem; misit ventilato-res, misit ventilato-res
43
24
et ventila----- bunt et demolientur
6
43
28
eam, et demolientur e---------am.
[𝄋]
Fugite, fugite
Fugite, fugite gentes, fugite
Fugite, fugite gentes,
♯
43

32
gentes, fugite populi, fugite, fugite, fugite, fugite, fugite, fugite po-puli,
populi, fugite, fugite, fugite, fugite, fugite, fugite, fugite, fugite po-puli,
fugite populi, fugite, fugite, fugite, fugite, fugite, fugite, fugite populi,
6
43
35
fugite gentes, fugite populi, fugite, fugite, fugite de me-dio Baby-
fugite gentes, fugite populi, fugite, fugite, fugite, fugite, fu-gite de medio Ba-by-
fugite gentes, fugite populi, fugite, fugite, fugite, fu-gite de medio Ba-by-
38
-lo - - nis, et salvet unus-
-lo - - - nis, et salvet unusquis-que a - - nimam su - - am,
-lo - - nis,
43
43
42
-quis-que a - - nimam su - am, et salvet unusquis - - que
et salvet unus-quis - - - que
et salvet unus-quisque, et salvet unusquis-que
43

46
V¹
V²
A
a - nimam su - - am, a - - - nimam suam, animam su - - am.
T
a - nimam su - - am, a - - nimam su - - am.
B
a - nimam su - - am, a - - - nimam su - - am.
vdg
bc
76 43 ♯ 43
50

54
Su- per muros e- ius levate
59
B
si- gnum, au- ge- te custo- diam, prepara- te in- si- dias, a-
bc
63
-cu- ite sagit- tas, im- ple- - te pha- - - - - re- tras; quia ul- tio
67
Do- mini est, mens e- ius est ut per- - - dat

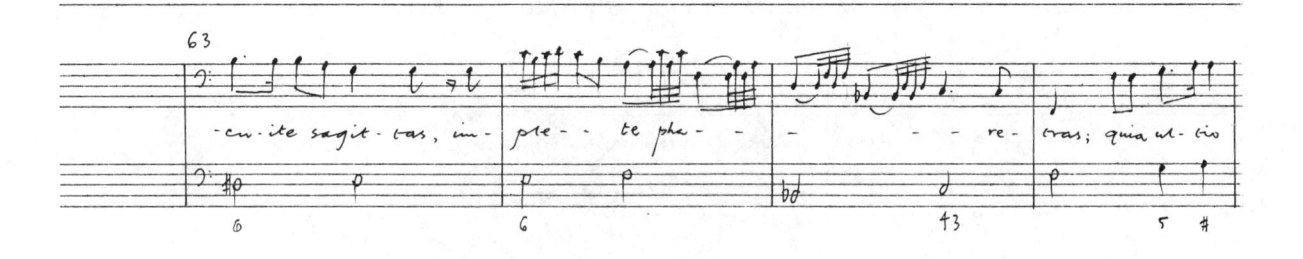

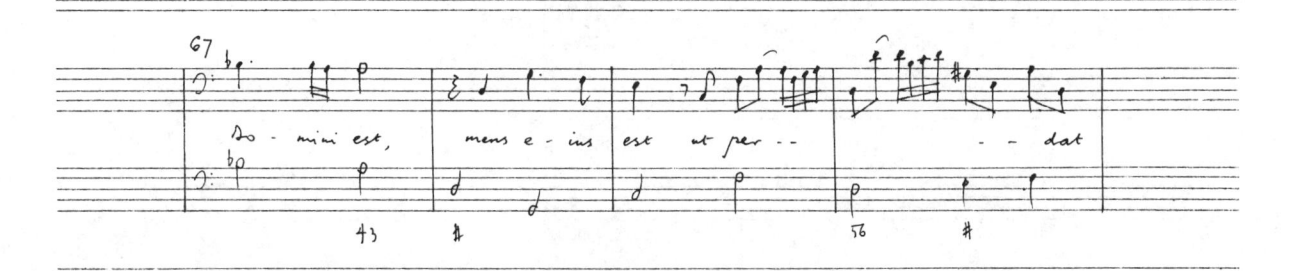

e - - am, et ponat urbem fortem in ru- inam, in rui[- -]
- - - - nam, et ponat urbem [fortem in ru- inam, in rui - -
- nam, in ru- i - - - - nam, in ru-] i - - - - - nam.
[Dal segno (31) al fine (56), = 80 - 105]
T
bc
Infelix Ba- bylon, infelix Ba- bylon, quae habitas super a- quas mul- tas
lo- cuples in thesau - - ris: venit, ve- nit finis e- ius, venit,
ve- nit inte- - ritus e- ius, venit di- es praecisio - - nis tu- ae, cessa-
- verunt fortes tu- i a prae- lio, habita- verunt in praesi- diis,

121
T
devora- tum est
ro- bur e- o- rum,
incensa sunt taber-
bc
124
V1
V2
A
Fugite, fugite
gentes, fugite populi, fugite,
T
-na- - cula tu- - a.
Fugite, fugite gentes, fugite
populi, fugite, fugite, fugite,
B
Fugite, fugite gentes,
fugite populi, fugite, fugite,
vdg
bc
128
fugite, fugite, fugite, fugite,
fugite po- puli,
fugite gentes,
fugite, fugite, fugite, fugite,
fugite po- pu- li,
fugite gentes, fugite, fugite,
fugite, fugite, fugite, fugite,
fugite po- puli,
fugite gentes, fugite

131
fugite populi, fugite, fugite, fu-gite de medio Ba-by-lo- - nis,
fugite, fugite, fugite, fugite, fu-gite de medio Ba-by-lo- - nis, [et]
populi, fugite, fugite, fugite, fu-gite de medio Ba-by-lo- - nis,
134
[et] salvet unus- quis-que a- - nimam
salvet unusquis-que a- - nimam su- - am,

138
su - - am, [et] salvet unus - quis - - que a - nimam su - - -
[et] salvet unus - quis - - - que a - nimam su - - -
et salvet unus - quis - que, et salvet unusquis - que a - - nimam su - - -
142
-am, a - - nimam suam, a - nimam su - - am, fugite, fugite, fugite
-am, a - - - nimam su - - am, fugite, fugite, fugite
-am, a - - - ni - mam su - - am, fugite, fugite, fugite

145
gentes, fugite, fugite, fugite populi, fugite, fu- gite de me-dio Babylo - -
gentes, fugite, fugite, fugite populi, fugite, fu- gite de me-dio Babylo - - -
gentes, fugite, fugite, fugite populi, fugite, fu- gite de me-dio Ba-bylo - - -
43
148
- nis, fu - - gite, fugite, fugite po - puli, fugite, fugite, fu - gite.
- nis, fu - - - gite, fugite, fugite, fugite, fugite po - puli, fugite, fugite, fu - gite.
- nis, fu - - gite, fugite, fugite, fugite po - puli, fugite, fugite, fu - gite.
6
43
43

TIMETE DOMINUM (SSATB bc)

BASIS OF THIS EDITION: I COd: ms I-V-14.

VARIANTS AND COMMENTS:

15.3	bc	Figured ♭.
19.3	bc	Figured ♭.
32	T	)
33	A	) Written ◯.
34	T	)
40.2 – 41.1	A	The underlay is ambiguous: the syllable '-um' could be under the e' or the d'. But the slur (which is original) clarifies the underlay.
54.3)	bc	Figured 76♭ – presumably as a precautionary measure.
56.3)		
55.1	bc	The natural in front of the b is written ♮ ; the tenor has the more usual ♯.
55.3	T	Written b. Cf. 59.3, 62.1, 66.1 and 68.3.
58.3)	bc	Figured 43♭.
60.3)		
65.1	bc	Figured 43♯.

70.1	bc	The left side of the first page of the bc part-book is faded. This bar is slightly affected, but the figuring appears to be 65 . The only slightly
		         43♭
		 doubtful figure is the 4. According to the movement of the voice parts, the figuring should be 76 .
		                         5
		                         43

71.1	T	Crotchet.
73.1	bc	Figured ♭.
86.3	bc	Semibreve.
91.3	bc	Figured ♭.
112		After bar 112 the original indication is 'Alleluia come sopra'.

Timete Dominum tacet
Timete Dominum tacet
Timete Do-mi-num om- - nes san-cti, om- - nes
Timete Dominum tacet
A
T
bc
Timete Do-mi-num om- - nes sancti, om- - nes
San - - cti e - - - ius,
san - - cti e - - - - ius, timete Do-mi-num,
timete Do-mi-num,
timete Do-mi-num
timete Do-mi-
-num om- - nes san - cti, om- - nes san - cti e - - - - ius,
om- - nes san-cti, om- - nes san-cti, om- - nes sancti e- - - ius,

18
om - - nes san - cti, om - - nes san - cti, om - - nes sancti e - -
om - - nes san - cti, om - - nes san - cti e - - -
21
- - ius: quo - niam nihil de - est ti - men - tibus e - - -
- - ius:
27
- um, nihil de - est
quo - niam nihil de - est ti - men - tibus e - - - um, nihil de -
34
quo - niam nihil de - est ti - men - tibus
- est quo - niam nihil de - est ti - - men - tibus
40
e - - - um, quo - niam nihil de - est
e - - um, quo - ni - am nihil de - est

47
ti- men-tibus e - - - um, ti- men-tibus e - - um.
ti- men-tibus e - - um, ti - - - men-tibus e - - - -
53
S1
S2
A
T
B
bc
Al-lelu - ia, alleluia, alle- lu - - - ia, alle-
Al-le-lu-ia, alleluia, alle-lu - - ia,
Allelu - - ia,
57
Al - lelu - - ia, alleluia, alle- lu - - ia,
- ia, alleluia, alle- lu - - ia,
alleluia, alle-lu-ia, al- - le luia, allelu - - ia, al-
al - lelu - ia, allelu - - ia, alle- lu - - ia, al-
alle-lu - ia, al-le- lu - - ia,
al - - lelu-

61
al - le-lu - ia, alle- luia, alle-lu - -
alleluia, al - le- lu - - - - ia, al-
- le-lu - - ia, alle- lu - - ia, alleluia, alle- luia, allelu - ia,
- leluia, allelu - - ia, allelu - - - ia, al - le-
- ia, alle-lu - - ia, al - le- lu - ia, allelu - - ia, al-lelu - - -
65
- ia, alle- lu - ia, alleluia, al - - le-lu - -
- lelu - - ia, alle- luia, alle-lu - - - ia,
al - - leluia, allelu - - ia, al - le-lu - - ia, alle- lu - -
- lu - ia, allelu - - ia, alle-lu - - ia, al - leluia, alle-lu - - ia, alle-
- ia, al - le lu - ia, alle- luia, alle-lu - -

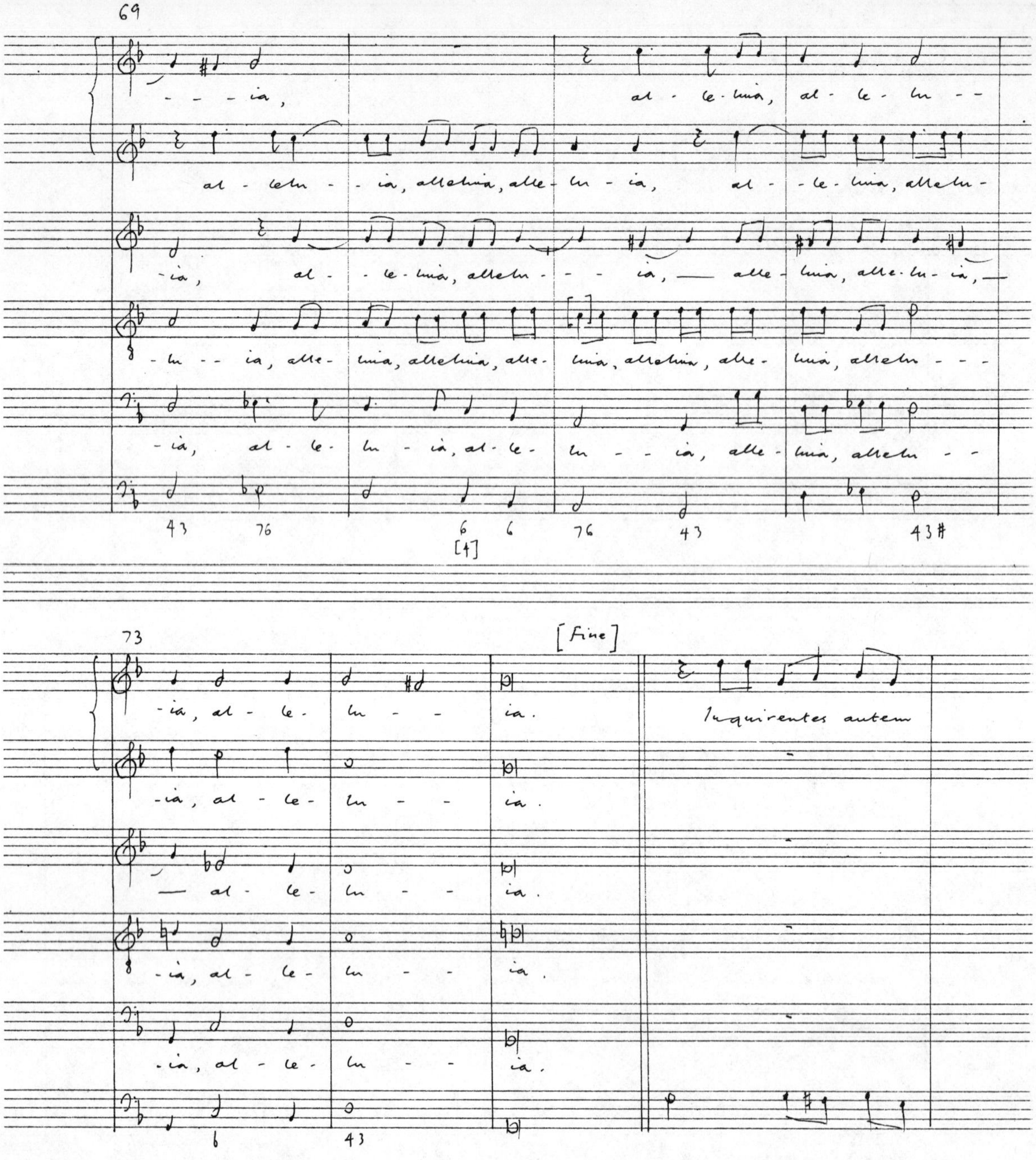

77
Do-minum, non de fi-cient omni bo - - - - - no, non de-ficient omni
Inqui- rentes autem Do-minum, non de - fi-cient omni bo - - -
43
80
bo - - no, inqui- rentes autem Do-minum, non de- fi-cient omni bo - - -
- - no,
inqui-rentes autem
6

502

94
- nes qui labo- ra - tis, qui labo- ra- tis et onera - ti e - stis, qui labo-
98
- ra - - - - tis et onera - ti e - stis: et e - go, et
102
e - go re - - - - - fi - ciam
106
vos, et e - go, et e - go re - - -
110
- - - fi - ciam vos.
[Dal segno al fine]

TURBABUNTUR IMPII (ATB bc)

BASIS OF THIS EDITION: Carissimi, *Sacri concerti musicali...*
(Rome: V. Mascardi, 1675). GB Och.

VARIANTS AND COMMENTS:

3	bc	A sharp is printed between the two minims. It should probably appear in bar 4.
15.1) 17.3)	bc	Figured 9♭8.
18.2	B	Second quaver: a. Cf. 31, 85, 104 and 141.
18.3	B	a
22.3	bc	Figured 5.
28.3	bc	Figured 6. 5
34.1-2	A	Rhythm: ♩.♪♪ Cf. 62, 88 and 144.
34.1 62.1 88.1 144.1	B B B B	) It is quite likely that b natural is) implied by the original notation (the) natural at the end of the preceding bar),) in which case the accidental should be in ( ), not [ ].
35.2) 48.4) 63.2)	bc	No figuring in these places; cf. 89.2 and 145.2, which are figured 5.
40	bc	The sharp (= natural) is placed between the two tied Gs. But the reason for tying the two notes must be to signify that the third is sharpened on beat 3; this could not be indicated with a single semibreve.
43	bc	Minim
47.3	A	Rhythm: ♩.♪ Cf. 62, 88 and 144.
62.2	T	Rhythm: ♪♪ Cf. 34, 47, 88 and 144.
78.1	bc	56
81.1	B	a
82.3	bc	F natural
83.1	T	Rhythm: ♩. ♪
99.2	B	B flat
103.4	B	c Cf. 17.4, 30.4, 84.4 and 140.4.
108.4	A	f'

110.1	A	f'
118.3	T	g
122.3	T	g
139.3 – 140.1	A	There is a slur from f' sharp to g', and the word 'heu' does not appear at 140.1. But cf. 16-17, 29-30, 83-84 and 102-03.

Turbabuntur tacet
Solo
Turbabuntur tacet
Tur - babuntur im - pii timo - re hor -
-ri - bili cum de - scen - dent in terram tene - bro - sam, et opertam
mor - tis cali - gine, u - bi nullus or - do sed sempiternus hor - ror inha - bi -
-tat, prae an - gu - stia spi - ritus ge - mentes, et dicen - - tes:

14
Heu, heu, heu nos miseros, heu, heu do-len-tes,
Heu, heu, heu nos mi-se-ros, heu, heu, heu do-
Heu nos, heu nos mi-seros, heu, heu, heu do-
18
heu dolen- - tes.
-len tes, do-len - tes.
Quo-modo praevene-runt nos ge-mitus
-len-tes, do-len - - tes.
22
quomodo dolo-res in-fer-ni circumde-de- -runt nos,
mor - tis,
quo-modo in hac flamma perenni cruci-
26
Heu, heu, heu, heu nos mi-seros, heu,
Heu, heu, heu, heu nos miseros, heu,
-a-mur incen-dio. Heu nos, heu nos mi-seros, heu,

30
heu dolentes, heu dolen- - tes. Pereat dies, pereat dies
heu, heu dolentes, dolen- - tes.
Pereat dies, pereat dies
heu, heu dolentes, dolen- - tes.
Pereat dies, pereat dies
34
in qua na-ti sumus; pereat nox, pereat nox in qua concepti fu-i-
in qua na-ti sumus; pereat nox, pereat, pereat nox in qua concepti fu-i-
in qua na-ti sumus; pereat nox, pereat nox in qua concepti fu-i-
37
-mus. Dies il-la ver-sa-tur in te-ne-bris, non illus-tre-tur lu-mine,
-mus.
-mus.
42
oc-cupet e-am ca-li-go, et invol-va- - -tur amari-tu-dine.

Pereat dies, pereat dies in qua na-ti sumus; pereat
Pereat dies, pereat dies in qua na-ti sumus; pereat nox,
Pereat dies, pereat dies in qua nati sumus; pereat nox,
nox, pereat nox in qua con-cepti fu-imus.
pereat, pereat nox in qua con-cepti fu-i-mus.
pereat nox in qua con-cepti fu-i-mus.
Noctem il-lam
tenebrosus tur-bo pos-si-de-at, obtene-bren-tur stel-lae ca-li-gine eius, ex-
-pec-tent nec vi-deant lu--cem, or-tum non vi-deant sur-gen-tis Auro--

Pereat dies, pereat dies in qua na-ti sumus;
Pereat dies, pereat dies in qua na-ti sumus; pereat
-rae. Pereat dies, pereat dies, pereat dies in qua na-ti sumus;
pereat nox, pereat nox in qua concepti fu-i-mus. Im-pie, im-pie,
nox, pereat, pereat nox in qua concepti fu-i-mus.
pereat nox, pereat nox in qua concepti fu-i-mus.
im-pie ge-ni-mus,
iniquita-tem, iniquita-tem fe-cimus,
lu-men iu-
-sti-tiae, sol intelli-gen-tiae non, non illuxit no-bis.
Lassati

75
ambu- la-vimus vi-as dif-
su-mus in vi-a iniqui- ta-tis et perditi- o - - nis;
79
-fi-ciles, vias Do-mini ignora - vi- mus. Heu, heu nos
Heu nos, heu nos
Heu, heu, heu nos
83
miseros, heu, heu do-len-tes heu dolen- - tes. Pereat dies,
miseros, heu, heu, heu do- len-tes dolen- - tes. Pereat
miseros, heu, heu, heu do- len-tes dolen- - tes. Pereat dies,
87
pereat dies in qua na-ti sumus; pereat nox, pereat
dies, pereat dies in qua na-ti sumus; pereat nox, pereat, pereat
pereat dies, pereat dies in qua na-ti sumus; pereat nox, pereat

90
nox in qua concepti fu- i- mus. Quid nobis pro-fuit su- perbia,
nox in qua concepti fu- i- mus.
nox in qua concepti fu- i- mus. quid diviti-
94
Transi- erunt
quid hu- manae sapien-tiae glo-ria? Transi-
-a- rum iactan-tia, Transi-
97
om-nia tamquam um- - - - - - bra, transierunt omnia tamquam um- bra.
-erunt om-nia tamquam umbra, transierunt omnia tamquam um- bra.
-erunt om-nia tamquam umbra, transierunt omnia, omnia tamquam um- bra.
100
Heu, heu, heu nos miseros, heu, heu do-len-tes, heu dolen- -
Heu, heu, heu nos miseros, heu, heu, heu do- lentes, dolen-tes.
Heu nos, heu nos miseros, heu, heu, heu do- lentes, dolen- -

105
-tes. Despera-ri- mus, despera- ri- mus, nequaquam ul-tra ri-
Despera-ri- mus,
-tes. Despera-rimus, despera-ri- mus, ne- -
108
-ve- - mus nec ri- de-bimus faciem De- - i, nec ri- de bimus faciem
ne - - quaquam ultra ri- ve- - mus nec ri-de bimus faciem
-quaquam ul-tra ri-ve- - mus nec ri- debimus faciem Dei, faciem
110
De - - i, despera-ri- mus.
De- - i, — despera-ri- mus, despera- ri- mus.
De - - i, despera-rimus, despera-ri- mus.
113
Un-dique terrent nos for- mi-dine,
un-dique in-va-dit nos hor-ror,
un-dique

116
un-dique, un-dique pavor, luctus,
undique, un-dique pavor, luctus,
tre- - - - mor oc-cupat, pavor, luctus,
119
et angu-sti-a, despera-vi-mus.
et an-gu-sti-a, despera-vi-mus, despera-vi-mus.
et angu-sti-a, despera-vimus, despera-vi-mus.
122
Quis stare po-terit cum igne devoran-te,
quis stare po-terit cum ar-
125
Qua-re non su-mus in u-tero mor-tui,
-do-ribus sempiter-nis?
qua-re, qua-re exce-pti

129
Cur, cur u- be-ribus la-cta-- ti,
Cur, cur u- be-ri-bus la-cta-- ti,
genibus? quare non ab u-tero transla-sti ad
132
qua-re mi-seris da-ta est lux,
qua- re miseris da- ta est lux,
tu-multum, qua-re da-ta est vi-ta his qui in amaritu-dine
136
Heu, heu, heu, heu nos miseros, heu, [heu] dolentes,
Heu, heu, heu, heu nos miseros, heu, heu, heu do-
a- nimae sunt? Heu nos, heu nos miseros, heu, heu, heu do-
141
heu dolen--- tes. Pereat dies, pereat dies
-lentes, do-len- tes. Pereat di-es, pereat dies
-lentes, do-len-- tes. Pereat dies, pereat dies, pereat dies

144
in quo na-ti sumus; pereat nox, pereat
in quo na-ti sumus; pereat nox pereat, pereat
in quo na-ti sumus; pereat nox, pereat, pereat
76 5
146
nox in qua concepti fu-i-mus, in qua concepti fu-i-mus.
nox in qua concepti fu-i-mus, in qua concepti fu-i-mus.
nox in qua concepti fu-i-mus, in qua concepti fu-i-mus.
76 [♭] 4 3

VIDERUNT TE DOMINE (SB bc)

BASIS OF THIS EDITION: <u>Floridus modulorum hortus...</u> (Rome: A. Fei, 1647). GB Lwa.

VARIANTS AND COMMENTS:

4.1	S	e'' quaver omitted (i.e. there is no dot on the preceding note).
9.3	bc	Figured 6♭.
10.4	S	The b' is printed as a quaver, and there is a sharp in front of it. There is a slur from this b' to the following c'' sharp semibreve. There is no slur at the corresponding place at the end of bar 14, and in both cases the syllable '-tes' is printed under the semibreve.
12.3	bc	Figured ♭.
16.3	S	Both notes are printed g'.
18.3	bc	Figured ♭43.
20.2	B	Quaver.
27.1) 29.3)	bc	Figured ♭.
28.1	S	d'' e''
32.1	bc	Figured 56♯.
49.2	bc	Figured ♭.
53.1	bc	Figured 4/3.
60.1	bc	Figured 4♯/2.
60.2	bc	Figured 6♭.
60.3) 64.2)	bc	Figured ♭.
66	B	Crotchet rest omitted.
72-73) 77-79) 89-91) 93-95)	SB	The rhythmic discrepancy between ♫ and ♩.♪ on the syllables '-stupe-' is <u>sic</u> in all cases. There is some vague consistency about the appearances of the two rhythmic figures, however:

    72-73 The appearance of the more 'interesting' rhythm second produces a climactic effect.

    77-79 Both B rhythms are ♫

517

		89-91 All ♪.♩
		93-95 All ♫
80.1	B	Dotted quaver.
80.4	S	Slur and discrepancy (of underlay) with bar 92 both sic.
91.4	S	Discrepancy with bar 90.2 (S) and 90.4 (B) on the syllable '-ci-' sic; at 91.4 the B counterpoint alters the musical context to make the different note in S (f') desirable.
95.4	S	Crotchet.
96.1	bc	Figured 4 . ♯3
97	bc	Figured 34 .

vi - - de - runt te, Do - - - - - - - - - - - - mine,
vi - - - de - - runt te, Do -
6
- - - - - mine,
et do - luerunt mon - - -
10
- - - tes,
et do - luerunt mon - - -
14
et do - luerunt mon - - - - - - - -
- - - tes, et do - luerunt mon -
18
- tes, et do - lu - e - runt mon - - - - tes; de - - dit a -
- - - - - - tes;

23
-bis - sus ro - - - cem su-am, altitudo manus
de - dit a - bis - sus ro - - - cem su-am.
27
su-as le - va - - - - - - - vit, le - va - - - -
altitudo manus su - as le - va - - - - - - vit, le -
31
- vit, le - va - - - - - - - vit, le-va - - - - - -
- - - - - - vit, le - - - - - vit, le - va - - - - -
35
- - - - - - - - vit. Sol et lu-na ste - te - - - runt
- - - - - - - - - vit. Sol et lu-na stete - -
39
in habita - cu - lo, in habita - - cu - lo su - - - - - o, in luce sagit -
- runt in habi - ta - - culo, in habi - ta - culo su - - - o,

82
- - - - mi-tu, in fre - - - - mitu
fre - - - - - - - - mi-tu, in fre - - - - mitu
85
conculcabis, conculcabis ter - - - ram, et in fu-ro - - -
conculcabis, concul- cabis ter-ram, et in fu-
76
88
- - - - - - re ob - - stupe- fa - - ci - es, ob - - stupefa - - ci-
- ro - - - - - - re ob - - stupe-fa - - ci- es gen - -
5 5
92
- es gen - - - tes, ob - - stupe- facies, ob-stupe-
- - - - tes, ob - - stupe- fa- cies gen - - -
43 76 56
96
-fa - cies gen - - - - - - tes.
- - - - - - tes.
[4 2] 343